'This comprehensive assessment of progress in liberalizing trade in services between ASEAN countries is a valuable contribution to the literature on trade agreements. It should be required reading for students and analysts interested in understanding the state of play and challenges in integrating ASEAN services markets.'

Bernard Hoekman
Professor and Director
European University Institute, Florence, Italy

'This is the finest volume on services trade in the ASEAN region. Its value, though, extends much beyond Southeast Asia. It is a model set up on how writings about trade in services should be approached. The reader will profit from the expertise reflected therein with respect to empirics, but also the deeper questions surrounding integration at the regional and multilateral levels.'

Petros C. Mavroidis, Edwin B. Parker
Professor of Law
Columbia Law School, New York City, USA

'A great book! Distinguished experts document services trade among ASEAN members, their aspirations for genuine integration, and their policy failures. This volume makes essential reading for firms, officials and scholars. A bonus chapter recounts the EU's successful creation of a single market for services, calling out lessons for ASEAN.'

Gary Clyde Hufbauer
Non-resident Senior Fellow
Peterson Institute for International Economics
Washington, DC, USA

SERVICES TRADE IN ASEAN

The Member States of the Association of Southeast Asian Nations (ASEAN) set themselves the ambitious aim of establishing a region-wide economic community by 2015 and to deepen it in the context of the ASEAN Economic Community (AEC) Blueprint 2025. To achieve these goals, service-sector reforms will keep occupying a central place in ASEAN's policy pantheon. This can be attributed to both ASEAN's integration process and its deepening ties within a dense layer of external economic partners. This book takes stock of the experience of ASEAN Member States in pursuing trade and investment liberalization in services. It identifies key challenges that the regional grouping can be expected to encounter in realizing its AEC Blueprint 2025 aims. Using a law and economics lens, the book assesses where ASEAN is and where it is headed in services trade, situating it alongside efforts at crafting a European Single Market for services.

DORA NEO is an associate professor at the Faculty of Law, National University of Singapore. She was part of the team that pioneered the first university course on World Trade Law in Singapore, and has given academic talks and conducted government training on trade in services. From 2007 to 2010, she was an instructor for the services module in the World Trade Organization's Regional Trade Policy Course for the Asia-Pacific. She has published on the outsourcing of services, and her most recent research focuses on the liberalization of trade in services in ASEAN. She graduated from both the universities of Oxford and Harvard.

PIERRE SAUVÉ is Senior Trade Specialist in the World Bank Group's Macroeconomics, Trade and Investment Global Practice. He has published extensively in leading journals and authored important books devoted to trade in services. He has lectured on trade and investment in services in leading universities (Harvard Kennedy School; London School of Economics and Political Science; Sciences Po, Paris; and the World Trade Institute, Bern); and led negotiations in services trade as a Canadian government official. Beyond his diplomatic service in Canada, he has served as a staff member of the Bank for International Settlements, the General Agreement on Tariffs and Trade, the Organisation for Economic Co-operation and Development and the World Bank Group.

IMOLA STREHO is an associate professor in the Law School at Sciences Po in Paris. Her research focuses on the liberalization of trade in services in the European Union. From 2001 to 2009, she was Référendaire at the European Court of Justice in Luxembourg, where she worked on numerous cases involving the free movement of services. She has delivered guest lectures on international economic law at the National University of Singapore; Melbourne University; the College of Europe; Central European University; and Católica University in Lisbon.

INTEGRATION THROUGH LAW

The Role of Law and the Rule of Law in ASEAN Integration

General Editors
J. H. H. Weiler, European University Institute
Tan Hsien-Li, National University of Singapore

The Association of Southeast Asian Nations (ASEAN), comprising the ten member states of Brunei Darussalam, Cambodia, Indonesia, Lao PDR, Malaysia, Myanmar, Philippines, Singapore, Thailand and Vietnam, has undertaken intensified integration into the ASEAN Community through the Rule of Law and Institutions in its 2007 Charter. This innovative book series evaluates the community-building processes of ASEAN to date and offers a conceptual and policy toolkit for broader Asian thinking and planning of different legal and institutional models of economic and political regional integration in the region. Participating scholars have been divided up into six separate thematic strands. The books combine a mix of Asian and Western scholars.

Centre for International Law, National University of Singapore (CIL-NUS)

The Centre for International Law (CIL) was established in 2009 at the National University of Singapore's Bukit Timah Campus in response to the growing need for international law expertise and capacity building in the Asia-Pacific region. CIL is a university-wide research centre that focuses on multidisciplinary research and works with other NUS or external centres of research and academic excellence. In particular, CIL collaborates very closely with the NUS Faculty of Law.

SERVICES TRADE IN ASEAN
The Road Taken and the Journey Ahead

DORA NEO
National University of Singapore

PIERRE SAUVÉ
World Bank Group

IMOLA STREHO
Sciences Po, Paris

CAMBRIDGE UNIVERSITY PRESS

CAMBRIDGE
UNIVERSITY PRESS

University Printing House, Cambridge CB2 8BS, United Kingdom

One Liberty Plaza, 20th Floor, New York, NY 10006, USA

477 Williamstown Road, Port Melbourne, VIC 3207, Australia

314–321, 3rd Floor, Plot 3, Splendor Forum, Jasola District Centre, New Delhi – 110025, India

79 Anson Road, #06-04/06, Singapore 079906

Cambridge University Press is part of the University of Cambridge.

It furthers the University's mission by disseminating knowledge in the pursuit of education, learning, and research at the highest international levels of excellence.

www.cambridge.org
Information on this title: www.cambridge.org/9781316645413
DOI: 10.1017/9781108151788

© Centre for International Law 2019

This publication is in copyright. Subject to statutory exception and to the provisions of relevant collective licensing agreements, no reproduction of any part may take place without the written permission of Cambridge University Press.

First published 2019

Printed and bound in Great Britain by Clays Ltd, Elcograf S.p.A.

A catalogue record for this publication is available from the British Library.

Library of Congress Cataloging-in-Publication Data
NAMES: Neo, Dora Swee Suan, author. | Sauve, Pierre, 1959– author. | Streho, Imola, author.
TITLE: Services trade in ASEAN: the road taken and the journey ahead / Dora Neo, National University of Singapore; Pierre Sauve, World Bank Group; Imola Streho, Sciences Po, Paris.
DESCRIPTION: Cambridge, United Kingdom; New York, NY, USA: Cambridge University Press, 2019. | Series: Integration through law: the role of law and the rule of law in Asean integration; 15
IDENTIFIERS: LCCN 2018056605 | ISBN 9781316645413 (paperback)
SUBJECTS: LCSH: Service industries – Law and legislation – Southeast Asia. | ASEAN. | BISAC: LAW / International.
CLASSIFICATION: LCC KNC850.5 .N46 2019 | DDC 382/.45000959–dc23
LC record available at https://lccn.loc.gov/2018056605

ISBN 978-1-316-64541-3 Paperback

Cambridge University Press has no responsibility for the persistence or accuracy of URLs for external or third-party internet websites referred to in this publication and does not guarantee that any content on such websites is, or will remain, accurate or appropriate.

CONTENTS

List of Figures *page* xiii
List of Tables xiv
List of Annexes xvi
General Editors' Preface xvii
Acknowledgements xxiii
List of Abbreviations xxiv

1 Introduction 1

2 Services and Services Trade in ASEAN: Trends and Policy Context 7
  2.1 Background 7
  2.2 Trends in Aggregate Output 8
  2.3 Trends in Employment 10
  2.4 Trends in Trade Integration 10
  2.5 Trends in Services Trade and Investment 12
    2.5.1 Trade 12
    2.5.2 Investment 17
  2.6 Services and ASEAN Value Chains 19
  2.7 Characterizing ASEAN's Openness in Services Markets 28

3 Is ASEAN an Optimal Regulatory Convergence Area in Services? 43

4 The Liberalization of Services Trade in ASEAN: Trends, Achievements and Prospects 54
  4.1 The ASEAN Framework Agreement on Services 54
    4.1.1 Aims of AFAS 55

ix

CONTENTS

   4.1.2 AFAS Provisions and Inter-relationship with the GATS 57
   4.1.3 Mutual Recognition Arrangements 69
   4.1.4 Denial of Benefits/Rules of Origin 70
   4.1.5 ASEAN Minus X 75
  4.2 Liberalization and Cooperation under AFAS 77
   4.2.1 ASEAN Policies Affecting Services 77
   4.2.2 The AEC Blueprint 2015 79
   4.2.3 Progress Report 85
  4.3 AFAS Negotiating History and Modalities 88
   4.3.1 Financial Services 92
   4.3.2 Air Transport Services 93
   4.3.3 Priority Integration Sectors 94
    e-ASEAN 95
    Tourism 96
    Healthcare 97
    Air Travel 97
    Logistics 98
  4.4 Mutual Recognition Agreements in Services 98
  4.5 Movement of Natural Persons 109
  4.6 ASEAN Qualifications Reference Framework 114
  4.7 Services Liberalization under AFAS 115
   4.7.1 AFAS Seventh Package 115
    AFAS versus GATS Commitments 116
   4.7.2 AFAS Eighth Package 126
   4.7.3 AFAS Ninth Package 133
  4.8 Assessment of Liberalization of Trade in Services under AFAS 148
   4.8.1 AFAS, GATS and AEC Blueprint 2015 148
   4.8.2 Looking to the Future 158
  4.9 Services Liberalization in ASEAN+ and ASEAN Member States' PTAs 159
   4.9.1 ASEAN+ Services PTAs 159
    The Regional Comprehensive Economic Partnership and Other Negotiations 162

CONTENTS

4.9.2 Services PTAs of Individual ASEAN Member States 167
4.10 Patterns of Commitment in ASEAN+ PTAs and Bilateral Agreements 176
4.11 Commitments and Rule-Making under ASEAN+ Agreements 186
   4.11.1 Commitments 186
      AFAS 7 196
      ASEAN–China Free Trade Agreement (First Package) 197
      ASEAN–Korea Free Trade Agreement 199
      ASEAN–Australia–New Zealand Free Trade Agreement 201
   4.11.2 Comparing Commitments in AFAS 7 and ASEAN+ Services Agreements 202
      AFAS as the Main Driver of Services Liberalization 202
      Comparing Overall and Sectoral Liberalization 203
      Differing Commitments across Different Agreements 203
   4.11.3 Rule-Making 204
4.12 Services Agreements of Individual ASEAN Member States 205
   4.12.1 Liberalization under AFAS versus Bilateral Agreements 206
   4.12.2 Services Agreements of Individual ASEAN Member States with the Same Third-Country Partner 208
   4.12.3 AFAS+ Features of Bilateral PTAs of ASEAN Member States with Third Countries 211
      Singapore–United States Free Trade Agreement 212
      New Zealand–Malaysia Free Trade Agreement 215
4.13 Comprehensive and Progressive Agreement for Trans-Pacific Partnership 216
4.14 Most Favoured Nation Clauses 218
4.15 Tentative Conclusions 225

CONTENTS

  5 Lessons from the EU Relevant to ASEAN Integration in Services 231
    5.1 The EU and Trade in Services: Some Contextual Considerations 231
    5.2 Building the European Internal Market for Services 233
      5.2.1 The Instruments Used 235
      5.2.2 The Steps to Build the Internal Market for Services 237
        The Origins: the First Soft Law Instrument: the Spaak Report 238
        The Founding Treaties: Hard Law Sources 240
        The Recurring Role of Soft Law Instruments 245
        The Case Law: The Input of the European Court of Justice 248
      5.2.3 Completing the Single Market for Services 257
        A New Set of Soft Law Instruments: the Strategies 258
        The Latest Hard Law Instrument: the Services Directive 260
        The Soft Law Instruments that Followed the Services Directive 265
        The Single Market in Services after Brexit 270
    5.3 The EU and Global Trade in Services 271
      5.3.1 The EU and a Multilateral Agreement for Trade in Services 272
      5.3.2 The EU and Bilateral Agreements on Trade in Services 279
      5.3.3 The EU and a Plurilateral Agreement on Services 288
    5.4 Implications for ASEAN: Tentative Conclusions 291
  6 Concluding Thoughts 294

  Index 305

FIGURES

2.1	ASEAN: Sectoral composition of GDP, 2000–16 (or latest available year)	*page* 9
2.2	ASEAN: Employment by sector, 2017 (in per cent)	11
2.3	ASEAN: FDI inflows, 2012–17 (US$bn and percentages)	19
2.4	ASEAN: Sectoral composition of FDI inflows in services, 2012–17 (US$bn)	20
2.5	ASEAN: STRI and per capita income levels, 2012	32
2.6	ASEAN: Overall STRI, 2008 and 2012	33
2.7	Overall STRI: ASEAN-6, ASEAN+3, ASEAN+6, TPP-11	35
2.8	ASEAN: STRI by mode of supply, 2012	35
2.9	ASEAN: Overall STRI by sector, 2008 and 2012	37
2.10	ASEAN: STRI in selected service sectors, 2008 and 2012	38
2.11	ASEAN: STRI by sector and Member State, 2012	40
2.12	STRI by sector: ASEAN and selected regional groupings, 2012	41
2.13	ASEAN: AFAS commitments, applied services regimes and AEC Blueprint goals	42

TABLES

2.1	ASEAN: Share of services trade (exports and imports of commercial services) in GDP, 2016 (or latest available year)	*page* 11
2.2	ASEAN: Exports of commercial services: 2000, 2005 and 2016 (millions of US$)	13
2.3	ASEAN: Logistics performance index (LPI) rankings, 2007–16	24
2.4	Enhanced Trade Index: Ranking of selected ASEAN Member States and RCEP partners, 2010–16	27
2.5	Open markets index: Selected ASEAN Member States, 2017	29
2.6	ASEAN: Global Competitiveness Index rankings, 2009–10 and 2017–18	30
3.1	ASEAN: Selected regulatory, governance and innovation-related indicators, 2017	47
3.2	ASEAN: Corruption perceptions index rankings, 2012–16	49
3.3	ASEAN: Human development index rankings, 2010–15	50
3.4	ASEAN: Judicial independence index rankings, 2017–18	51
3.5	ASEAN: Selected governance indicator rankings, 2016	52

LIST OF TABLES

4.1	AFAS package of commitments and negotiation modalities under ASEAN Economic Ministers	91
4.2	Level of services liberalization in ASEAN and the GATS	118
4.3	Services liberalization in AFAS 7 and gains compared with the GATS	120
4.4	Most liberalized sub-sectors for each ASEAN Member State under AFAS 7	124
4.5	Summary of selected targets set by AEC Blueprint 2015	150
4.6	Number of sub-sectors committed in AFAS Packages 7, 8 and 9	154
4.7	Selected services agreements between ASEAN Member States and third countries	177
4.8	Services liberalization in ASEAN services agreements and ASEAN+ FTAs	190
4.9	Level of liberalization in ASEAN services agreements compared with the GATS	192
4.10	Level of services liberalization of ASEAN Members in selected trade agreements	207
4.11	Level of services liberalization of selected non-ASEAN partners	209

ANNEXES

Annex 4.1 Hoekman Index of Services Liberalization in AFAS and ASEAN FTAs per Sector/Member   *page* 227

GENERAL EDITORS' PREFACE

This monograph is published within the context of a wide-ranging research project entitled 'Integration Through Law: The Role of Law and the Rule of Law in ASEAN Integration' (ITL), undertaken by the Centre for International Law at the National University of Singapore and directed by J. H. H. Weiler and Tan Hsien-Li.

The Preamble to the ASEAN Charter concludes with a single decision: 'We, the Peoples of the Member States of the Association of Southeast Asian Nations ... [h]ereby decide to establish, through this Charter, the legal and institutional framework for ASEAN.' For the first time in its history of over four decades, the Legal and the Institutional were brought to the forefront of ASEAN discourse. The gravitas of the medium, a Charter: the substantive ambition of its content, the creation of three interlocking Communities, and the turn to law and institutions as instruments for realization provide ample justification for this wide-ranging project, to which this monograph is one contribution, examining ASEAN in a comparative context.

That same substantive and, indeed, political ambition means that any single study, illuminating as it may be, will cover but a fraction of the phenomena. Our *modus operandi* in this project was to create teams of researchers from Asia and elsewhere who would contribute individual monographs within an overall framework which we had designed. The project framework, involving several thematic clusters within each monograph, is thus determined by the framework and the place of each monograph within it.

As regards the specific content, however, the authors were free – indeed, encouraged, to define their own understanding of the problem and their own methodology and reach their own conclusions. The thematic structure of the entire project may be found at the end of this Preface.

The project as a whole, and each monograph within it, display several methodological sensibilities.

First, law, in our view, can only be understood and evaluated when situated in its political and economic context. Thus, the first studies in the overall project design are intended to provide the political, economic, cultural and historical context against which one must understand ASEAN, and are written by specialists in these respective disciplines. This context, to a greater or lesser degree, also informs the sensibility of each monograph. There are no 'black-letter law' studies to be found in this project, and, indeed, even in the most technical of areas we encouraged our authors to make their writing accessible to readers of diverse disciplines.

Comparative experience suggests that the success of achieving some of the more ambitious objectives outlined in Article 1 of the Charter will depend in no small measure on the effectiveness of legal principles, legal rules and legal institutions. This is particularly true as regards the success of establishing 'an ASEAN Community comprising the ASEAN Security Community, the ASEAN Economic Community and the ASEAN Socio-Cultural Community as provided for in the Bali Declaration of ASEAN Concord II'. Article 2(2)(n) stipulates the commitment of ASEAN member states to act in accordance with the principle of 'adherence to multilateral trade rules and ASEAN's rules-based regimes for effective implementation of economic commitments and progressive reduction towards elimination of all barriers to regional economic integration.' The ASEAN member states therefore envisage that rules of law and the Rule of Law will become a major feature in the future of ASEAN.

Although, as seen, the Charter understands itself as providing an institutional and legal framework for ASEAN, the question of the 'role of law and the rule of law' is not advocacy but a genuine enquiry in the various substantive areas of the project as to:

- the substantive legal principles and substantive rules of the various ASEAN communities;
- the procedural legal principles and rules governing institutional structures and decision-making processes;
- implementation, enforcement and dispute settlement.

One should not expect a mechanical application of this scheme in each study; rather, a sensibility that refuses to content itself with legal enactments as such and looks to a 'living' notion of law and institutions is ubiquitous in all the studies. Likewise, the project is sensitive to 'non Law'. It variously attempts to locate the appropriate province of the law in this experience. That is, not only the role of law, but also the areas that are and should remain outside the reach of legal institutionalization, with due sensitivity to ASEAN and Asian particularism and political and cultural identities.

The project, and the monographs of which it is made, are not normatively thick. They do not advocate. They are designed, for the most part, to offer reflection, discuss the pros and cons, and in this way enrich public awareness, deepen understanding of different options and in that respect contribute indirectly to policymaking.

This decisive development of ASEAN has been accompanied by a growing Asian interest in various legal and institutional forms of transnational economic and political cooperation, notably the various voices discussing and showing an interest in an East Asia Integration project. The number of Free Trade Agreements (FTAs) and Regional Trade Agreements (RTAs) has increased from six in 1991 to 166 in 2013, with a further 62 in various stages of negotiations.

Methodologically, the project and many of the monographs are comparative in their orientation. Comparative law is one of the few real-life laboratories that we have in which to assess and understand the operation of different legal and institutional models designed to tackle similar objectives and problems. One should not need to put one's own hand in the fire to learn that it scorches. With that in mind a couple of monographs offer both conceptual reflection and pragmatic 'tool boxing' on some of the key elements featuring in all regional integration systems.

Comparative law is in part about divergence: it is a potent tool and means to understand one's own uniqueness. One understands better the uniqueness of Apples by comparing them to Oranges. You understand better the specialness of a Toyota by comparing it to a Ford.

GENERAL EDITORS' PREFACE

Comparative law is also about convergence: it is a potent tool and means to understand how what are seemingly different phenomena are part of a broader trend, an insight which may enhance both self-understanding and policy potentialities.

Although many studies in the project could have almost immediate policy implications, as would the project as a whole, this is not its only or even principal purpose. There is a rich theory of federalism which covers many countries around the world. There is an equally rich theory of European integration, which has been associated with the advent Union. There is also considerable learning on Free Trade Areas and the like.

To date, the study of the legal aspects of ASEAN specifically and other forms of Asian legal integration has been derivative of, and dependent on, theoretical and conceptual insight which were developed in different contexts.

One principal objective of ITL and these monographs will be to put in place the building blocks for an authentic body of ASEAN and Asian integration theory developed in, and with sensitivity to, the particularities and peculiarities of the region and continent. A theory and conceptual framework of Asian legal integration will signal the coming of age of research of and in the region itself.

Although the monographs form part of an overarching project, we asked our authors to write each as a 'standalone' – not assuming that their readers would have consulted any of the other titles. Indeed, the project is rich and few will read all monographs. We encourage readers to pick and choose from the various monographs and design their own menu. There is, on occasion, some overlap in providing, for example, background information on ASEAN in different studies. That is not only inevitable but desirable in a project of this amplitude.

The world is increasingly witnessing a phenomenon of interlocking regional organization where the experience of one feeds on the others. In some way, the intellectual, disciplinary and comparative sensibility of this project is a microcosm of the world it describes.

The range of topics covered in this series comprises:

The General Architecture and Aspirations of ASEAN
The Governance and Management of ASEAN: Instruments, Institutions, Monitoring, Compliance and Dispute Resolution
Legal Regimes in ASEAN
The ASEAN Economic Community ASEAN and the World
The Substantive Law of ASEAN

ACKNOWLEDGEMENTS

The authors are grateful to Federico Lupo Pasini, Yaxuan Chen, Bharti Lamba, Simon Lacey and Justine Lan for their helpful background research and suggestions; to members of the ASEAN Secretariat and researchers at ERIA for helpful discussions; and to participants at seminars and conferences at which various elements of this study have been presented during the course of its preparation. The authors are also grateful to two anonymous referees for their helpful comments on an earlier version of this manuscript. All remaining errors are the authors'.

ABBREVIATIONS

AANZFTA	Agreement Establishing the ASEAN–Australia–New Zealand Free Trade Area
ABIF	ASEAN Banking Integration Framework
ACFTA	Trade in Services Agreement of the Framework Agreement on Comprehensive Economic Cooperation between ASEAN and the People's Republic of China
ACIA	ASEAN Comprehensive Investment Agreement
ACP	African–Caribbean–Pacific
AEC	ASEAN Economic Community
AEM	ASEAN Economic Ministers
AFAS	ASEAN Framework Agreement on Services
AFTA	ASEAN Free Trade Area
AIA	ASEAN Investment Area
AIFTA	Framework Agreement on Comprehensive Economic Co-operation between the Republic of India and ASEAN

LIST OF ABBREVIATIONS

AJCEP	ASEAN–Japan Comprehensive Economic Partnership
AKFTA	Trade in Services Agreement under the Framework Agreement on Comprehensive Economic Cooperation among the Governments of the Member Countries of ASEAN and the Republic of Korea
AMS	ASEAN Member States
ANZSCEP	Agreement between New Zealand and Singapore on a Closer Economic Partnership
APEC	Asia-Pacific Economic Cooperation
APTA	Asia-Pacific Trade Agreement
AQRF	ASEAN Qualifications Reference Framework
ASEAN	Association of South East Asian Nations
ATIGA	ASEAN Trade in Goods Agreement
ATISA	ASEAN Trade in Services Agreement
ATPRS	ASEAN Tourism Professionals Registration System
BIMSTEC	Bay of Bengal Initiative for Multi-Sectorial Technical and Economic Cooperation
BJEPA	Brunei–Japan Economic Partnership Agreement
BTA	bilateral trade agreement

xxv

LIST OF ABBREVIATIONS

CAFTA-DR	Central American Common Market, the Dominican Republic and the United States
CCI	Coordinating Committee on Investment
CCP	common commercial policy
CCS	Coordinating Committee on Services
CECA	India–Singapore Comprehensive Economic Cooperation Agreement
CEPT	Common Effective Preferential Tariff
CETA	EU–Canada Comprehensive Economic and Trade Agreement
CFTA	Continental Free Trade Area
CLMV	Cambodia, Laos, Myanmar and Vietnam
CPTPP	Comprehensive and Progressive Agreement for Trans-Pacific Partnership
CSFTA	China–Singapore Free Trade Agreement
DCFTA	Deep and Comprehensive Free Trade Areas
ECJ	European Court of Justice
EEC	European Economic Community
EFTA	European Free Trade Association/ European Free Trade Area
EPA	economic partnership agreement
ERIA	Economic Research Institute for ASEAN and East Asia

LIST OF ABBREVIATIONS

ESFTA	European Free Trade Association–Singapore Free Trade Agreement
ETI	Enhanced Trade Index
EU	European Union
EUSAFTA	European Union–Singapore Free Trade Agreement
EVFTA	Free Trade Agreement between the European Union and Vietnam
FDI	foreign direct investment
GATS	General Agreement on Trade in Services
GATT	General Agreement on Tariffs and Trade
GDP	gross domestic product
GSFTA	Gulf Co-operation Council Singapore Free Trade Agreement
HRD	human resource development
ICC Index	International Chamber of Commerce's Open Markets Index
ICT	information and communications technology
IJEPA	Agreement between Japan and the Republic of Indonesia for an Economic Partnership
IPA	investment promotion agencies
IT	information technology
JPEPA	Japan–Philippine Economic Partnership Agreement

LIST OF ABBREVIATIONS

JSEPA	Agreement between Japan and the Republic of Singapore for a New-Age Economic Partnership Agreement
JTEPA	Agreement between Japan and the Kingdom of Thailand for an Economic Partnership
KSFTA	Korea–Singapore Free Trade Agreement
MAFTA	Malaysia–Australia Free Trade Agreement
MFN	most-favoured-nation
MICECA	Malaysia–India Comprehensive Economic Cooperation Agreement
MJEPA	Malaysia–Japan Economic Partnership Agreement
MNE	multinational enterprise
MNP	movement of natural persons
MNZFTA	Malaysia–New Zealand FTA
MPCEPA	Malaysia–Pakistan Closer Economic Partnership Agreement
MRA	mutual recognition agreement
NAFTA	North American Free Trade Agreement
NTA	New Transatlantic Agenda
NTMA	New Transatlantic Marketplace
OECE	Organization for European Economic Co-operation
PDR	People's Democratic Republic
PeSFTA	Peru–Singapore Free Trade Agreement

LIST OF ABBREVIATIONS

PSFTA	Panama–Singapore Free Trade Agreement
PTA	preferential trade agreement
R&D	research and development
RCEP	Regional Comprehensive Economic Partnership
SAFTA	Singapore–Australia Free Trade Agreement
SCP	Single Contact Points
SCRFTA	Singapore–Costa Rica Free Trade Agreement
SEOM	Senior Economic Officials Meeting
SJFTA	Singapore–Jordan Free Trade Agreement
STRI	Services Trade Restrictiveness Index
TAFTA	Thailand–Australia Closer Free Trade Agreement
TFEU	Treaty on the Functioning of the European Union
TiSA	Trade in Services Agreement
TPSEP	Trans Pacific Strategic Economic Partnership Agreement involving Brunei Darussalam, Chile, New Zealand and Singapore
Trans-Pacific SEP	Trans-Pacific Strategic Economic Partnership Agreement
TRSFTA	Turkey–Singapore Free Trade Agreement
TTIP	Transatlantic Trade and Investment Partnership

LIST OF ABBREVIATIONS

UK	United Kingdom
US	United States
USSFTA	US–Singapore Free Trade Agreement
USTR	US Trade Representative
VJEP	Agreement between Japan and the Socialist Republic of Viet Nam for an Economic Partnership
VKFTA	Vietnam–Korea Free Trade Agreement
VN-EAEU FTA	Free Trade Agreement between Vietnam and the Eurasian Economic Union
WTO	World Trade Organization

Chapter 1

Introduction

The Member States of the Association of South East Asian Nations (ASEAN) set themselves the ambitious aim of establishing a region-wide economic community by 2015, and to deepen it in the context of the ASEAN Economic Community (AEC) Blueprint 2025. In striving to achieve such ambitious objectives, there are strong reasons, both internal to ASEAN's own integration process and linked to the region's deepening ties with a dense layer of external economic partners, to believe that service sector reforms – and trade and investment in services more particularly – will occupy a place of choice in the region's policy pantheon.

The region's rapid economic advance and the steady rise in living standards that have been achieved in recent decades have largely been anchored in a growth model assigning to external demand and insertion into global value chains, particularly in manufacturing, dominant roles. Such progress could not have proven possible without marked improvements in the efficiency with which the region's underlying services infrastructure has sustained productivity growth in upstream and downstream industries, from natural resource extraction and agriculture to manufacturing and services themselves. For the most part, however, such efficiency gains appear to have resulted more from unilateral policy benevolence than from concerted collective action initiatives, though negotiated and more institutionalized policy approaches have exerted an increasing influence on policy trajectories in recent years, particularly in the wake both of the 1997–98 financial crisis that engulfed several ASEAN Member States and as a more recent response to the growing economic and political ascendency of China and India as regional powers.

The AEC Blueprint spells out a comprehensive set of treaty-based objectives through which Member States aim to work together in freeing up trade and investment in services. To date, they have pursued such objectives under the ASEAN Framework Agreement on Services (AFAS), an incomplete framework of rules and market opening commitments that is set to be deepened under the proposed development of an ASEAN Trade in Services Agreement (ATISA) as well as through the ASEAN Comprehensive Investment Agreement (ACIA).

This volume takes stock of the experience of ASEAN Member States (AMS) in pursuing trade and investment liberalization in services. It identifies a number of the challenges that the regional grouping can be expected to encounter on the way to realizing the AEC Blueprint 2025 aims. The volume is structured as five chapters. Following a brief introduction in Chapter 1, Chapter 2 situates the role of services and services trade in the ASEAN economic landscape, providing a range of contextual metrics with which to gauge the contribution that services and services trade are making to the region's insertion into regional and global value chains and the overall regulatory and institutional setting in which such efforts proceed. The chapter further investigates the *actual* (as opposed to *negotiated*) degree of openness of service regimes maintained in a sample of leading AMS, using a database developed by the World Bank Group.[1]

Despite the considerable progress that has been achieved under AFAS, as well as under a growing network of preferential trade and investment agreements entered into by AMS with countries in the immediate neighbourhood and beyond (trends which Chapter 4 probes in detail), the empirical evidence adduced on *applied* regulatory regimes in Chapter 2 depicts a region that paradoxically still ranks among the world's most restrictive in the services field alongside South Asia and the Middle East and North African region, with a policy stance towards services trade that is some 38 per cent more restrictive than the world average. ASEAN is also, alongside Sub-Saharan Africa, the integration process that displays the greatest intra-regional policy variance, suggesting that the various liberalization packages that have been pursued under AFAS have yet to translate into significant region-wide policy convergence.

Chapter 3 explores whether ASEAN displays the attributes of an optimal regulatory convergence area for services, examining a number of factors likely to challenge the pursuit of an integration agenda in policy environment characterized by a continued aversion towards more institutionalized forms of normative convergence and the regional pooling of regulatory sovereignty that a sustained commitment to deep integration generally requires in the services field.

[1] See the World Bank's Services Trade Restrictiveness Index at http://iresearch.worldbank.org/servicetrade/home.htm

INTRODUCTION

As intimated above, Chapter 4 offers readers a detailed reading of the progress achieved to date in the *negotiated* opening of services markets under both AFAS and preferential trade agreements (PTAs) entered into (or currently being negotiated) with third parties both by ASEAN as a whole and by individual AMS. The discussion uncovers a rich and novel trajectory of progressive liberalization under AFAS, with extensive recourse made to an evolving set of negotiating parameters designed explicitly to account – and respond to the political demand – for variable geometry in market opening given prevailing ASEAN-wide income and implementation gaps. ASEAN's development of various formula-based approaches to market opening stands out among the regional grouping's most innovative contributions to services rule-making – one that has been increasingly replicated in other PTAs as well as at the World Trade Organization (WTO) level.

Chapter 4 further discusses the need for AMS to revisit and complete a rule-making template in services that has remained incomplete and is likely to be no longer attuned to the exigencies of modern tradecraft in a sector that has experienced significant structural change since the AFAS rule-book was designed and adopted in the early days of the WTO's General Agreement on Trade in Services. This is presumably what ASEAN Member States aim to achieve under ATISA. Chapter 4 concludes by exploring the iterative relationship between internal (i.e. intra-ASEAN) and external liberalization of services markets, highlighting some of the challenges and risks arising from ASEAN's negotiation of a multiplicity of potentially overlapping agreements, culminating most recently with the Comprehensive and Progressive Trans Pacific Partnership (CPTPP) whose WTO and AFAS+ content is sure to exert an important influence on both the nature and pace of future intra-ASEAN integration in the services field.

Chapter 5 chronicles the richness of the European Union's (EU) journey on services trade and investment, drawing possible lessons for the future of ASEAN institutional design in this area. The chapter retraces the historical origins and jurisprudence-led evolution of the internal market rules governing trade and investment in services among an expanding group of advanced nations, and explores how the experience gained in building the internal market both influenced and paralleled the EU's engagement with the rest of the world in services trade. In particular, Chapter 5 documents how the EU experiment helped to shape the nascent multilateral body of rules governing services trade in the WTO, which was subsequently replicated in a large number of services PTAs, including AFAS.

The depth and range of legal instruments and institutions deployed in the EU in pursuit of market integration objectives in services markets knows no equivalent. Such uniqueness needs to be borne in mind in pondering whether, how and to what extent lessons from the EU's ongoing experiments in market integration are replicable in other regional settings and policy contexts, including within ASEAN.

In most instances, the analysis on offer in Chapter 5 suggests that the EU model is not easily transposable, resting as it does on a degree of pooling of regulatory sovereignty that few regional groupings appear willing to replicate or even aspire to. This most certainly is the case for ASEAN. Chapter 5 also recalls that EU advances relate in no small measure to the Union's first-mover advantages, with progress rooted in over six decades of policy- and rule-making experimentation on the internal front and close to three decades of external experimentation. Such a path afforded all key EU stakeholders – Member States, the European Commission, regulatory agencies and the European Court of Justice (ECJ), as well as private actors – considerable space in which to learn by doing, make mistakes, learn from them and iterate an evolving governance regime for services production, trade and investment.

Chapter 6 closes the work by offering a number of concluding remarks.

Chapter 2

Services and Services Trade in ASEAN: Trends and Policy Context

2.1 Background

The process of economic modernization typically entails a number of structural shifts that assign to services a growing role in output, employment and income growth, as well as in international trade and investment. In recent decades, much of the world has witnessed a steady shift of resources away from agricultural production towards manufacturing and services as technology evolves, human capital is enhanced and incomes rise.

Although cross-country differences in the pace and texture of structural change remain pronounced in some instances, the member countries of the Association of Southeast Asian Nations (ASEAN) are no exception to the trends depicted above. Indeed, as the data reviewed in this study's opening section attests, services show every sign of assuming a more central and dynamic role in the region's development process.

The section that follows provides empirical and political economy context to the study's subsequent analysis by reviewing salient developments in service-sector reforms and the growing role that trade and investment in services is assuming in ASEAN's development trajectory and the attainment of the regional grouping's AEC 2025 Blueprint objectives.

2.2 Trends in Aggregate Output

Figure 2.1 traces the evolution of services in ASEAN value-added, offering a snapshot of the structural composition of output and its evolution over the period from 2000 to 2016.

The figures reveal that a number of pronounced inter-sectoral shifts are currently under way within ASEAN. For one, the region as a whole has witnessed a significant drop in the share of agriculture in gross domestic product (GDP), whose share in aggregate output contracted markedly – from 21 per cent to 9 per cent – over the period. As might be expected, the steepest declines were observed, among the region's poorest members – Cambodia, Lao People's Democratic Republic (PDR), Myanmar and Vietnam – as the sub-grouping's income growth accelerated and agricultural productivity increased.

ASEAN's aggregate shift away from agriculture was directed in part towards manufacturing output, whose share in GDP increased from 36 per cent to 38 per cent over the last decade and a half, with services experiencing the greatest structural shift, as tertiary sector output grew from 43 per cent to just over 50 per cent of aggregate GDP. Over the decade to 2016, the share of services in the GDP of individual ASEAN Member States increased by between 2 and 4 percentage points on average, with Malaysia recording the largest structural shift with a rise of 7.6 percentage points, followed by Myanmar and Indonesia with 4.7 and

TRENDS IN AGGREGATE OUTPUT

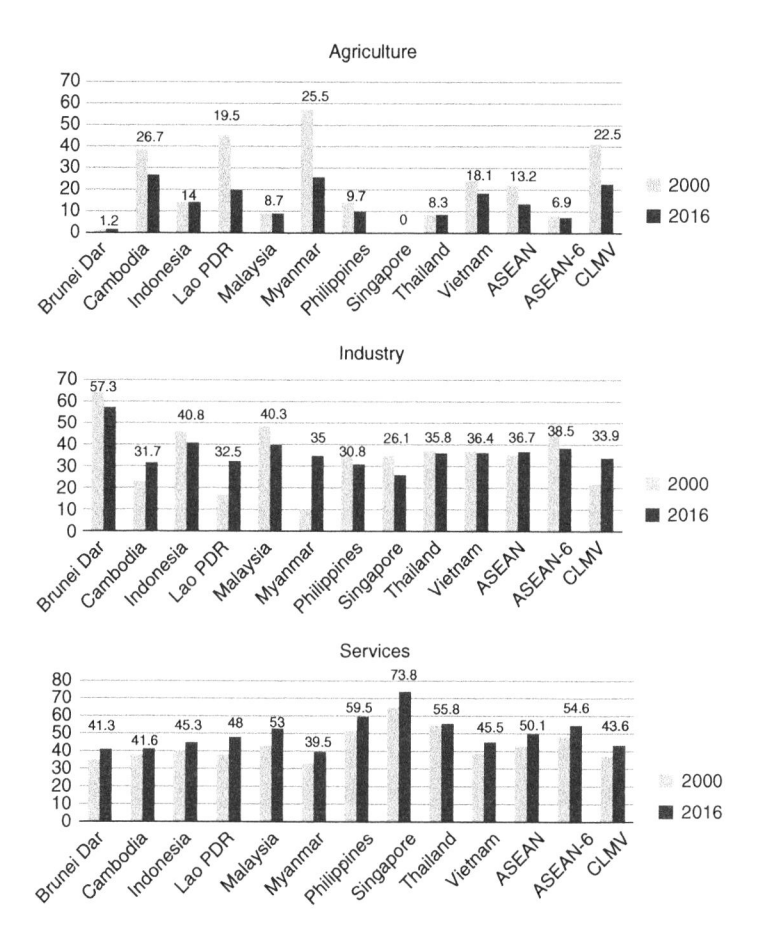

Figure 2.1 ASEAN: Sectoral composition of GDP, 2000–16 (or latest available year)

4.5 percentage points, respectively. Placing the focus on ASEAN as a whole masks important intra-regional differences, with Cambodia, Laos, Myanmar and Vietnam (CLMV) countries exhibiting far more pronounced shifts in aggregate output relative to their more mature ASEAN-6 brethren. Ranging from a low of 39 per cent in Myanmar to a high of 74 per cent in Singapore, services account for 55 per cent of output among the ASEAN-6 sub-grouping, compared with a contribution of 44 per cent of GDP for the region's CLMV members.

2.3 Trends in Employment

Figure 2.2 shows that, for the region as a whole, services supply over a third (35.2 per cent) of total employment.

However, as in the case of aggregate output, trends within the region exhibit stark variance, with services employment ranging from a low of 18 per cent in Lao PDR to a high of 83 per cent in Singapore. Throughout the region, the relatively high share of employment in public services and in wholesale and retail trade appear suggestive of services markets that are still somewhat biased towards domestic rather than foreign (i.e. export) markets, though the retail sector does exhibit a greater trade intensity as a result of higher intra- and extra-regional foreign direct investment (FDI) in recent years.

2.4 Trends in Trade Integration

Table 2.1 measures the level of trade integration in ASEAN services markets by calculating the share of commercial services exports and imports in GDP.

ASEAN's level of trade integration in services averaged 24.4 per cent in 2016 – a level that, as elsewhere, stands markedly lower than the service sector's contribution to output and

TRENDS IN TRADE INTEGRATION

Table 2.1 *ASEAN: Share of services trade (exports and imports of commercial services) in GDP, 2016 (or latest available year)*

Country	Share of services trade in GDP (%)
Brunei Darussalam	19
Cambodia	29
Indonesia	6
Lao PDR*	10
Myanmar*	10
Malaysia	25
Philippines	18
Singapore	103
Thailand	27
Vietnam	15

Source: Trade data was retrieved from WTO Statistics Database (accessed 21 January 2018), available at: http://stat.wto.org/Home/WSDBHome.aspx?Language=GDP data was retrieved from the World Bank Data (accessed 21 January 2018), available at: http://databank.worldbank.org/data/reports.aspx?source=world-development-indicators

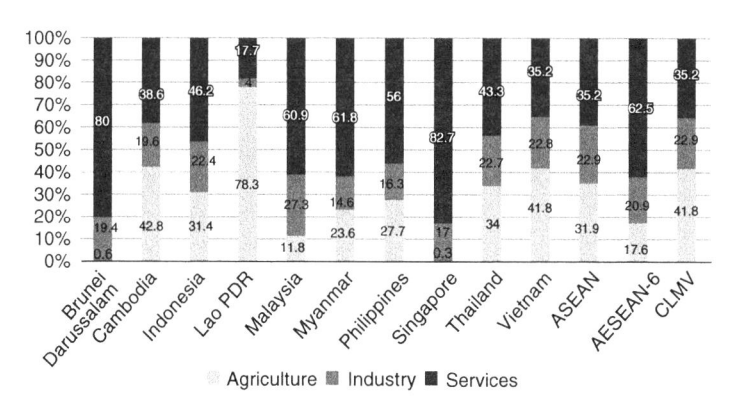

Figure 2.2 ASEAN: Employment by sector, 2017 (in per cent)

11

employment. Once more, ASEAN is characterized by marked internal divergence, with trade integration levels in services ranging from a high of 103 per cent in Singapore to a low of 5.79 per cent in Indonesia – numbers that parallel important differences in the make-up of regional economies, relative factor endowments and resulting specialization patterns. Absent Singapore's outlying performance, trade integration levels within ASEAN stood at 16.95 per cent at year end 2016.

2.5 Trends in Services Trade and Investment

2.5.1 Trade

Table 2.2 traces the evolution of ASEAN's exports of commercial services over the period from 2000 to 2016[1] and situates such trends against performances observed in China, India and the rest of the world.

The data reveals a number of contrasting trends. Among these is the fact that ASEAN services exports have grown markedly over the period, rising in nominal value by an aggregate factor of 4.8.

---

[1] It needs to be borne in mind that the data presented in Table 2.2 captures cross-border trade in services transactions (so-called 'Mode 1' trade in services) as recorded in national balance of payments statistics. If one recalls that the definition of 'trade' in services used in a negotiating context covers four modes of supply (chief among which is trade occurring through the establishment of a commercial presence in a foreign territory, which, according to World Trade Organization (WTO) estimates, accounts for some 60 per cent of aggregate services trade), the data presented in Table 2.2 represents a markedly lower bound of the true level of services trade.

Table 2.2 ASEAN: Exports of commercial services: 2000, 2005 and 2016 (millions of US$)

Reporter	Exports of commercial services (2000)	Share of world exports (%)	Exports of commercial services (2005)	Share of world exports (%)	Exports of commercial services (2016)	Share of world export (%)s	2000–16 export value ratio
Brunei Darussalam	198	0.01	616	0.02	482	0.01	2.43
Cambodia	423	0.03	1 064	0.04	3 850	0.08	9.10
Indonesia	5 061	0.34	12 642	0.49	23 473	0.49	4.64
Lao PDR*	134	0.01	184	0.01	798	0.02	5.96
Myanmar*	13 812	0.93	19 637	0.76	33 837	0.70	2.45
Malaysia	453	0.03	259	0.01	3 800	0.08	8.39
Philippines	3 377	0.23	8 611	0.33	31 340	0.65	9.28
Singapore	28 427	1.91	46 243	1.78	149 360	3.11	5.25
Thailand	13 785	0.92	19 773	0.76	66 128	1.38	4.80
Vietnam	2 702	0.18	4 232	0.16	12 236	0.25	4.53
ASEAN	68 372	4.58	113 261	4.36	325 304	6.77	4.76
China	30 146	2.02	77 974	3.00	207 275	4.31	6.88
India	16 031	1.07	51 851	2.00	161 250	3.35	10.06
World	1 491 320	100.00	2 597 200	100.00	4 807 690	100.00	3.22

Sources: Trade data was retrieved from WTO Statistics Database (accessed 21 January 2018), available at: http://stat.wto.org/Home/WSDBHome.aspx?Language= GDP data was retrieved from the World Bank Data (accessed 21 January 2018), available at: http://databank.worldbank.org/data/reports.aspx?source=world-development-indicators

Note: Figures from 2000 follows BPM5, while the rest follow BPM6.

* 2015 (instead of 2016) figures are used in the case of Lao PDR and Myanmar (the latest available data)

At the end of 2016, ASEAN exports of commercial services stood at US$325 billion, accounting for 6.8 per cent of the world's total – a level 48 per cent higher than that obtaining in 2000 (4.6 per cent). Within the regional grouping, the most notable gains in export growth were registered by the Philippines, whose nominal exports grew in value by a factor of 9.3 over the period. Other notable export performances were those of Cambodia, whose services exports grew more than nine-fold over the period (9.1), followed by Malaysia (8.4) and Lao PDR (6.0). Meanwhile, services imports in ASEAN have also grown at a brisk pace, reaching US$317 billion at the end of 2016 – double the level of a decade earlier. The above trends have transformed the region as a whole into a net exporter of services, with evidence of significant underlying structural transformation, sustained value-chain insertion and steady gains in export competitiveness in services.

While the trends depicted above show that ASEAN as a whole has experienced a non-trivial gain in export competitiveness in services relative to the rest of the world over the last decade, such gains need to be seen against those observed in China and India – two regional powers with whom ASEAN has close economic and commercial links and with whose firms ASEAN service providers compete directly in a number of important market segments. Both China and India registered sharply higher relative export gains over the same period. Indeed, whereas aggregate ASEAN exports of commercial services stood 48 per cent higher than the *combined* value of Chinese and Indian exports in 2000, by 2016 ASEAN's total exports of commercial services were 12 per cent lower than the aggregate total of those of its two powerful neighbours.

The data presented in Table 2.2 indicates a prevalence of asymmetrical export capacity within ASEAN. This is a likely source of policy concern, as it is symptomatic of important development gaps that are likely to stand in the way of the full realization of the potential gains from an ASEAN-wide single market and production base. What is more, the last decade has witnessed little change in the share of *intra*-ASEAN trade in services, with both exports and (less so) imports of services *among* members today at roughly the level that they were in 2005. Among the possible reasons that could be adduced in explaining such an observed discrepancy is the generally weaker – and more generally 'back loaded' – pace of market opening under the ASEAN Framework Agreement on Services (AFAS) relative to the progress achieved for trade in goods under ASEAN Trade in Goods Agreement (ATIGA) as well as the regional grouping's still-dominant reliance on manufactures as a source of export-driven growth. ASEAN's services trade remains relatively small when compared with merchandise exports. However, the gap is narrowing. By 2016, services export represented 14.7 per cent of the regional grouping's merchandise exports, which is a marked increase over the 9.50 per cent level attained a decade earlier. Meanwhile, ASEAN services imports represented 27.7 per cent of the volume of goods imports in 2016 – also a sizeable increase from the 21.2 per cent level observed a decade earlier.

Data on the sectoral composition of ASEAN services trade shows that ASEAN Member States continue to export mainly 'traditional services', such as transportation, travel and tourism services. On the whole, they have been less successful in tapping into new services opportunities, such as information technology (IT) and business-related services. The Philippines and Singapore – and, to a lesser degree, Malaysia – are the main exceptions in the region. In the case of the Philippines, its business processing outsourcing and IT-enabled services exports have witnessed explosive growth, with cross-border sales of some IT-related services exceeding those of India. Meanwhile, Singapore's exports of modern services, such as professional, education, finance and other business services, have developed steadily since the mid-1990s, transforming the country into the region's undisputed knowledge service hub.[2]

When looked at in terms of recent growth performance, a more upbeat measure of the region's ongoing structural transformation towards higher value-adding activities emerges. ASEAN's three fastest-growing service sectors over the period from 2006 to 2016 related, on the export side, to services linked to intellectual property (royalty payments and associated fees), insurance- and pension-related services, as well as telecommunications and information and communications technology (ICT) services. On the import side, where transportation services naturally predominate, given the region's reliance on exports of manufactured goods within regional and global production networks, telecommunications

---

[2] ASEAN Secretariat and World Bank Group (2015), *ASEAN Services Integration Report* (Jakarta and Washington, DC: ASEAN Secretariat and World Bank Group), p. ii.

and ICT, and maintenance and repair services, as well as financial services, have exhibited the fastest growth over the past decade.

The buoyancy of the ASEAN tourism sector helps to explain why the region as a whole was able to cushion the impact of the 2008–09 global financial crisis, the effects of which manifested themselves in a contraction of manufactured goods exports rather than in services, even as the region registered a dip in services trade during this period.

2.5.2 Investment

No discussion of services trade is complete without accounting for the central role that has been assumed by cross-border investment as the leading vector of service sector internationalization. As it is in much of the rest of the world, such a trend is much in evidence in Southeast Asia. ASEAN as a whole absorbed an estimated US$137 billion of FDI inflows in 2017 – a record amount for the region – which placed it as the leading recipient in the world. Intra-ASEAN investment remained strong, accounting for a quarter of total inflows to the grouping. This reflected growing regional investment opportunities, as well as the financial strength of ASEAN-based multinational enterprises (MNEs) and their intensified drive to internationalize in manufacturing and services alike.[3] Meanwhile, FDI outflows from the region, originating

---

[3] ASEAN Secretariat and UNCTAD (2017). *ASEAN Investment Report 2017: Foreign Direct Investment and Economic Zones in ASEAN* (Jakarta: ASEAN Secretariat and Geneva: UNCTAD), pp. XVII–XVIII.

mainly from Singapore, Thailand and Malaysia, stood at US$55 billion at the end of 2017 – a 38 per cent contraction over the record level achieved in 2014.[4]

The ASEAN Secretariat reports that a preponderant share of FDI directed towards the sub-region goes to service industries. This share has rarely dipped below 60 per cent over the past decade, replicating levels commonly associated with the world's most advanced economies (see Figure 2.3).

Four sectors – finance; wholesale and retail trade; transport and storage; and real estate services – have attracted the largest annual volumes of FDI inflows in the service sector over the 2012–17 period (see Figure 2.4).

Such trends have tended to reinforce the dominance of Singapore as a regional services hub, as the island state alone has absorbed close to 60 per cent of ASEAN-wide FDI inflows over the last decade. They are furthermore illustrative of persistent region-wide disparities that may pose obstacles in fulfilling ASEAN's aim of promoting an inclusive regional development path.

The absence of detailed disaggregated bilateral data on intra-ASEAN trade and investment in services continues to inhibit informed policy research on the region's unfolding economic transformation. Correcting such an informational deficit needs to command far greater resolve among regional policy makers as ASEAN Trade in Services Agreement (ATISA) negotiations get under way and as strategies for addressing the development gaps identified above and for

---

[4] UNCTAD (2018), *World Investment Report 2018: Investment and New Industrial Policies* (Geneva: United Nations), pp. 202–3.

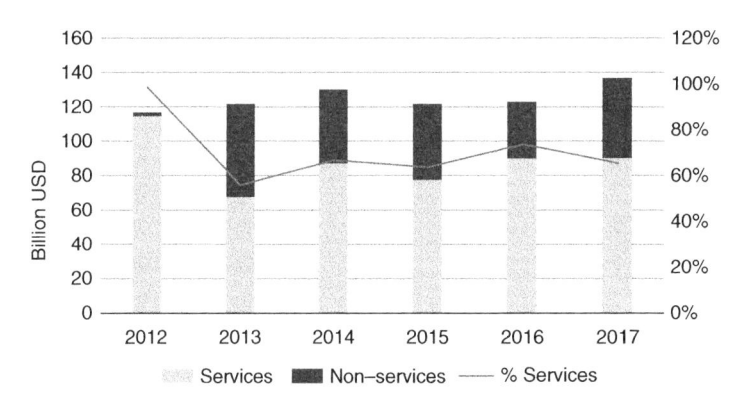

Figure 2.3 ASEAN: FDI inflows, 2012–17 (US$bn and percentages)

nurturing a more robust supply and employment response in domestic and regional service markets through targeted reform measures become ever more pressing.

2.6 Services and ASEAN Value Chains

The fact that ASEAN services imports have broadly kept pace with the region's exports over the past decade, and the steady growth in intra-ASEAN FDI, both lend support to the increasing fragmentation of production and the growing intensity of trade in intermediate products – both goods and services – that has come in its wake regionally. The growth of ASEAN imports may also be attributed in part to the steady pursuit of market opening under both AFAS and the ASEAN Economic Community (AEC) as well as under a mushrooming number of preferential trade agreements (PTAs) covering services that ASEAN as a whole, and individual Member States, have

SERVICES AND SERVICES TRADE IN ASEAN

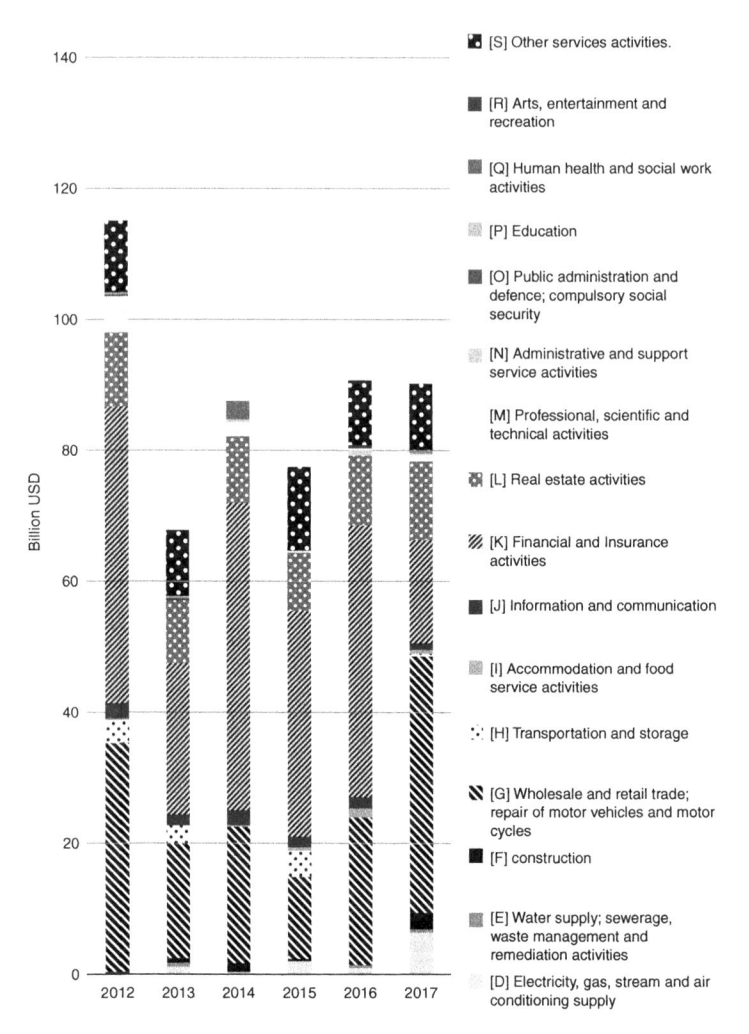

Figure 2.4 ASEAN: Sectoral composition of FDI inflows in services, 2012–17 (US$bn)

concluded with third countries in recent years.[5] The rising demand for regional governance, both within ASEAN and in its immediate neighbourhood, and the growing institutionalization of an integration process long driven more by the invisible hand of markets than by treaty-based instruments, can be seen as a direct corollary of the growing insertion of ASEAN producers in international production networks, often referred to as 'global value chains' even if, in most instances, their regional dimension predominates.

The rising salience of supply chain production is much at work in ASEAN – more so than in most developing regions of the world. The increasing 'servicification' of the ASEAN ecosystem, characterized by the growing share of services in the value of final output and exports, holds important implications for services trade and investment and an acceleration of service sector reforms, both region-wide and within individual ASEAN Member States (AMS).

Evidence of ongoing changes in the composition of trade is indeed particularly noticeable when trade data is expressed in value-added rather than in gross terms. Such

[5] For a fuller discussion of services PTAs in Asia, see ASEAN (2017), 'ASEAN Services Report 2017: The Evolving Landscape' (Jakarta: ASEAN Secretariat (August)). See also Rupa Chanda, 'Mapping the Universe of Services Disciplines in Asian PTAs' (2011) NCCR Working Paper No. 2011/34 (Bern: World Trade Institute); PECC and ADBI, 'Services Trade: Approaches for the 21st Century, Singapore and Tokyo: Pacific Economic Cooperation Council and Asian Development Bank Institute' (2012); and Ben Shepherd and Gloria O. Pasadilla, 'Services as a New Engine of Growth for ASEAN, the People's Republic of China, and India' (2012), ADBI Working Paper Series No. 349 (Asian Development Bank Institute).

revised calculations offer tangible signs of the greater role that services are playing in ASEAN's overall export performance.

In much of those ASEAN countries in which data is available, the share of services in total exports has essentially doubled over the past decade – a trend that has been even more pronounced in the cases of Indonesia, Singapore and Vietnam.[6] Here again, the growing demand for services liberalization, both within ASEAN under AFAS and through the pursuit of a number of negotiating targets under the AEC Blueprint, can be understood in the context of the increasing 'servicification' of ASEAN economies.

As is now increasingly appreciated by policy makers, moving intermediate goods and services across borders multiple times prior to final assembly requires well-developed transport and logistics services, underpinned by modern infrastructure and trade-facilitating regulatory ecosystems. The recent theoretical interest in trade costs and its trade facilitation policy and rule-making corollary have done much to sensitize policy makers to the critical nexus between service sector efficiency and export competitiveness, particularly in the context of production networks and supply-chain assembly.

Using machinery parts and components as a percentage of total exports as a proxy for the degree of participation in internationalized production, recent

---

[6] Gloria O. Pasadilla and Christopher Findlay. 'APEC, Services and Supply Chains: Taking Stock of Services-Related Activities in APEC' (2014) APEC Policy Support Unit Policy Brief No. 9 (Asia-Pacific Economic Co-operation: http://publications.apec.org/publication-detail.php?pub_id=1506 (accessed 14 March 2015).

empirical work has shown, somewhat reassuringly from the perspective of deepened integration, that ASEAN countries over-perform their peers from other regions with respect to the average relationship between services sector development and participation in production networks.

There is, similarly, growing empirical evidence confirming the strong links between international production networks and logistics performance.[7] Recent work has indeed shown trade in machinery parts and components to be significantly more sensitive to improvements in logistics performance than is the case for trade in finished goods. Such effects have traditionally been found to be particularly strong in the Asia-Pacific region, which is consistent with the importance of internationalized production throughout the region.[8]

Table 2.3 offers a glimpse of recent changes in ASEAN's logistics performance over the 2007–16 period.

Somewhat preoccupying is the fact that, of the nine AMS for which data from the World Bank's Logistics Performance Index is available, only two countries –

---

[7] Daniel Saslavsky and Ben Shepherd (2012), 'Facilitating International Production Networks: The Role of Trade Logistics', World Bank Policy Research Working Paper No. 6224 (Washington, DC: The World Bank).

[8] See Martin Roy, Pierre Sauvé and Anirudh Shingal (2017), 'Do WTO+ commitments in services trade agreements reflect a quest for optimal regulatory convergence? Evidence from Asia' *The World Economy*, 10(11) (18 October 2017), 123–50. Available at: http://dx.doi.org/10.1111/twec.12574. See also Pierre Sauvé and Anirudh Shingal (2016), 'Why do countries enter into preferential agreements on trade in services? Assessing the potential for negotiated regulatory convergence in Asian services markets' *Asian Development Review*, 33(1) (March 2016), available at: www.mitpressjournals.org/doi/pdf/10.1162/ADEV_a_00061

Table 2.3 *ASEAN: Logistics performance index (LPI) rankings, 2007–16*

Country	2016 Ranking	2016 LPI score	2007 Ranking	2007 LPI score	Score difference (2017–16)	Change in ranking (2007–16)
Brunei Darussalam	70	2.87	n.a.	n.a.	n.a.	n.a.
Cambodia	73	2.8	81	2.5	0.3	8
Indonesia	63	2.98	43	3.01	−0.03	−20
Lao PDR	152	2.07	117	2.25	−0.18	−35
Myanmar	113	2.46	147	1.86	0.6	34
Malaysia	32	3.43	27	3.48	−0.05	−5
Philippines	71	2.86	65	2.69	0.17	−6
Singapore	5	4.14	1	4.19	−0.05	−4
Thailand	45	3.26	31	3.31	−0.05	−14
Vietnam	64	2.98	53	2.89	0.09	−11

Source: World Bank Logistics Performance Index Database (accessed 21 January 2018), available at: https://lpi.worldbank.org

Note: LPI is a summary indicator of logistics sector performance. It is rated from 1 (lowest) to 5 (highest). The 2016 data covers 160 economies and the 2015 data covers 150 economies

Cambodia and Myanmar – have registered an improvement in their global ranking over the reporting period, with Singapore retaining its enviable position as world leader.

Sustaining ASEAN's edge as a single production area implies that priority attention continues to be given to a region-wide connectivity agenda through sustained improvements in both the hardware (i.e. physical infrastructure) and software (i.e. policy and institutional environment) dimensions of transport, logistics and customs-related performance. Doing so is all the more important in the light of the recent region-wide slippages noted above.

Focusing on a broader range of metrics of overall border management, Table 2.4 documents how selected Asian economies have fared under the Enhanced Trade Index (ETI) developed by the World Economic Forum.

This index measures the extent to which individual economies have developed institutions, policies and services facilitating the free flow of goods over borders and to destination.[9] ETI data for eight of the ten AMS shows

---

[9] The Enabling Trade Index (ETI) was developed within the context of the World Economic Forum's Supply Chain and Transportation Industry Partnership programme and was first published in the Global Enabling Trade Report 2008. The ETI measures the extent to which individual economies have developed institutions, policies and services facilitating the free flow of goods over borders and to destination. The structure of the Index reflects the main enablers of trade, breaking them into four overall issue areas that are captured in sub-indexes A, B, C and D and nine pillars that are attributed to the sub-indexes as follows: A. The market access sub-index measures the extent to which the policy framework of the country welcomes foreign goods into the country and enables access to foreign market for its exporters. It includes the following pillar: Pillar 1 – Domestic

improvement over the 2010–16 period in only two cases: those of Cambodia and the Philippines, alongside Singapore's continued stellar performance as world leader. All other AMS have seen a drop in global rankings that, even when not markedly pronounced, must remain a source of policy concern. Still, it bears noting that even when excluding Singapore's outlying performance, ASEAN as a whole offers a more attractive setting for value chain production than does India (but slightly less than China), both of whose own ETI rankings slipped noticeably over the reporting period (see Table 2.4).

> and foreign market access; B. The border administration sub-index assesses the extent to which the administration at the border facilitates the entry and exit of goods through the following pillars: Pillar 2 – Efficiency of customs administration; Pillar 3 – Efficiency of import-export procedures and Pillar 4 – Transparency of border administration; C. The transport and communications infrastructure sub-index takes into account whether the country has in place the transport and communications infrastructure necessary to facilitate the movement of goods within the country and across the border through the following pillars: Pillar 5 – Availability and quality of transport infrastructure; Pillar 6 – Availability and quality of transport services and Pillar 7 – Availability and use of ICTs; and D. The business environment sub-index looks at the quality of governance as well as at the overarching regulatory and security environment impacting the business of importers and exporters active in the country through the following pillars: Pillar 8 – Regulatory environment and Pillar 9 – Physical security. Each of the above pillars is made up of a number of individual variables. The dataset includes both hard data and survey data from the World Economic Forum's Executive Opinion Survey. The hard data were obtained from publicly available sources and international organizations active in the area of trade (e.g. the International Air Transport Association (IATA), the International Trade Centre (ITC), the International Telecommunication Union (ITU), the United Nations Conference on Trade and Development (UNCTAD), the United Nations (UN) and the World Bank).

Table 2.4 *Enhanced Trade Index: Ranking of selected ASEAN Member States and RCEP partners, 2010–16*

Country/grouping	2010 Score	2010 Ranking	2016 Score	2016 Ranking	Change in score	Change in ranking
Brunei Darussalam	n.a.	n.a.	4.3	72	n.a.	n.a.
Cambodia	3.6	102	4.0	98	0.4	4
Indonesia	4.0	68	4.3	70	0.3	−2
Malaysia	4.7	30	4.9	37	0.2	−7
Philippines	3.7	92	4.1	82	0.4	10
Singapore	6.1	1	6.0	1	−0.1	0
Thailand	4.1	60	4.4	63	0.3	−3
Vietnam	4.0	71	4.3	73	0.3	−2
ASEAN-8 average	4.3	60.6	4.5	62.0	0.3	0.0
China	4.3	48	4.5	61	0.2	−13
India	3.8	84	3.9	102	0.1	−18

Sources: World Economic Forum and Global Alliance for Trade Facilitation, The Global Enabling Trade Report 2016 (accessed 21 January 2018), available at: http://reports.weforum.org/global-enabling-trade-report-2016/enabling-trade-rankings/ World Economic Forum, The Global Enabling Trade Report 2010 (accessed 21 January 2018), available at www.weforum.org/agenda/2010/05/enabling-trade-paves-the-way-to-recovery-from-global-economic-crisis/

Note: Data for Lao PDR and Myanmar are not available

A measure of the distance that ASEAN Member States still need to travel on the road to establishing a regionally integrated single production area can be gleaned from Tables 2.5 and 2.6, which situate selected AMS (those for which data is available) within the International Chamber of Commerce's (ICC's) Open Markets Index (Table 2.5) and rank all ten ASEAN economies according to the World Economic Forum's Global Competitiveness Index (Table 2.6).

Of the six AMS covered by the ICC index, only two – Singapore (ranked second behind Hong Kong, China) and Malaysia (ranked thirty-first out of seventy-five countries in the ICC sample) score above the sample median, with particular weaknesses found in regard to the level of openness towards FDI, most notably in Indonesia and the Philippines: the two ASEAN Member States with the highest aggregate levels of service sector restrictiveness.

On the competitiveness front, ASEAN countries exhibited marked improvements over the 2009–10 and 2017–18 periods, with the exception of Brunei Darussalam, which registered a notable deterioration in its global ranking. The most significant gains in overall competitiveness were registered in the Philippines and in Vietnam, followed by Indonesia and Cambodia.

2.7 Characterizing ASEAN's Openness in Services Markets

The following section takes stock of the *actual* degree of openness prevailing in ASEAN service markets, as reflected not in the legally binding negotiated undertakings of AMS

Table 2.5 *Open markets index: Selected ASEAN Member States, 2017*

Country	Trade openness 2013	Trade openness 2017	Trade openness Change	FDI openness 2013	FDI openness 2017	FDI openness Change	Trade-enabling infrastructure 2013	Trade-enabling infrastructure 2017	Trade-enabling infrastructure Change	Overall ranking 2013	Overall ranking 2017	Overall ranking Change
Indonesia	2.6	2.2	−0.4	2.2	2.2	0.0	2.8	2.5	−0.3	53	63	−10
Malaysia	3.8	2.9	−0.9	3.8	3.7	−0.1	4.2	3.9	−0.3	30	31	−1
Philippines	1.9	1.9	0.0	1.8	2.3	0.5	3.0	2.4	−0.6	58	62	−4
Singapore	5.2	5.5	0.3	5.7	5.7	0.0	5.5	5.2	−0.3	2	1	1
Thailand	3.5	2.9	−0.6	3.3	3.3	0.0	3.3	3.1	−0.2	49	48	1
Vietnam	4.2	3.9	−0.3	3.5	3.5	0.0	3.2	2.8	−0.4	46	33	13
ASEAN-6	3.5	3.2	−0.3	3.4	3.5	0.1	3.7	3.3	−0.4	40	40	0

Sources: International Chamber of Commerce (2013). ICC Open Markets Index 2nd Edition 2013 (accessed 21 January 2018), available at: https://iccwbo.org/publication/icc-open-markets-index-2nd-edition-2013/
International Chamber of Commerce (2017). ICC Open Markets Index 2017 (accessed 21 January 2018), available at: https://iccwbo.org/publication/icc-open-markets-index-2017/

Note: Data is unavailable for Brunei Darussalam, Cambodia, Lao PDR and Myanmar. Scores fall between 1 (least open) and 6 (most open). This index covers 75 economies

Table 2.6 ASEAN: Global Competitiveness Index rankings, 2009–10 and 2017–18[10]

Country/grouping	2009–10 Score	2009–10 Ranking	2017–18 Score	2017–18 Ranking	Change in score (2010–18)	Change in ranking (2010–18)
Brunei Darussalam	4.6	32	4.5	46	−0.1	−14
Cambodia	3.5	110	3.9	94	0.4	16
Indonesia	4.3	54	4.7	36	0.4	18
Lao PDR	n.a.	n.a.	3.9	98	n.a.	n.a.
Malaysia	4.9	24	5.2	23	0.3	1
Philippines	3.9	87	4.4	56	0.5	31
Singapore	5.6	3	5.7	3	0.2	0
Thailand	4.6	36	4.7	32	0.1	4
Vietnam	4.0	75	4.4	55	0.4	20
ASEAN average	4.4	53	4.6	49	0.3	9.5

Sources: World Economic Forum (2017). The Global Competitiveness Report 2009–10 (accessed 21 January 2018), available at: http://reports.weforum.org/global-competitiveness-index-2017-2018/competitiveness-rankings/
World Economic Forum (2009). The Global Competitiveness Report 2017–18 (accessed 21 January 2018), available at: www3.weforum.org/docs/WEF_GlobalCompetitivenessReport_2009-10.pdf
World Economic Forum (2006). The Global Competitiveness Report 2006–07 (accessed 21 January 2018), available at: www3.weforum.org/docs/WEF_GlobalCompetitivenessReport_2006-07.pdf

Note: GCI 2006 covers 125 economies. GCI 2009–10 covers 133 economies. GCI 2017–18 covers 137 economies. The ASEAN average does not take into account missing values. Data is unavailable for Myanmar in all periods

[10] Out of 138 countries.

found in various bilateral, regional or multilateral agreements analysed later on in this volume but in what is publicly known about the regulatory status quo prevailing in the economies of the region. The empirical evidence on offer draws on the World Bank's Services Trade Restrictiveness Index (STRI) database.[11]

A first measure of the policy stance of ASEAN Member States' towards services can be found in Figure 2.5, which tracks the level of services restrictiveness relative to the income level of a group of ASEAN+6 (Regional Comprehensive Economic Partnership) countries. Countries above the fitted line are those whose level of services trade restrictiveness exceeds that normally associated with their income levels, while those below it are more open than predicted by their level of per capita GDP.

Of the six AMS for which 2012 STRI data is reported in Figure 2.5 (the last year for which World Bank data is currently available), four economies – Indonesia, the Philippines, Thailand and Malaysia lie – above the fitted line, with the Philippines appearing as the most restrictive ASEAN Member State, though still a far cry from regional competitor India, whose STRI data appear starkly at odds with the country's 'back office of the world' narrative.

Among ASEAN Member States, only Vietnam and Cambodia lie below the regression line, which is indicative of

---

[11] For a fuller description of the database and its methodology, see Ingo Borchert, Batshur Gootiiz and Aaditya Mattoo, 'Guide to the Services Trade Restrictions Database' (2012) World Bank Policy Research Working Paper WPS6108.

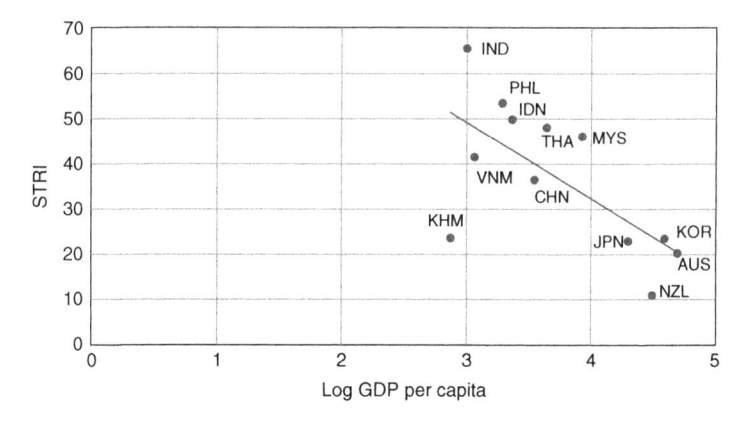

Figure 2.5 ASEAN: STRI and per capita income levels, 2012

a level of openness in services that exceeds that commonly associated with countries at their level of development. Along with China, whose per capita STRI level broadly straddles the fitted line, it is noteworthy that Cambodia and Vietnam both acceded to the WTO rather than being founding members. Accordingly, they were subject to considerably greater pressure to adopt pro-competitive policy stances and undertake a wider set of liberalization commitments in services (typically reflecting the regulatory status quo) than the other AMS in the sample. In tariff parlance, both are countries with significantly less 'water' in their services-related regulatory space.

The data in Figure 2.6 reveals positive overall improvements in the policy stance of ASEAN Member States, both individually and collectively, in the services field over the 2008–12 interval between which STRI indices were computed by the World Bank. On a scale from 0 to 100, where 0 connotes full openness and 100 a fully restrictive policy

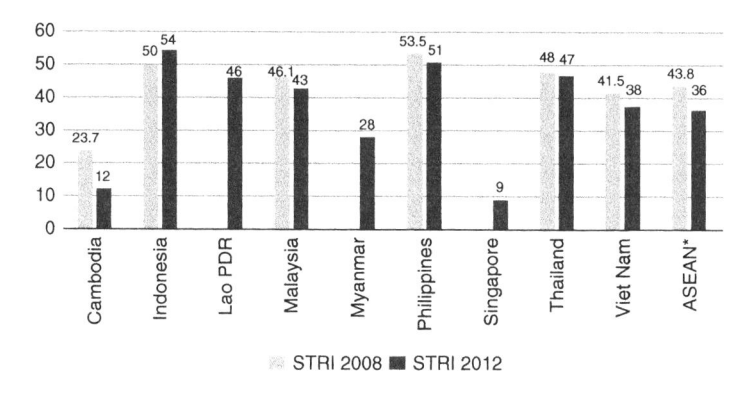

Figure 2.6 ASEAN: Overall STRI, 2008 and 2012

stance, the overall STRI level dropped significantly, from 43.8 to 36. For the most part, however, this reflects the addition of Singapore's highly liberal services regime (with an overall STRI of 9) to the World Bank's STRI 2012 sample rather than AFAS-driven changes, even if the latter have incrementally steered AMS in the direction of more open policies. Absent Singapore, ASEAN's 2012 STRI stands at 40, connoting a still restrictive internal policy stance after two decades of AFAS-induced liberalization.

Figure 2.6 shows that all AMS except Indonesia registered a drop in their policy restrictiveness between the two STRI surveys. With the exception of Singapore, whose STRI ranks among the lowest globally, and Cambodia, whose STRI was almost halved between 2008 and 2012, the applied services regimes of most other ASEAN Member States registered only modest gains in levels of market openness between the two reporting periods. Figure 2.6 reveals significant variance in levels of policy restrictiveness among the ASEAN sub-group, with Cambodia displaying the greatest degree of openness on the one hand, while Indonesia and the Philippines maintain highly restrictive overall policy regimes in services. Apart from Singapore, all four other founding members of ASEAN – Indonesia, Malaysia, the Philippines and Thailand – maintain significant restrictions across a host of sectors.

Figure 2.7 offers a measure of the policy 'distance' separating ASEAN from some of the sub-region's main trading partners and the negotiating pressure that the regional grouping confronted when embarking on the two mega-regional agreements with which its Member States have been involved over the past decade with key trading partners in the immediate neighbourhood and globally under the (still ongoing) Regional Comprehensive Economic Partnership negotiations and the (recently concluded) Comprehensive and Progressive Trans-Pacific Partnership (CPTPP) agreement.

Reducing such distance is of some significance if ASEAN Member States are to align more closely their regulatory regimes in services to those of their main external partners with a view to facilitating two-way trade and investment flows and to reduce regulatory compliance and associated transaction costs. In the case of the CPTPP, the openness gap – i.e. the ratio of STRI indices – stood some 75 per cent higher within ASEAN in 2012.

Figure 2.8 measures the level of ASEAN services restrictiveness across Modes 1 (cross-border supply), 3

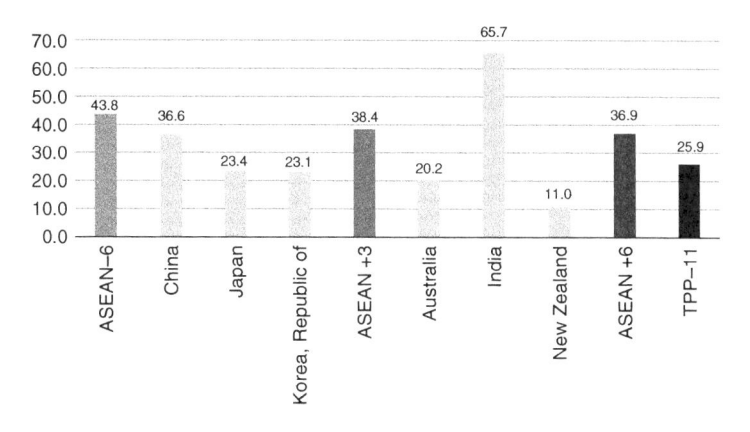

Figure 2.7 Overall STRI: ASEAN-6, ASEAN+3, ASEAN+6, TPP-11

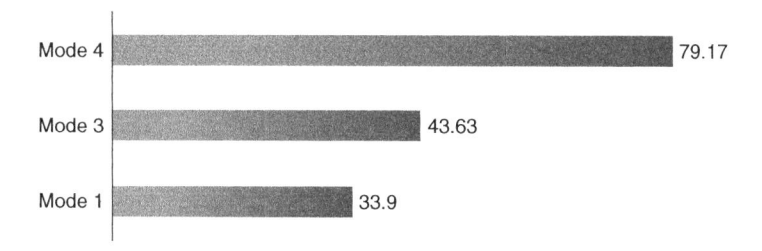

Figure 2.8 ASEAN: STRI by mode of supply, 2012

(commercial presence) and 4 (movement of natural persons).

Paralleling trends obtaining in all regions of the world, ASEAN Member States maintain their highest policy restrictions against the movement of foreign services suppliers. However, ASEAN deviates from all other regional groupings by maintaining a level of restrictiveness against foreign investors under Mode 3 that is higher than that which it maintains towards services supplied remotely through Mode 1. Such policy unease towards foreign ownership and the control that it may allow is illustrative of the decision (which is somewhat paradoxical, given the stated aim to establish an AEC-wide single production area) to cap intra-ASEAN foreign equity limitations at 70 per cent under the AEC.

With the exception of India for Modes 1 and 3, which is seen as maintaining punitively high levels of service sector restrictiveness affecting trade under both modes of supply, ASEAN Member States are generally more restrictive than their regional peers across all three modes of supply for which comparative data is available.

Figures 2.9, 2.10 and 2.11 offer a disaggregated sector- and AMS-specific breakdown of the overall trends described above. The data confirms the uneven pace of service sector reforms between the two STRI intervals, with the most impressive declines in policy restrictions observed in professional services (driven in part by the mobility-enhancing properties of the mutual recognition agreements concluded among ASEAN Member States in a number of professions), followed by financial services.

Meanwhile, the ASEAN policy regime became more restrictive in retail trade and telecommunications services between 2008 and 2012. The latter trend raises potentially troubling questions about the region's commitment to harnessing the full potential of the ongoing digital revolution and to making a success of stated e-ASEAN aims.

Apart from trade in professional services (legal and accountancy services), where the policy restrictiveness of

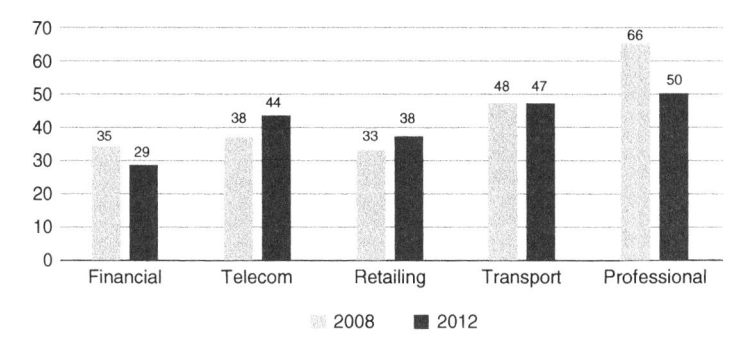

Figure 2.9 ASEAN: Overall STRI by sector, 2008 and 2012
Note: Data is unavailable for Brunei Darussalam. 2008 data is unavailable for Lao PDR, Myanmar and Singapore
Source: World Bank STRI Database (accessed 21 January 2018), available at: http://iresearch.worldbank.org/servicetrade/

ASEAN Member States remains, as it does in most parts of the world and even if on declining path regionally, the highest overall, the sub-region as a whole is characterized by levels of restrictiveness in all other sectors that remain high. STRI levels range from a low of 30.63 (out of 100) in aviation services, in which ASEAN has registered a measure region-wide advances through targeted steps aimed at relaxing a number of policy restrictions affecting intra-regional air transportation, to highs of 47 for all transport modes and 44 for fixed and mobile telecommunications.

While the various liberalization packages pursued under AFAS (a process that is analysed in greater detail in Chapter 4) have resulted in a progressive lowering of levels of policy restrictiveness within ASEAN, the pace of service sector reforms and market liberalization has, with the exception

SERVICES AND SERVICES TRADE IN ASEAN

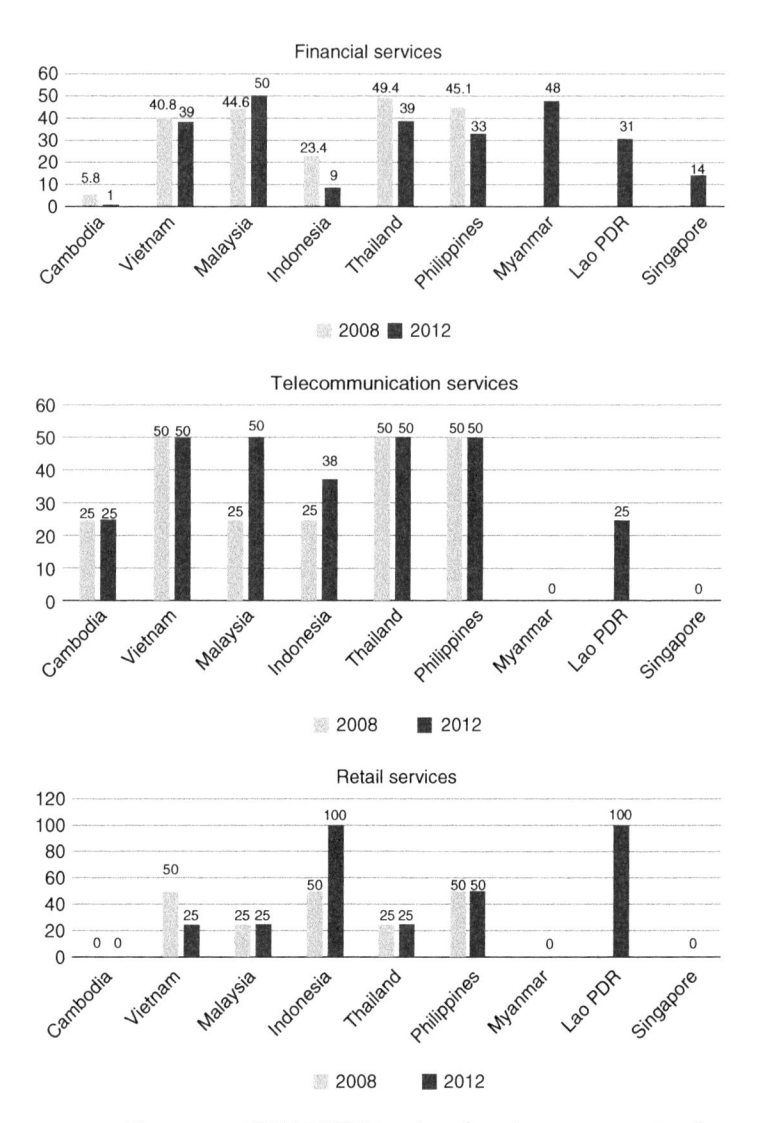

Figure 2.10 ASEAN: STRI in selected service sectors, 2008 and 2012

Transport services

Country	2008	2012
Cambodia	35.5	28
Vietnam	38.6	50
Malaysia	55.4	50
Indonesia	66.4	48
Thailand	47.1	50
Philippines	44.2	58
Myanmar		53
Lao PDR		50
Singapore		0

Professional services

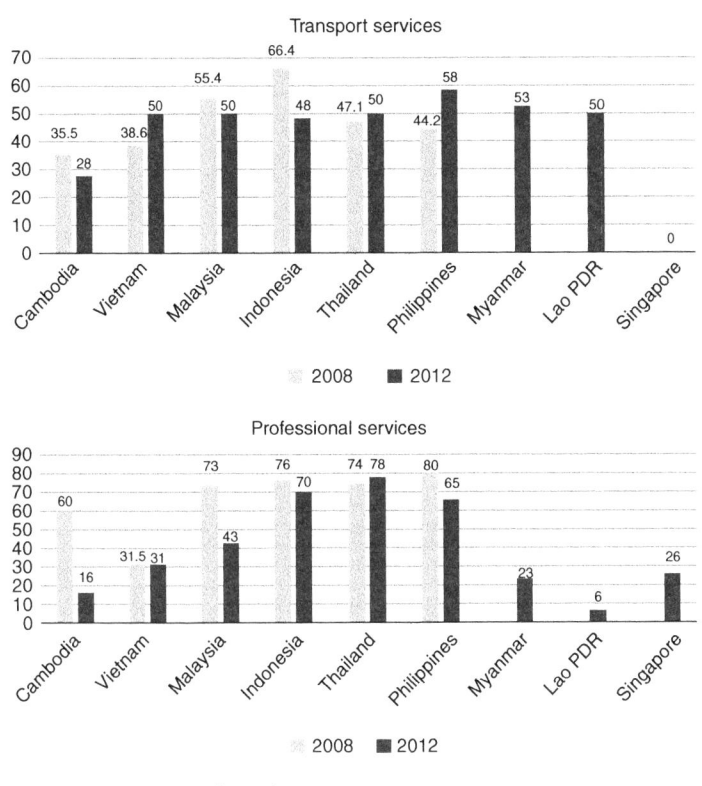

Country	2008	2012
Cambodia	60	16
Vietnam	31.5	31
Malaysia	73	43
Indonesia	76	70
Thailand	74	78
Philippines	80	65
Myanmar		23
Lao PDR		6
Singapore		26

Figure 2.10 (Cont.)

of India, been even more pronounced among ASEAN's main regional trading partners.

Situating ASEAN-wide levels of policy restrictiveness in services compared with other regional groupings helps to provide a finer sense both of comparative dynamics and the extent to which service sector regimes in ASEAN can be seen as promoting economy-wide gains in efficiency and sustaining the emergence of competitive value chain production in

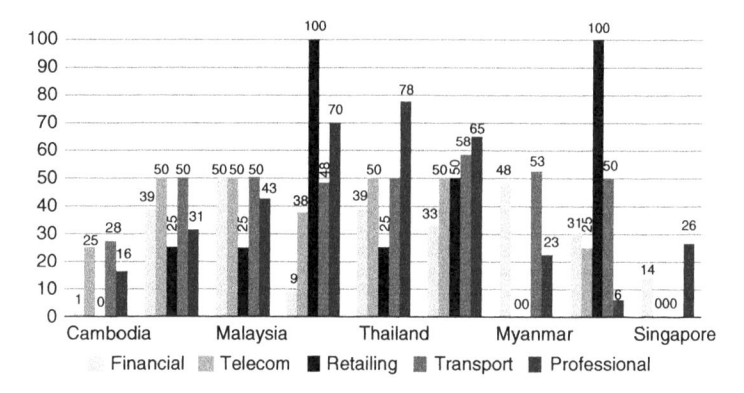

Figure 2.11 ASEAN: STRI by sector and Member State, 2012

a region characterized by increasingly contestable markets, particularly for export-oriented (i.e. so-called 'efficiency-seeking') FDI.

A recent comprehensive look at the applied services regime of major regional groupings showed that ASEAN maintained more restrictive regimes than any other region of the world except for the Gulf Cooperation Council. ASEAN's overall policy restrictiveness matches that of South Asia as the second most restrictive regional pact (see Figure 2.12). The average STRI for ASEAN was found to be some 60 per cent higher than the global average.[12]

Looked at from a sectoral angle, ASEAN typically ranks among the world's second or third most highly

---

[12] B. Gootiz and A. Mattoo (2015), 'Regionalism in Services: A Study of ASEAN', Policy Research Working Paper No. 7498, Washington, DC: World Bank: http://documents.worldbank.org/curated/en/616071467987821046/pdf/WPS7498.pdf

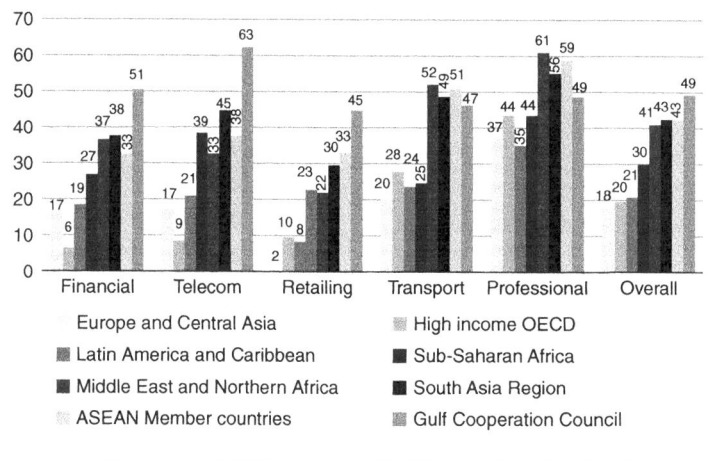

Figure 2.12 STRI by sector: ASEAN and selected regional groupings, 2012

restrictive integration hubs in most sectors other than international air transport. It is also unenviably found to top the restrictiveness index in the areas of international maritime transport, accountancy and legal services.

Among the main impediments to more contestable service markets in ASEAN reported by Gootiz and Mattoo are the widespread prevalence of unduly discretionary licensing regimes and opaque regulatory procedures, implicit and explicit limits placed on market entry conditions in key sectors such as banking and transport, and regulatory regimes that are either weakly developed or non-existent or involve several agencies and ministries in manners that can both deter and raise entry and operating costs for new firms, both domestic and foreign. The high level of regulatory discretion found within several countries of the regional grouping create

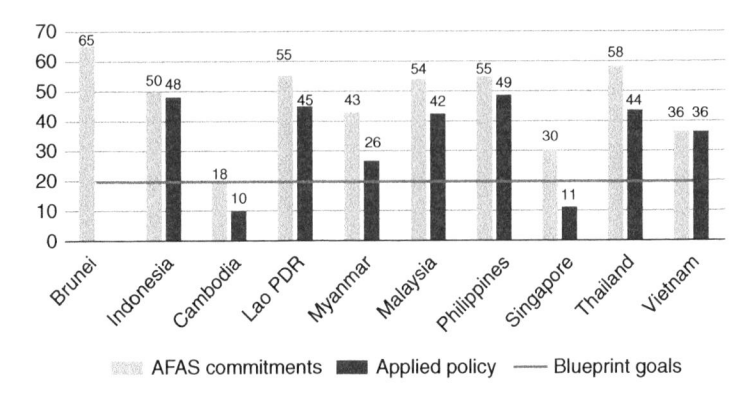

Figure 2.13 ASEAN: AFAS commitments, applied services regimes and AEC Blueprint goals

policy uncertainty that makes it hard for would-be entrants to assess actual policy regimes.[13]

Figure 2.13 provides a measure of the road that lies ahead if ASEAN Member States are to achieve the ambitious aims that they have set for themselves under the AEC 2025 Blueprint. At the time when the 2015 AEC thresholds were being passed, only two AMS – Cambodia and Singapore – had applied policies exceeding Blueprint aims. Meanwhile, all AMS except Cambodia maintained AFAS commitments far above the level of openness that was called for by the AEC.

[13] For instance, Gootiz and Mattoo recall that Myanmar, Malaysia, the Philippines, Singapore and Thailand do not require regulators to provide reasons for licence rejection. Appeals are not allowed in Cambodia, Myanmar and Malaysia. While prior notice mechanisms help the private sector to prepare for policy changes and allow for private-sector input into policy formulation, so such processes exist in Indonesia, the Philippines, Thailand, Myanmar and Lao PDR.

Chapter 3

Is ASEAN an Optimal Regulatory Convergence Area in Services?

Given the insignificance of tariffs as instruments of protection in services trade, regulatory requirements and the degree to which they diverge among trading partners assume central significance. Trade and investment agreements devoted to services typically pursue a range of objectives. These include: first, to bring down the level and incidence of restrictive regulation on a reciprocal basis; second, to provide greater predictability and security of access and market operation through the undertaking of legally binding commitments, thereby exploiting the 'signalling' properties of enforceable treaty instruments; and, third, to reap the trade- and investment-facilitating benefits stemming from convergence, approximation (including through mutual recognition) and ultimately (but less frequently) harmonization of regulatory practices between trading partners.

The gains from preferential trade agreements (PTAs) are likely to be significant in areas in which there is scope for attaining economies of scale and promoting increased competition. While such gains can, in principle, be realized through most-favoured nation (MFN) liberalization conducted at the multilateral level, in practice, the integration of service markets often requires some degree of prior or concomitant convergence in regulatory regimes. Such convergence is likely to prove more feasible in a preferential (bilateral or regional) context in which proximity – whether geographic or in terms of income levels, language, common colonial legacies or legal traditions – favours closer institutional and regulatory ties and repeat interaction among regional officials and institutions.

The regulatory intensity of services trade prompts the question of whether and how PTAs can be conduits for trade- and investment-facilitating convergence in domestic regulatory practices. Simply put, under what circumstances is a country (or a country grouping such as the Association of Southeast Asian Nations (ASEAN)) more likely to benefit from cooperation in a preferential setting than in a multilateral one? And what attributes are most likely to prompt pairs or groups of countries to aim for deeper integration through regional or preferential approaches to regulatory convergence?

There is much in both the public goods and monetary theory literature (regarding the pre-conditions for the establishment of optimal currency areas) to suggest that regulatory cooperation may well be more desirable among a subset of countries than if pursued on a global scale.[1] There is, however, little, if any, empirical guidance on the payoffs to regulatory cooperation – i.e. on the costs and benefits of mutual recognition agreements or the deeper harmonization or approximation of regulatory standards, particularly in service industries, not least for reasons of generalized data paucity. Such a dearth

---

[1] Richard Cooper, 'Worldwide versus Regional Integration: Is there an Optimum Size of the Integration Area?' in F. Matchlup (ed.), *Economic Integration: Worldwide, Regional, Sectoral* (Macmillan, 1976), pp. 41–53. See also Sandler Todd, 'Global and Regional Public Goods: A Prognosis for Collective', *Fiscal Studies*, 19(3) (1998), 221–47.

of empirical evidence hinders the task of determining the appropriate scope and depth, as well as the proper geographical confines or optimal institutional forms, of regulatory cooperation.

Optimal regulatory convergence areas can be thought of as defining sets of countries whose aggregate welfare would be maximized as a result of the adoption of convergent regulatory norms and practices.[2] Such an area would balance the benefits and costs of participation in a preferential agreement. The gains from eliminating policy differences through regulatory approximation or harmonization will ultimately depend on the scope for creating truly integrated markets, which, as noted above, is most often conditioned by 'natural' ties between countries as well as contingent on factors such as geographic and linguistic proximity. The costs of pursuing a regulatory convergence agenda will depend for their part on the *ex ante* similarities (or divergences) in regulatory or collective preferences and the compatibility of the regulatory regimes and institutions designed in response to such preferences.

In the very definition of an optimal regulatory convergence area is the notion that cooperation can be an important means of sharing information and experience on regulatory reform initiatives and of identifying good regulatory practices with a view to their eventual diffusion among parties to an integration process. Such diffusion can be especially useful for regulating novel services in sectors

---

[2] Aditya Mattoo and Pierre Sauvé, 'Services' in J. P. Chauffour and J. C. Maur (eds.), *Preferential Trade Agreement Policies for Development: A Handbook* (The World Bank, 2011), pp. 235–74.

characterized by continuous technical or regulatory change, such as in digital trade or financial services. In Asia, both the Asia-Pacific Economic Cooperation (APEC) grouping and ASEAN have assumed such a role through the establishment of numerous dialogue (and typically soft law) platforms among Member States on various dimensions of a regional connectivity agenda.

Whether or not a country or country grouping benefits from regulatory convergence, its willingness to participate in such efforts and in PTAs designed for this purpose will thus likely hinge on where regulatory standards are set, the level at which they are set and the regulatory environment to which the standards respond. Such considerations will, in turn, determine who must ultimately bear the costs associated with adopting agreed standards.

Table 3.1 offers a measure of the extent of prevailing ASEAN heterogeneity across a range of regulatory, governance and innovation-related indicators of particular relevance to services markets.[3] Taken as a whole, the picture on offer suggests that, apart from a common geography that gives coherence to production sharing and the elaboration of connectivity and trade facilitation agendas centred on the provision of a number of regional public goods of an infrastructural nature, ASEAN appears to possess few of the attributes of an optimal regulatory convergence area. In large measure, such an observation traces its origin in the pronounced development gap characterizing the region, with a per capita gross

---

[3] The figures in Table 3.1 exclude Lao People's Democratic Republic (PDR) and Myanmar, for which comparable data is not available.

Table 3.1 ASEAN: Selected regulatory, governance and innovation-related indicators, 2017

	Brunei Darussalam		Cambodia		Indonesia		Malaysia		Philippines		Singapore		Thailand		Vietnam	
	Rank	Score	Rank	Score	Rank	Score	Rank	Score	Rank	Score	Rank	Score	Rank	Score	Rank	Score
Institutions	31	77.2	98	49.1	120	41.2	53	67	89	52	1	94.4	75	55.8	87	52.8
Government effectiveness	30	69.2	109	24.4	83	36.4	37	66.9	65	44.9	1	100	50	51.3	68	44.1
Regulatory environment	27	79	101	49.3	126	16.7	75	58.3	105	48.4	1	98.6	110	43.8	103	48.9
Business environment	62	71.4	115	55	79	64	50	75.1	81	63.3	11	87.5	37	77.6	113	55.4
Human capital and research	69	31.1	118	14.2	92	23	35	41.9	95	22.3	5	63.7	72	30.8	70	31
Education	68	46.3	119	24.6	103	33.5	77	43.9	113	26.9	76	44	85	40.6	17	61.2
Tertiary education	27	47	105	17.9	87	27.5	24	48.4	74	32.7	1	80.5	90	26.7	86	27.8
Knowledge workers	7	71	117	15.4	123	9.7	93	26.9	45	45.5	4	73.2	85	29.2	102	23.3
Research and development (R&D)	115	0	115	0	63	8.1	35	33.3	64	7.4	11	66.5	40	25.2	80	4.1
Infrastructure	55	49.4	113	26.9	81	42	45	52.4	72	44.6	2	69.1	71	45	77	42.7
ICT access	47	72.1	99	42.1	88	47.1	59	67.5	89	47	11	87	75	55	90	46
Investment	28	51.7	88	34.1	96	33.2	22	55.1	111	30.2	1	75	50	43.3	109	30.5
	86	51.7	92	48.3	67	56.7	3	80	105	41.7	1	83.3	26	66.7	80	53.3

Table 3.1 (cont.)

	Brunei Darussalam Rank	Brunei Darussalam Score	Cambodia Rank	Cambodia Score	Indonesia Rank	Indonesia Score	Malaysia Rank	Malaysia Score	Philippines Rank	Philippines Score	Singapore Rank	Singapore Score	Thailand Rank	Thailand Score	Vietnam Rank	Vietnam Score
Ease of protecting minority investors	102	60	93	62.1	50	71.2	39	73.1	59	70.2	19	76.9	43	71.9	77	65.9
Intensity of local competition	105	19.4	92	24.4	77	28.1	45	37.3	94	22.8	32	42.9	53	34.6	52	34.8
Creative outputs	110	4.5	74	14.7	52	22.3	13	38.4	115	3.7	16	36	20	34.4	36	27.4
Creative goods and services	78	15.6	99	9.8	79	15.2	69	18.5	92	12.4	30	37.8	67	18.8	64	19.3
Online creativity	71	32.9	101	27	87	30.1	37	42.7	73	32.5	7	58.7	51	37.6	47	38.3
Global Innovation Index																

Source: Global Innovation Index 2017 Interactive Database, available at: www.globalinnovationindex.org/ (accessed 21 January 2018)
Note: Data from Myanmar and Lao PDR is unavailable

Table 3.2 *ASEAN: Corruption perceptions index rankings, 2012–16*

Country	2016 rank	2012 score	2016 score	Change in score 2012–16
Brunei	41	55	58	3
Cambodia	156	22	21	−1
Indonesia	90	32	37	5
Laos	123	21	30	9
Malaysia	55	49	49	0
Myanmar	136	15	28	13
Philippines	101	34	35	1
Singapore	7	87	84	−3
Thailand	101	37	35	−2
Vietnam	113	31	33	2

Source: Transparency International (2017), Corruption Perceptions Index 2017, Berlin: Transparency International, available at: www.transparency.org/whatwedo/publication/corruption_perceptions_index_2017 (accessed 25 January 2018)

Note: 2016 ranks cover 176 economies. The score follows a scale from 0 (highly corrupt) to 100 (very clean)

domestic product (GDP) ratio of almost 60 to 1 between the region's richest and poorest countries (or 45 to 1 in purchasing power parity terms).[4] Such diversity helps to explain why convergence towards a common ASEAN norm is a process that is feasible only with significant doses of variable geometry and on the basis of liberalization allowing for intra-ASEAN

---

[4] It bears noting, however, that, once stripped of the region's per capita GDP outliers – Singapore and Brunei Darussalam – the income gap in the remaining ASEAN-8 Member States is actually lower than that prevailing in the European Union (EU), since its two poorest members – Bulgaria and Romania – joined the Union.

Table 3.3 *ASEAN: Human development index rankings[5], 2010–15*

ASEAN Member	Ranking in 2015	Δ 2010–15
Brunei Darussalam	30	+1
Cambodia	143	+1
Indonesia	113	+3
Lao PDR	138	+5
Malaysia	59	+1
Myanmar	145	+2
Philippines	116	−7
Singapore	5	0
Thailand	87	+4
Vietnam	115	+2

Source: UNDP, Human Development Indicator, available at: http://hdr.undp.org/en/composite/HDI (accessed 6 January 2018)

forms of special and differential treatment directed towards the regional grouping's weakest members.

Of greater concern from a services trade and investment perspective is the weak overall performance of ASEAN Member States (AMS) in regard to core indicators of regulatory and institutional performance, with several Member States being ranked within the world's bottom third in regard to the overall quality of institutions and regulatory environment. Weaknesses are also noticeable in regard to human capital and research-related indicators (such as general and tertiary education, the supply of knowledge workers and research and development), as well as information and

[5] Out of 188 countries.

Table 3.4 *ASEAN: Judicial independence index rankings,*[6] *2017–18*

Country	Rank
Brunei Darussalam	60
Cambodia	122
Indonesia	52
Lao PDR	69
Malaysia	41
Myanmar*	117
Philippines	88
Singapore	19
Thailand	62
Vietnam	84

Source: World Economic Forum, 'The Global Competitiveness Index 2017–2018', available at: http://reports.weforum.org/global-competitiveness-index-2017-2018/competitiveness-rankings/#series=EOSQ144 (accessed 6 January 2018)
* 2014 data for Myanmar

communications technology (ICT) access, all of which may hold back the skills (including in terms of digital literacy) upgrading required to sustain the insertion of workers and firms into higher value-added supply chains and promote resilience-enhancing diversification efforts.

Tables 3.2 to 3.5, detailing the region's uneven overall performance in the areas of corruption perceptions, human development, judicial freedom, and rule of law-related indicators, evidence a number of further constraints weighing on

[6] Out of 138 economies.

Table 3.5 *ASEAN: Selected governance indicator rankings, 2016*[7]

Countries	Rule of law index ranking[8]	Regulatory enforcement index ranking[9]
Cambodia	112	112
Indonesia	61	53
Malaysia	56	74
Myanmar	98	87
Philippines	70	55
Singapore	9	1
Thailand	64	56
Vietnam	67	91

Source: World Justice Project (2017), Rule of Law Index 2016, Washington, DC: World Justice Project, available at: https://worldjusticeproject.org/our-work/publications/rule-law-index-reports/wjp-rule-law-index%C2%AE-2016-report (accessed 22 January 2018)

[7] Out of 113 economies.
[8] The 2016 edition of the World Justice Project's Rule of Law Index expands coverage to 113 countries and jurisdictions (from 102 in 2015), relying on more than 110,000 household and expert surveys to measure how the rule of law is experienced and perceived in practical, everyday situations by the general public worldwide. Performance is measured using forty-four indicators across eight primary rule of law factors, each of which is scored and ranked globally and against regional and income peers: constraints on government powers; absence of corruption; open government; fundamental rights; order and security; regulatory enforcement; civil justice; and criminal justice.
[9] The Regulatory Enforcement Index Factor 6 measures the extent to which regulations are effectively implemented and enforced without improper influence by public officials or private interests. It also includes whether administrative proceedings are conducted in a timely manner, without unreasonable delays, and whether due process is respected in administrative proceedings. This factor also addresses whether the government respects the property rights of people and corporations.

ASEAN's ability to perform a region-wide structural shift towards a more service-centric growth and development model.

The persistence of marked intra-regional diversity in regulatory and institutional performance places important limitations on the degree of policy convergence that can be secured on a ASEAN-wide basis, confirming once more the need for formula-based flexibilities in the design and implementation of service sector reforms that engage the region as a whole. The persistence of widespread development, income and implementation gaps likely fuels the growing interest shown by several of ASEAN's more advanced economies to seek deeper forms of services liberalization with external partners in the Asia-Pacific region and beyond.

Chapter 4

The Liberalization of Services Trade in ASEAN: Trends, Achievements and Prospects

4.1 The ASEAN Framework Agreement on Services

The liberalization of services trade leading to the establishment of the ASEAN Economic Community in 2015 took place under the ASEAN Framework Agreement on Services (AFAS). This agreement was signed on 15 December 1995 in Bangkok, Thailand, at the 5th ASEAN Summit, by the Economic Ministers of Brunei Darussalam, Indonesia, Malaysia, Philippines, Singapore, Thailand and Vietnam. It came into force on 30 December 1998. Lao People's Democratic Republic (PDR) and Myanmar acceded to this agreement in 1997, and Cambodia in 1999, when they became ASEAN members. This agreement formalized ASEAN's commitment to integration in respect of trade in services, complementing the earlier agreement signed at the 4th ASEAN Summit in 1992 to adopt a Common Effective Preferential Tariff (CEPT) Scheme in order to create the ASEAN Free Trade Area (AFTA) for goods (largely superseded by the ASEAN Trade in Goods Agreement (ATIGA) in 2010). An agreement covering investment, the Framework Agreement on the ASEAN Investment Area (AIA), was signed in 1998. Post-2015, the next step for services liberalization in ASEAN is the enhancement of AFAS to create the ASEAN Trade in

Services Agreement (ATISA).[1] This chapter provides a detailed analysis of the substantive provisions of AFAS, which has been the primary vehicle for ASEAN services liberalization for some twenty years.

4.1.1 Aims of AFAS

The objectives of AFAs are threefold:[2]
(1) to enhance cooperation in services among Member States in order to improve the efficiency and competitiveness, diversify production capacity and supply and distribution of services of their service suppliers within and outside ASEAN;
(2) to eliminate substantially restrictions to trade in services among Member States; and
(3) to liberalize trade in services by expanding the depth and scope of liberalization beyond those undertaken by Member States under the General Agreement on Trade in Services (GATS) with the aim of realizing a free trade area in services.

Under the first aim of enhancing cooperation, Member States must identify service sectors for cooperation and formulate detailed plans and programmes in order to carry this out.[3] Existing cooperation efforts were to be enhanced and new efforts made in sectors that were not covered by existing

---

[1] Negotiations for ATISA were concluded in November 2018. See www.mti.gov.sg/-/media/MTI/Newsroom/Press-Releases/2018/11/17th-AECC/Media-Release-17th-AECC-12-Nov-2018.pdf
[2] AFAS, Art. 1(a), (b) and (c).   [3] AFAS, Art. 2(3).

cooperation arrangements. Methods through which this might be done include establishing or improving infrastructural facilities; making joint production, marketing and purchasing arrangements; engaging in research and development; and exchanging information.[4]

The second aim of AFAS, the elimination of restrictions hampering services trade, and its third aim, the liberalization of services trade, are overlapping and somewhat tautological in character. The elimination of any restrictions would automatically result in liberalization, while liberalization would, of necessity, entail the elimination, progressively or fully, of restrictions. Admittedly, the latter may not always and everywhere be the case, as liberalization could result from the grant of a privilege not hitherto enjoyed. A question could be raised in relation to the relative degree of liberalization envisaged by the second and third objectives. Although GATS+ liberalization is not expressly stated as an aim of the second objective, this can be implied by its reference to 'substantially' eliminating restrictions to trade in services among Member States. This objective is more ambitious than the stated aspirations of the GATS, whose preamble and text merely refer to the 'achievement of progressively higher levels of liberalization of trade in services' without mentioning an ultimate target substantially to eliminate restrictions. It is consistent with the third objective of AFAS in Article I(c), which expressly aims to achieve liberalization beyond the GATS. Article I(c) also states the ultimate aim of realizing an ASEAN-wide free trade area in services. This does not necessarily mean that a state of total

[4] AFAS, Art. 2(2).

absence of restrictions or a complete elimination of all impediments to services trade is targeted. Such a degree of market opening is not explicitly envisaged even in key ASEAN documents such as the ASEAN Economic Community Blueprint 2015, published some ten years after AFAS came into force. The Blueprint provides that 'the free flow of trade in services is one of the important elements in realizing an ASEAN Economic Community, where there will be substantially no restriction to ASEAN service suppliers in providing services and in establishing companies across national borders within the region, subject to domestic regulations'.[5]

Consistent with AFAS, in the Blueprint, ASEAN Member States aim to facilitate the free flow of services by 2015 by, *inter alia*, taking action to 'remove substantially all restrictions on trade in services' for all service sectors by 2015.[6] The aim of ASEAN Member States might therefore be understood to be one of eliminating all barriers to trade in services if possible, but with the acknowledgement that the ultimate goal that can realistically be achieved might be the elimination of substantially, but not all, such barriers.

4.1.2 *AFAS Provisions and Inter-relationship with the GATS*

While AFAS appears not to have elaborated specifically on the Article I(b) aim of eliminating substantially restrictions to

---

[5] See ASEAN Economic Community Blueprint (ASEAN Secretariat, Jakarta, 2008), para. 20.
[6] See ibid., para. 21.

trade in services, the Article I(c) aim of liberalization is expanded upon in Articles III and IV of AFAS, both of which merit detailed analysis. Article III provides as follows:

> Pursuant to Article I(c), Member States shall liberalize trade in services in a substantial number of sectors within a reasonable time-frame by:
>
> (a) eliminating substantially all existing discriminatory measures and market access limitations amongst Member States; and
>
> (b) prohibiting new or more discriminatory measures and market access limitations.

The express reference in Article III to Article I(c) reinforces the fact that the liberalization mandated by Article III is to be based on, measured against, and surpass the depth and scope of liberalization achieved by ASEAN Member States under the GATS. Under Article III, liberalization is to take place in a 'substantial' number of sectors, and within a 'reasonable' time frame, by eliminating 'substantially all' existing discriminatory measures and market access limitations and prohibiting new or more such measures or limitations.

General terms such as 'substantial' and 'reasonable' could be criticized as being vague, but it is understandably difficult to specify an exact quantity or time frame. Such a challenge is arguably no lesser in a preferential context than it has proven to be at the multilateral level. If the language of Article III seems familiar, this is explained by a cross-reference to Article V of the GATS, which sets out the circumstances under which economic integration agreements are allowed under the World Trade Organization (WTO) regime for services. Almost all the matters mandated by Article III of AFAS (e.g. substantial sectoral coverage, elimination of substantially all discrimination, and the deadline of a reasonable time frame) are those which are required in order to satisfy the exigencies of Article V of the GATS.[7] The language and content of Article III were probably carefully chosen by the drafters of AFAS to show that this was a GATS-compliant agreement. It should be noted that Article V of the GATS details the minimum standards that preferential trade agreements in services must satisfy. However, that AFAS uses language that serves to align itself with this minimum standard does not mean that it is necessarily limited by it. This can be seen clearly in Article III's inclusion of the requirement that ASEAN Member States should eliminate, among themselves, substantially all existing market access limitations relating to trade in services. Market access is not an element that is required in order for an economic integration agreement to qualify under Article V of the GATS, whose

---

[7] GATS, Art. V(1) provides as follows:
   This Agreement shall not prevent any of its Members from being a party to or entering into an agreement liberalizing trade in services between or among the parties to such an agreement, provided that such an agreement:
   (a) has substantial sectoral coverage, and
   (b) provides for the absence or elimination of substantially all discrimination, in the sense of Article XVII, between or among the parties, in the sectors covered under subparagraph (a), through:
       (i) elimination of existing discriminatory measures, and/or
       (ii) prohibition of new or more discriminatory measures,
   either at the entry into force of that agreement or on the basis of a reasonable time-frame ... .

central remit lies with discriminatory measures violating the National Treatment provision (Article XVII) of GATS. Nor is the elimination of substantially all market access limitations a requisite condition in order to satisfy the market access requirements of Article XVI of the GATS, as that article merely requires each WTO Member to adhere to the market access undertakings made in its GATS Schedule under the principle of progressive liberalization, and such undertakings will vary in ambition depending on the commitments made by the WTO Member concerned.

Article IV of AFAS requires Member States to enter into negotiations on measures affecting trade in specific service sectors with a view to 'achieving commitments which are beyond those inscribed in each Member State's schedule of specific commitments under the GATS and for which Member States shall accord preferential treatment to one another on an MFN basis'.[8] It also provides that these new commitments are to be set out by each Member State in a schedule.[9] Such an approach represents an economical means of incorporating two key GATS disciplines into AFAS, in the sense that the reference to improving upon the commitments in each Member State's GATS schedule clearly makes the rules of national treatment and market access, which are key components of these schedules, applicable also to AFAS. This confirms the importance of market access, which is expressly stated as a mandatory principle in Article III of AFAS.

The term 'national treatment', however, is not mentioned at all in AFAS, although it is implicitly mandated by

[8] AFAS, Art. 4(1).   [9] AFAS, Art. 4(2).

the requirement for Member States to eliminate and prohibit 'discriminatory measures' under Article III. The cross-reference to the GATS schedules of Member States also serves to incorporate various features of the GATS into AFAS – for instance, liberalization by specific-service sectors according to each of the four modes of supply.

AFAS contains an even more general and sweeping cross-reference to the GATS in Article XIV(1), which provides that the 'terms and definitions and other provisions of the GATS shall be referred to and applied to matters arising under this Framework Agreement for which no specific provision has been made under it'. Two observations can be made in this regard. First, such a reference explains why the drafters of AFAS did not see a need to define the content of the rules of market access, national treatment or non-discrimination in AFAS, since the GATS already provided a ready-made definition of these core principles. Second, all GATS disciplines and provisions relating to matters for which no specific provision has been made under AFAS would end up applying also to AFAS. This may be of limited significance now that all ASEAN Member States have become WTO Members, with Lao PDR being the last to do so on 2 February 2013. In any case, GATS rules relating to measures affecting trade in services would provide the default position for all ASEAN Member States by virtue of the fact that, as WTO Members, GATS disciplines automatically applies to them.

Because of Article XIV(1) of AFAS, an important task is to identify matters for which specific provision have been made in AFAS, compared with those for which AFAS makes no specific provision and which would fall under GATS rules.

AFAS specifically refers to the key GATS disciplines of market access and non-discrimination and the coverage of these matters under AFAS has been discussed above. Whether such AFAS coverage qualifies as having already made 'specific provision' for these matters or not, as a practical matter, the cursory treatment given to market access and non-discrimination under AFAS requires that GATS provisions be used to supplement their meaning,

A third key discipline of the GATS that is specifically mentioned in AFAS is that relating to most favoured nation (MFN) treatment. The main reference to MFN is found in Article IV(1) of AFAS, which requires that Member States enter into negotiations on measures affecting trade in services with a view to achieving commitments beyond each of their GATS commitments, 'and for which Member States shall accord preferential treatment to one another on an (intra-ASEAN) MFN basis'.[10] This is a narrow MFN provision, under which a preference accorded under any commitment made in a Member State's AFAS schedule will have to be extended to all the other AFAS Member States equally. It offers no protection against preferences that a Member State may accord to other Member States or to non-Member States in respect of measures affecting trade in services that lie outside AFAS schedule of commitments – for instance, those falling under other preferential trade agreements. In contrast, the MFN obligation in the GATS is much wider, and requires MFN treatment in relation not only to the GATS

---

[10] The wording of Art IV(1) suggests that this refers to MFN on an intra-ASEAN basis.

commitments made by each WTO Member, but also to treatment with respect to any measures affecting trade in services. Specifically, Article II of the GATS provides that, '[w]ith respect to any measure covered by this Agreement, each Member shall accord immediately and unconditionally to services and service suppliers of any other Member treatment no less favourable than that it accords to like services and service suppliers of any other country'.

As AFAS already features an MFN provision, it is unclear whether, as a result of Article XIV(1) of AFAS, the GATS MFN provision should also apply to AFAS, concurrently with the MFN provision found in AFAS itself. If it did, this would mean that an ASEAN Member State that enters into a preferential trade agreement (PTA) with another country containing more favourable services commitments than its AFAS commitments would have to extend these better commitments to all other ASEAN Member States, in common with other WTO members, as well, unless an exception to this requirement can be found. One important exception to the MFN requirement in the GATS is, of course, preferential treatment accorded under economic integration agreements that satisfy Article V of the GATS, which need not be extended to other WTO Members outside the PTA grouping. It is not clear whether Article XIV(1) of AFAS would make the principles of Article V of the GATS applicable in the context of AFAS, but a legitimate argument can be made that it would. If so, ASEAN Member States that enter into GATS-compliant PTAs need not extend those benefits to other ASEAN Member States under AFAS.

In addition to possibly relying on the MFN provisions of the GATS to supplement the provisions of AFAS, the protocols to implement the Sixth, Seventh and Eighth Packages of commitments under AFAS each contain a provision stating that, subject to each Member State's schedules of commitments and lists of MFN exemptions, 'Member States shall accord preferential treatment to one another on a Most-Favoured-Nation basis'.[11] It is not clear whether this provision should be interpreted to refer to MFN treatment vis-à-vis all other countries in respect of any measure covered in the GATS, or MFN treatment vis-à-vis other ASEAN Member States in respect of AFAS commitments only. The first interpretation would more closely approximate the GATS position, while the second would mirror the narrow MFN provision in Article IV(1) of AFAS discussed above.

In addition to market access, non-discrimination and MFN, AFAS contains specific provisions dealing with the following: mutual recognition (Article V); denial of benefits (Article VI); settlement of disputes (Article VII); supplementary agreements (Article VIII); other agreements (Article IX); modification of schedules of specific commitments (Article X); institutional arrangements (Article XI); amendments (Article XII); and accession of new members (Article XIII), as well as final provisions such as a cross-reference to the GATS and deposit instructions (Article XIV). A few of these specific provisions are further discussed below. For present purposes, the foregoing list of AFAS provisions allows us to identify, by elimination, those issues, as a result of Article XIV (1) of AFAS, that are dealt with by default under the GATS provisions since they are not dealt with under AFAS. These

[11] See Art. 3 of the respective Protocols.

include the key GATS provisions on transparency; domestic regulation; monopolies; business practices; payments and transfers; balance of payment safeguards; general exceptions; and security exceptions, all of which are not addressed by AFAS.

While many of the foregoing provisions address complex issues for which negotiating experience, even multilaterally, was scant at the time AFAS was developed, all have subsequently been addressed and, in some cases, substantively enhanced, in a large number of post-AFAS preferential agreements governing services trade. A significant development has been the decision in 2012 by ASEAN Member States to start negotiations to enhance AFAS, with the stated aim of further broadening and deepening integration within ASEAN and ASEAN's integration into the global supply chain.[12] This new agreement will be known as ATISA, and it was stated as aiming to be completed by the end of 2015 to lay the foundation for the post-2015 ASEAN policy on trade in services, but this was delayed[13] until November 2018. Such a development is long overdue. The seeming lack of appetite, in the past, of ASEAN Member States to revisit and update their services rule-book and codify best PTA practices on the rule-making front was somewhat paradoxical, given the regional grouping's otherwise professed acknowledgement of the service

---

[12] This was first mentioned at the 44th ASEAN Economic Ministers' Meeting, 27–28 August 2012, Siem Reap, Cambodia, and reiterated at the 45th ASEAN Economic Ministers' Meeting, 19 August 2013, Brunei Darussalam.

[13] See Chairman's Statement of the 24th ASEAN Summit, Nay Pyi Daw, 11 May 2014.

sector's central importance to the achievement of the ASEAN Economic Community objectives. This recent decision in relation to services rule-making has the potential to lead to important changes that might be comparable to the major substantive overhaul that ASEAN Member States agreed to perform in the area of investment policy by replacing the AIA by the ACIA.

GATS provisions need to be resorted to in relation to matters that are specifically mentioned in AFAS, but for which AFAS does not provide sufficient guidance, and these would include the GATS provisions on MFN, market access, national treatment and additional commitments. For instance, the treatment under AFAS of the key GATS disciplines of market access and non-discrimination has been discussed above. As the content of market access and non-discrimination and matters incidental to both disciplines have not been set out in AFAS, this would mean that these terms are to bear the same meaning as under the GATS. Therefore, when a Member State schedules market access commitments under AFAS, it is not allowed to maintain any of the restrictive measures set out in Article XVI of the GATS (unless they are scheduled). Similarly, the obligation to eliminate and prohibit discriminatory measures is not defined in AFAS, but non-discrimination might be understood in the light of Article V(1)(b) of the GATS to refer to the obligation of national treatment under Article XVII of the GATS, whereby each Member must accord to services and service providers of any other Member treatment no less favourable than it accords to its own like services and service providers. On the other hand, this definition could be argued to apply only to Article V of the GATS, leaving open the possibility that a wider meaning of non-discrimination, meaning not just national treatment but also MFN treatment, might have been intended under AFAS. Precisely how much further the commitments made by each Member State under AFAS to give market access and national treatment reach as compared with their GATS commitments will depend on what each Member State is willing to undertake in its respective AFAS schedule. As a matter of aspiration, however, it has already been observed that the market access rule under AFAS ultimately mandates a higher level of liberalization than under the GATS, as it requires AFAS Member States to eliminate substantially all market access limitations among Member States – something that is not required under the flexible approach of the GATS. The same is true of the ultimate AFAS aim of eliminating substantially all existing discriminatory measures among Member States, as compared with the national treatment obligation in Article XVII of the GATS, which mandates a Member's obligations by reference to 'the sectors inscribed in its Schedule, and subject to any conditions and qualifications set out therein', without mandating any particular level or nature of non-conforming measures to be eliminated.

It is well known that GATS commitments do not necessarily reflect the applied measures affecting trade in services. This leads to the question how to interpret the seemingly GATS+ requirement[14] in Article III(b) of AFAS that Member States must prohibit new or more discriminatory

---

[14] This is a requirement for an FTA to qualify as an economic integration agreement under Art. V of the GATS, but it is not a general requirement of the GATS agreement itself.

measures and market access limitations. Should the question whether a discriminatory measure is 'new' or 'more' (and therefore prohibited under AFAS) be gauged against the limitations and measures that are in existence and actually applied by each Member at the time of the AFAS agreement, or the possibly less generous commitments made in a Member's AFAS schedule that may reflect a higher level of discrimination or limitation than is actually applied by the Member State? Practically speaking, as there is no formal method to record the regulatory status quo applied in each Member State regarding discriminatory measures or market access limitations, which, in addition, could change from time to time, any deviations from the status quo would be difficult to monitor or police. Therefore, it is more likely that the application of – and adherence to – Article III of AFAS by Member States would be measured in relation to their formal AFAS commitments, and this may not necessarily result in their applying a more favourable regime regarding trade in services than they already do in reality.

In terms of rule-making, as stated earlier, AFAS goes no further than the GATS, except possibly in its 'ASEAN minus X' formula. However, it must be remembered that AFAS was signed at the end of 1995, within a year of the coming into force of the GATS on 1 January 1995. In these circumstances, it is likely that not enough time had elapsed for the GATS rules to be properly tested and for improvements to be conceived. Since ASEAN Member States have not proven particularly successful in – or keen on – devising new rules or developing existing rules for the liberalization of trade in services, any GATS+ liberalization attained by AFAS is to be achieved not so much through innovative rule-making but rather via the scheduling of broader and deeper commitments under the existing GATS rules. The extent to which AFAS commitments made by ASEAN Member States goes beyond their GATS commitments is analysed later in this study.

4.1.3 *Mutual Recognition Arrangements*

Article V of AFAS can be seen as an abbreviated version of the recognition provision found in Article VII of the GATS. As AFAS did not see the need to reproduce any part of Article VI of the GATS on domestic regulation or even to refer to this provision expressly, it seems significant that the topic of recognition, which is one aspect of the rules on domestic regulation, is specifically provided for under AFAS. Article V.1 allows each Member State to recognize, whether based on an agreement or autonomously, 'the education or experience obtained, requirements met, or licenses or certifications granted in another Member State, for the purpose of licensing or certification of service suppliers'. However, Article V.2 makes clear that a Member State is not required 'to accept or enter into such mutual recognition agreements or arrangements'.

A footnote to Article V further provides that these agreements 'are concluded for Member State only' and that '[i]n the event a Member State wishes to join such agreements or arrangements, it should be given equal opportunity to do at any time'. The inclusiveness of this provision is in line with Article VII of the GATS, though stated in summary form. There are elements of Article VII of the GATS that are missing, however. For instance, AFAS does not contain a provision that the opening of negotiations on mutual recognition agreements should be notified to a general body such as the ASEAN Secretariat. This might limit the ability of other states to join an agreement at its inception, as they might not know of these potential arrangements until the agreement is concluded. Further, unlike the GATS, there is no provision, albeit hortatory, that recognition should, where appropriate, be based on common international standards or regionally-agreed criteria. While it may be thought that the absence of these details might prevent AFAS from moving as fast as it potentially could in facilitating ASEAN-wide mutual recognition agreements, this does not appear to be the case in practice. ASEAN Member States have concluded seven services mutual recognition agreements (MRAs) under the ASEAN Economic Ministers and one under the ASEAN Tourism Ministers. These will be discussed later in this study.

4.1.4 Denial of Benefits/Rules of Origin

Unlike the GATS, in which rules of origin apply to both services[15] and services providers, the rules in AFAS apply to service providers but not to services per se. Although this may seem to have the effect of limiting the scope of ASEAN Member States to apply potentially restrictive rules of origin to services supplied on a cross-border basis (via Mode 1)

---

[15] Under GATS, Art. XXVII(b), a Member may deny the benefits of the Agreement to the supply of a service that is supplied from or in the territory of a non-Member.

without the movement of either people (service providers) or capital (i.e. through an established or commercial presence), the restrictive rule that affects a service supplier of a non-state will inevitably affect the services provided by this supplier.

Under Article VI of AFAS, the benefits of AFAS shall be denied to a service supplier who is a natural person of a non-Member State. However, there are no provisions in AFAS to help to determine when a service supplier will be considered to be a 'natural person of a non-Member State'. In such circumstances, the definitions contained in the GATS may be resorted to under Article XIV(1) of AFAS to interpret such a provision. Although the GATS contains a definition of 'natural person of another Member' in Article XXVIII(k),[16] it does not define the term 'natural person of a non-Member State', and the meaning of the latter term has to be extrapolated from the definition of the former. Since 'natural person

---

[16] GATS, Art. XXVIII(k) provides: 'natural person of another Member' means a natural person who resides in the territory of that other Member or any other Member, and who under the law of that other Member:
   (i) is a national of that other Member; or
   (ii) has the right of permanent residence in that other Member, in the case of a Member which:
   1. does not have nationals; or
   2. accords substantially the same treatment to its permanent residents as it does to its nationals in respect of measures affecting trade in services, as notified in its acceptance of or accession to the WTO Agreement, provided that no Member is obligated to accord to such permanent residents treatment more favourable than would be accorded by that other Member to such permanent residents. Such notification shall include the assurance to assume, with respect to those permanent residents, in accordance with its laws and regulations, the same responsibilities that other Member bears with respect to its nationals.

of another Member' means a natural person who resides in the territory of that other Member or any other Member, and who under the law of that other Member is a national of that other Member, the corollary should be that 'natural person of a non-Member State' means someone who resides in the territory of that non-Member State or any other non-Member State and who is a national of that non-Member State. But what would be the position if the service supplier resides in a Member State despite being a national of a non-Member State? This could arguably take the service supplier outside the meaning of 'natural person of a non-Member State', as this term could be argued to require both elements of residence in and nationality of a non-Member State. On this interpretation, it is possible that a natural person who is a national of a non-Member State could qualify for the benefits of AFAS by virtue of his or her residence in a Member State. However, this is unclear.

As regards juridical persons, the benefits of AFAS can be denied to 'a juridical person owned or controlled by persons of a non-Member State constituted under the laws of a Member State, but not engaged in substantive business operations in the territory of Member State(s)'. The group of persons falling within this restriction is relatively narrow and, taking the provision literally, it would seem that it will not prevent the benefits of AFAS to be enjoyed by (i) a juridical person owned or controlled by persons of a non-Member State constituted under the laws of a Member State, *but engaged in substantive business operations in the territory of Member State(s)* or (ii) *a juridical person owned or controlled by persons of a Member State,* regardless of whether it is constituted under the laws of a Member or non-Member State, and regardless of whether it is engaged in substantive business operations in the territory of Member State(s).

By way of illustration, the AFAS denial of benefits clause would prevent a United States person or company (ownership or control 'by persons of a non-Member State') that sets up a locally incorporated company in Malaysia ('constituted under the laws of a Member State') from taking advantage of AFAS if the Malaysian company is not engaged in substantive business operations in Malaysia or another ASEAN Member State. While this may be one disincentive for US companies to invest in Malaysia, it is unlikely to have adverse economic effects for Malaysia, as AFAS benefits would be denied only if the US-controlled local company did not engage in substantive business operations in Malaysia or another ASEAN Member State and, in that sense, amounts to a shell company. Looked at from the opposite perspective, a Malaysian company owned or controlled by US persons will still be able to enjoy the benefits of AFAS so long as it carries on substantive business operations in Malaysia or another ASEAN Member State.

Economic integration agreements form an exception to the MFN principle in the GATS and are allowed only under the terms laid out in Article V of the GATS. Article V.6 provides that a 'service supplier of any other Member that is a juridical person constituted under the laws of a party to an agreement referred to in paragraph 1 shall be entitled to treatment granted under such agreement, provided that it engages in substantive business operations in the territory of the parties to such agreement'. This provision makes clear that the constitution of a service supplier under the laws of a party to the economic integration agreement, and not the control or ownership of that service supplier, is the determining factor for enjoying the benefits of a qualifying economic integration agreement. The only other requirement in Article V.6 of the GATS is that the service supplier should engage in substantive business operations in the territory of the parties to the agreement. However, more restrictive rules of origin are possible in economic integration agreements that involve only developing country members. Arguably, all ASEAN countries are developing countries.[17] Article V(3)(b) of the GATS provides that, in such cases, notwithstanding paragraph 6 of Article V, 'more favourable treatment may be granted to juridical persons owned or controlled by natural persons of the parties to such an agreement'. In the case of AFAS, the difference in treatment is manifested by the opposite phenomenon of less favourable treatment being given under the agreement to juridical persons owned or controlled

---

[17] Some have suggested that it might be uncertain whether Singapore would qualify as a developing country under the GATS. As there is no definition of what constitutes a developing country in the WTO, Members self-select whether they are developed or developing. However, an attempt by a Member to take advantage of a GATS provision that is for the benefit of developing countries may be challenged by other WTO Members. Singapore has used the more stringent rules of origin allowed for developing countries under the Comprehensive Economic Cooperation Agreement with India, in which Art. 7.23(1)(c) provides that a Party can deny the benefits of the services chapter to 'the supply of a service through commercial presence, if the Party establishes at any time that persons of a non-Party own or control, or have acquired ownership or control over through subsequent transactions, the service supplier.

by persons of a non-Member State. There is, however, no requirement in AFAS that a juridical person who is entitled to enjoy the benefits of AFAS needs to be owned or controlled by a natural as opposed to a juridical person of a Member State.

4.1.5 ASEAN Minus X

An important, variable geometry-promoting, market-opening innovation that AFAS has over the GATS stems from the adoption of the so-called 'ASEAN minus X' formula. Article II(1) of AFAS obliges all Member States to participate in cooperation agreements under the Framework Agreement, but with the understanding that 'two or more Member States may proceed first if other Member States are not ready to implement these arrangements'.[18] Following the decision by ASEAN Economic Ministers to accelerate services liberalization among Member States, AFAS was amended in 2003 to expand the 'ASEAN minus X' approach to cover also the conduct of negotiations and the liberalization of trade in services. This was done through a Protocol to Amend the ASEAN Framework Agreement on Services (the 'Amendment Protocol'), signed on 2 September 2003,[19] which inserted a new Article IV*bis* into AFAS. This new article states that

---

[18] This approach was set out in para. 3 of Art. I of the Framework Agreement on Enhancing ASEAN Economic Cooperation, signed on 28 January 1992 in Singapore.

[19] Entered into force on 31 December 2004.

'[n]otwithstanding the provisions of Article IV of this Framework Agreement, two or more Member States may conduct negotiations and agree to liberalize trade in services for specific sectors or sub-sectors (hereinafter referred to as "the participating Member States")'. Significantly, Article IV*bis* does not require that such preferential treatment be extended to the remaining Member States, providing instead that '[a]ny extension of such preferential treatment to the remaining Member States on an MFN basis shall be applied voluntary on the part of the participating Member States'. It would seem from this provision that although participating Member States are not obliged to extend preferences negotiated and agreed upon under the 'ASEAN minus X' formula to the remaining Member States, if the participating Member States decide to extend such preferences voluntarily to other Member States, this cannot be done selectively but must be granted to all remaining Member States on an MFN basis. This is confirmed by the interpretative notes at the end of the AFAS Amendment Protocol, which state that 'any preferential treatment extended to the remaining Member States on a voluntary basis shall be unconditional, non-discriminatory and without the need for reciprocity'.

Inclusiveness is one of the operative principles in the implementation of the 'ASEAN minus X' formula. Article IV*bis* paragraph 3 requires participating Member States to keep the remaining Member States informed of the progress or results of their negotiations, including the scheduling of commitments in the specific sectors or sub-sectors concerned, and Member States who wish to join any ongoing negotiations among the participating Member States may do so in consultation with the participating Member States. Where an agreement has been reached pursuant to the 'ASEAN minus X' formula, any Member State who is not a party to this agreement may in due course become a party by 'making offers at similar or acceptable levels to the participating Member States'.[20]

What might be deemed to be 'acceptable' by the participating Member States in an existing agreement could vary depending on developmental differences (in terms of both economic development and stage of development of the particular sector) in the Member State wishing to join the agreement. However, while the acceptable level of commitments by aspiring members can be lower than the commitments made by the participating Member States, the converse is not true. The interpretative notes to the AFAS Amendment Protocol state that 'participating Member States shall not require a higher level of commitments from the remaining Member States than their respective commitments under the agreement'.

4.2 Liberalization and Cooperation under AFAS

4.2.1 ASEAN Policies Affecting Services

The Singapore Declaration of 1992 provided that ASEAN should move towards a higher overall level of economic

---

[20] AFAS, Art. IV*bis*, para. 3.

cooperation to secure regional peace and prosperity, in conjunction with which the Framework Agreement on Enhancing ASEAN Economic Cooperation was signed on 28 January 1992.[21] This Agreement called upon ASEAN Member States to explore further measures on border and non-border areas of cooperation to supplement and complement the liberalization of trade. As a result, AFAS was signed by ASEAN Economic Ministers on 15 December 1995. Greater ambitions were affirmed when the ASEAN Leaders decided at their Summit in Kuala Lumpur in December 1997 to transform ASEAN into a stable, prosperous and highly competitive region with equitable economic development, reduced poverty and socio-economic disparities in the year 2020 (ASEAN Vision 2020).

The 9th ASEAN Summit ('Bali Concord II') held in October 2003 saw the emergence of the concept of an 'ASEAN Community' comprising three pillars of cooperation respectively in the political and security, economics and socio-cultural fields. The ASEAN Economic Community (AEC) was stated to be the ultimate aim of economic integration as outlined in the ASEAN Vision 2020. On 13 January 2007, the 12th ASEAN Summit accelerated the time frame for the establishment of the ASEAN Community to 2015, and on 20 November 2007 the 13th ASEAN Summit adopted the AEC Blueprint to implement the AEC by 2015. The free flow of services was identified as one of the key means of realizing the AEC, and specific time frames and targets were set under the AEC Blueprint to achieve this by 2015. It was later clarified that the deadline was to be at the end, and not the beginning, of 2015. On 22 November 2015, the ASEAN Heads of State/

Government signed a declaration formally to establish the AEC on 31 December 2015.[21]

4.2.2 The AEC Blueprint 2015

The provisions of the AEC Blueprint 2015 have been of the utmost importance in guiding the liberalization of trade in services in ASEAN. It sets out the specific end goals of the AEC in achieving the 'free flow of trade in services' by 2015 and also lays out interim goals for various aspects of the process. By the phrase 'free flow of trade in services', which is a key element in realizing the AEC, the ASEAN Member States envisage a situation in which 'there will be substantially no restriction to ASEAN services suppliers in providing services and in establishing companies across national borders within the region, subject to domestic regulations'.[22]

Any assessment of services trade liberalization under AFAS must be done not just by looking at the state of liberalization at a particular point in time (which will reflect only the incomplete picture of a work in progress), but also always bearing in mind the end goals stated in the AEC Blueprint 2015. It is useful to remember that the main negotiations in relation to the free flow of services in ASEAN took place at the time that the Blueprint was being prepared and the results of these negotiations laid out therein.

---

[21] 2015 Kuala Lumpur Declaration on the Establishment of the ASEAN Community, available at www.asean.org/wp-content/uploads/2015/12/K L-Declaration-on-Establishment-of-ASEAN-Community-2015.pdf
[22] AEC Blueprint 2015, para. 20.

In the run-up to the AEC in 2015, the focus of ASEAN Member States was largely on implementing the plans (as periodically reviewed) that had already been agreed upon in the Blueprint. The principles to be applied and aims and actions to be taken under the AEC Blueprint 2015 relating to trade in services are as follows:

1. Remove substantially all restrictions on trade in services:[23]
   - by 2010 for the four priority services sectors of air transport, e-ASEAN, healthcare and tourism;
   - by 2013 for the fifth priority sector of logistics services;
   - by 2015 for all other service sectors.
2. Undertake liberalization through consecutive rounds every two years from 2008 to 2015, with a target to schedule minimum numbers of new sub-sectors for each round[24] (expressly based on GATS W/120 classification and taking into account only the sub-sectors negotiated under the purview of ASEAN Economic Ministers). The targets set in the Blueprint were subsequently updated and are as follows:[25]
   - 2009 (AFAS Package 7): ten new sub-sectors (total sixty-five sub-sectors);[26]

---

[23] Ibid., item 21(i) and (ii).   [24] Ibid., item 21(iii) and (iv).
[25] See *ASEAN Integration Report 2015* (Jakarta: ASEAN Secretariat, November 2015), p. 29.
[26] The total number of sub-sectors shown in this list is not expressly stated in the AEC Blueprint 2015 but has been mentioned in other official publications by the ASEAN Secretariat and referred to in writings by third parties. An example from an official source is the ASEAN Secretariat's publication *ASEAN Integration in Services* (2009), which

- 2011 (AFAS Package 8): fifteen new sub-sectors (total eighty sub-sectors);
- 2013 (AFAS Package 9): twenty-four new sub-sectors (total 104 sub-sectors);
- 2015 (AFAS Package 10): twenty-four new sub-sectors (total 128 sub-sectors).

3. Schedule packages of commitments for every round, according to the following parameters:[27]
    (i) Modes 1 and 2: No restrictions except due to *bona fide* regulatory reasons (such as public safety) which are subject to agreement by all Member Countries on a case-by-case basis;
    (ii) Mode 3:[28]
        (a) Allow for minimum foreign (ASEAN) equity participation targets;
        By 2009: four earlier priority sectors not less than 51 percent; Logistics: not less than 49 percent; Other services sectors: not less than 49 percent
        By 2011: four earlier priority sectors not less than 70 percent; Logistics: not less than 51 percent; Other services sectors: not less than 51 percent

---

states at p. 10 that liberalizing an additional ten new sub-sectors for the seventh package of commitments would make a total of sixty-five sub-sectors based on the W/120 classification. From this starting point, the total number of sub-sectors to be liberalized with each successive package can be calculated.

[27] AEC Blueprint 2015, item 21(v), (vi) and (vii).
[28] As updated subsequently. See *ASEAN Integration Report 2015* (Jakarta: ASEAN Secretariat, November 2015), p. 29.

By 2013: four earlier priority sectors and logistics: not less than 70 percent;
By 2015: Other services sectors: not less than 70 percent

(b) Progressively remove other Mode 3 market access limitations by 2015.

(iii) Mode 4, national treatment limitations and limitations in the horizontal commitments: set the parameters of liberalization for each round by 2009 and thereafter schedule commitments according to such agreed parameters.

4. Complete the compilation of an inventory of barriers to services by August 2008.[29]

5. There shall be no back loading of commitments but ASEAN Member Countries are to be accorded overall flexibilities and scheduling flexibilities in each round:[30]

(i) Allow for overall flexibilities (of 15 percent) that cover the sub-sectors totally excluded from liberalization and the sub-sectors in which not all the agreed parameters of liberalization of the modes of supply are met, in scheduling liberalization commitments.

(ii) Allow the following flexibilities for the scheduling of liberalization commitments in each round:
- possibility of catching up in the next round if a Member Country is not able to meet the parameters of commitments set for the previous round;
- allowing for substituting sub-sectors that have been agreed to be liberalized in a round but for which a

[29] AEC Blueprint 2015, item 21(viii).   [30] Ibid., items 20 and 21(ix).

Member Country is not able to make commitments with sub-sectors outside the agreed sub-sectors; and
- liberalization through the ASEAN minus X formula.
6. Complete, implement and develop MRAs:[31]
   (i) complete MRAs currently under negotiation, i.e. architectural services, accountancy services, surveying qualifications, medical practitioners by 2008, and dental practitioners by 2009; and implement them expeditiously according to the provisions of each respective MRA by 2015;
   (ii) identify and develop MRAs for other professional services by 2012, to be completed by 2015; and
7. Strengthen human resource development and capacity building in the area of services.[32]
8. Liberalize the financial services sector according to certain principles and targets:[33]
   - Liberalization measures will be subject to prudential measures and balance of payment safeguards as provided for under the GATS, and these should allow members to ensure orderly financial sector development and the maintenance of financial and socio-economic stability.
   - Liberalization can take place through the ASEAN minus X formula where countries that are ready to liberalize can proceed first and be joined by others later.
   - The process of liberalization should take place with due respect for national policy objectives and the level of

---

[31] Ibid., item 21(x), (xi) and (xii).   [32] Ibid., item 21(xiii).
[33] Ibid., item 22.

economic and financial sector development of the individual members.
- There should be progressive liberalization of restrictions in sub-sectors or modes as identified by each Member Country[34] by 2015, and progressive liberalization of restrictions in the remaining sub-sectors or modes by 2020. In both instances, Member States can maintain restrictions that fall within 'pre-agreed flexibilities' developed and agreed to earlier according to a schedule laid down by the Blueprint.

9. Supporting the Priority Integration Sectors (PIS):[35]
   (i) Conduct a bi-annual review to monitor the status, progress and effectiveness of PIS road maps to ensure their timely implementation; and
   (ii) Identify sector-specific projects or initiatives through regular dialogues or consultation with stakeholders, particularly the private sector.

10. Expeditiously implement the enabling framework for the full liberalization of air services in ASEAN:

   (i) Implement the ASEAN Open Sky Policy (Road map for Integration of the Air Travel Sector); and
   (ii) Implement the ASEAN Single Aviation Market.[36]

After the establishment of the AEC in 2015, liberalization of services trade in ASEAN continues under the AEC Blueprint 2025, the primary focus of which is the negotiation and implementation of the ATISA. Under the AEC Blueprint 2025, continued efforts will also be made to:[37]

---

[34] Ibid., Annex 1.   [35] Ibid., item 37(i) and (ii).
[36] Ibid., items 47 and 49.   [37] Ibid., item 13.

i. review existing flexibilities, limitations, thresholds and carve-outs, as appropriate;
ii. enhance mechanisms to attract foreign direct investment (FDI) in the services sectors, including but not limited to foreign equity participation to support global value chain (GVC) activities;
iii. explore alternative approaches for further liberalization of services;
iv. establish possible disciplines on domestic regulations to ensure competitiveness of the services sector, taking into consideration other non-economic or development or regulatory objectives;
v. consider the development of sectoral annexes; and
vi. enhance technical cooperation in the services sector for human resource development (HRD), joint promotion activities to attract FDI in the services sector, and the exchange of best practices.

4.2.3 Progress Report

The liberalization of trade in services under AFAS has been pursued under successive packages of commitments, with target completion dates set under the AEC Blueprint 2015 from the seventh package onwards. The ten packages of commitments were signed in 1997, 1998, 2001, 2004, 2006, 2007, 2009, 2010, 2015 and 2018.[38] There was a time lag of five years between

---

[38] First package, signed on 15 December 1997 in Kuala Lumpur, Malaysia; second package, signed on 16 December 1998 in Ha Noi, Vietnam; third package, signed by 31 December 2001 (Ad-Referendum Signing); fourth package, signed on 3 September 2004 in Jakarta, Indonesia; fifth package,

the eighth and ninth packages, reflecting the progressive difficulty of agreeing on the commitments. This was despite the political will shown by ASEAN Member States to keep to the AEC target dates. At the 44th ASEAN Economic Ministers (AEM) Meeting in August 2012, the Ministers tasked the Senior Officials with liberalizing the remaining services subsectors through the ninth and tenth AFAS Packages by 2013 and 2015, respectively. But it was not until November 2015 that the ninth package was signed. The tenth package had not been completed at the time the AEC was established at the end of 2015, and was only signed in August 2018.[39]

AFAS covers all service sectors and generally comes under the Coordinating Committee on Services (CCS), which reports to AEM through the Senior Economic Officials Meeting (SEOM). Since June 1999, the liberalization of trade in financial services and air transport services under AFAS has been negotiated separately and is overseen by the ASEAN Finance Ministers Meeting[40] and the ASEAN Transport Ministers,[41] respectively. Among the possible reasons for such separate

---

signed on 8 December 2006 in Cebu, the Philippines; sixth package, signed on 19 November 2007 in Singapore; seventh package, signed on 26 February 2009 in Cha-am, Thailand; eighth package, signed on 28 October 2010 in Ha Noi, Vietnam; and ninth package, signed on 27 November 2015 in Makati City, the Philippines.

[39] www.asean2018.sg/Newsroom/Press-Releases/Press-Release-Details/20180829_Signing_Ceremony_of_ASEAN_Agreements

[40] This is overseen by the Working Committee on ASEAN Financial Services Liberalization under the ASEAN Framework Agreement on Services (WC-FSL/AFAS).

[41] This is overseen by the Air Transport Sectoral Negotiation (ATSN) of the Air Transport Working Group.

treatment are considerations of bureaucratic turf that prevail in sectors that feature particular economy-wide or security-related concerns of a systemic nature. Such turf-related issues are far from unique to the ASEAN context. Progress has been registered in these sectors under the aegis of ASEAN Finance and Transport Ministers, who have signed six protocols on financial services and six on air transport services.

In September 2001, services incidental to the five sectors of manufacturing, agriculture, fishery, forestry, and mining and quarrying were taken out of the ambit of AFAS and made subject to the AIA Framework Agreement (and subsequently the ACIA) under the Coordinating Committee on Investment (CCI) instead.[42]

A quantitative view can be taken of the sectoral responsibilities of the different regional authorities. Based on the W/120 classification of services sectors,[43] there are a total of 155 sub-sectors. In summary, of the allocation of responsibilities described above, 128 sub-sectors are within the purview of the ASEAN Economic Ministers, 17 are within that of the ASEAN Finance Ministers, six are within that of the ASEAN Transport Ministers and four are within that of the Central Coordination Committee on Investment.[44]

---

[42] The CCI also reports to the AEM through the SEOM. The AIA Framework Agreement was updated and subsumed under the ASEAN Comprehensive Investment Agreement (ACIA) in February 2009, together with the 1996 Agreement for the Promotion and Protection of Investments.

[43] 'W/120' refers to WTO document MTN.GNS/W/120, dated 10 July 1991.

[44] See *ASEAN Services Report 2017: The Evolving Landscape* (Jakarta, ASEAN Secretariat, August 2017) at p. 28, n. 17.

Meanwhile, ASEAN Member States have entered into eight MRAs. Seven of these of these fall within the purview of the ASEAN Economic Ministers and are aimed at enabling professional services suppliers certified or registered by the relevant authorities in their home country to be mutually recognized by other signatory Member States. The eighth relates to tourism services that are within the purview of the ASEAN Tourism Ministers.

4.3 AFAS Negotiating History and Modalities

Negotiations to liberalize trade in services under AFAS initially took place under various rounds of negotiations.[46] From 1996 to 2007, four such negotiating rounds were held under AFAS, through which ASEAN Member States used increasingly innovative approaches and criteria by adopting formula-based routes to market opening in services and requiring the attainment of mode-specific objectives. The first round (1996–8) used a GATS-style 'request and offer approach' in which the negotiation process started with an exchange of information among Member States on their existing GATS and other services commitments. This resulted in the first and second packages of AFAS commitments.

The second round (1999–2001) used a 'common sub-sector approach' and resulted in the third package of AFAS commitments. Under this approach, sub-sectors in which four or more Member States had made commitments under the GATS or previous AFAS packages were identified and Member States were asked to schedule commitments in these identified sub-sectors.

In the third round (2002–4), a 'modified common sub-sector approach' was used, resulting in the fourth package of AFAS commitments. This was a more rigorous version of the 'common sub-sector approach' in that the identified sub-sectors were those in which three or more Member States had made commitments under the GATS or previous AFAS packages, so that an increased number of sub-sectors had to be scheduled.

In the fourth round of negotiations (2005–7), Member States were asked to schedule a minimum number of sub-sectors from two sets of sub-sectors: a mandatory list consisting of sixty-five sub-sectors and a list of nineteen sub-sectors from which Member States had to choose to schedule at least five. The scheduling was to be based on certain threshold levels, consisting of (i) scheduling 'none' for Mode 1 and 2 commitments (i.e. no limitations on market access and national treatment in these two modes of supply) unless justifiable reasons could be provided, and (ii) scheduling Mode 3 foreign equity participation threshold limitations of 49 percent for the priority services sub-sectors, 51 percent for the construction sub-sector, and 30 percent for the other services sectors. This round resulted in the fifth and sixth packages of AFAS commitments.

The fifth AFAS package saw a further change in scheduling methodology. The first to fourth AFAS packages only recorded changes in commitments from previous packages, making it necessary to refer to past packages to get a total picture of all the commitments scheduled under AFAS. From the fifth AFAS package onwards, all previous AFAS and GATS commitments (other than those taken out from AFAS or those in finance and air transport services, which had been removed from the purview of the ASEAN Economic Ministers) were consolidated into a single comprehensive schedule together with the new commitments made under subsequent packages.[45] This was more convenient and user friendly, except that it became more difficult to identify any improvements over previous commitments.

When the AEC Blueprint 2015 was adopted in November 2007, the approach taken towards services liberalization changed yet again and the commitments were not negotiated in the same way as before. Instead, ASEAN Member States had to comply with pre-determined targets and timelines, involving a set of objectives and formulae across modes and priority sectors as laid out in the Blueprint, discussed in more detail below. This approach was taken for the seventh, eighth, ninth and tenth AFAS packages. Table 4.1 offers a synoptic review of the various market-opening packages and negotiating modalities under AFAS to date.

It should be noted that negotiation of (i) financial services and air transport services and (ii) services incidental to manufacturing, agriculture, fishery, forestry, and mining and quarrying were subject to the above negotiating

---

[45] ASEAN Secretariat Paper, *ASEAN Integration in Trade in Services: Development, Challenges and Way Forward*, presented at ADBI-PECC Conference on 'Strategies to Enhance Competitiveness and Facilitate Regional Trade and Investment in Services' Hong Kong, China, 1–3 June 2011, draft of 22 May 2011, available at: www.pecc.org/resources/doc_view/1715-asean-integration-in-trade-in-services-development-challenges-and-way-forward-paper

Table 4.1 *AFAS package of commitments and negotiation modalities under ASEAN Economic Ministers*

Package of commitments	Round	Protocol signed	Negotiation modality
First package	First round (1996–8)	15 Dec 1997	Request and offer approach
Second package		16 Dec 1998	Request and offer approach
Third package	Second round (1999–2001)	31 Dec 2001	Common sub-sector approach
Fourth package	Third round (2002–4)	3 Sept 2004	Modified common sub-sector approach
Fifth package	Fourth round (2005–7)	8 Dec 2006	Minimum sub-sectors from two tables of sub-sectors
Sixth package		19 Nov 2007	Minimum sub-sectors from two tables of sub-sectors
Seventh package (2008–9)		26 Feb 2009	Pre-set parameters under AEC Blueprint and any subsequent ministerial decisions
Eighth package (2009–10)		28 Oct 2010	Pre-set parameters under AEC Blueprint and any subsequent ministerial decisions
Ninth package (2010–15)		27 Nov 2015	Pre-set parameters under AEC Blueprint and any subsequent ministerial decisions
Tenth package (2015–18)		29 Aug 2018	Pre-set parameters under AEC Blueprint and any subsequent ministerial decisions

modalities only until June 1999 and September 2001, respectively, before being removed from the purview of the ASEAN Economic Ministers as discussed earlier.

4.3.1 *Financial Services*

The first package of financial services commitments under AFAS were contained in the second AFAS package signed by the ASEAN Economic Ministers in 1998. Subsequent commitments on financial services can be found in six protocols signed by the ASEAN Finance Ministers as follows:

second package, signed on 6 April 2002 in Yangon, Myanmar
third package, signed on 6 April 2005 in Vientiane, Lao PDR
fourth package, signed on 4 April 2008 in Da Nang, Vietnam
fifth package, signed on 4 May 2011 in Ha Noi, Vietnam
sixth package, signed on 20 March 2015 in Kuala Lumpur, Malaysia
seventh package, signed on 23 June 2016 in Hanoi, Vietnam.

The protocols to implement the sixth and seventh packages on financial services include an important provision related to the ASEAN Banking Integration Framework (ABIF) conducted by the ASEAN Central Bank Governors, which allows two or more ASEAN Member States to liberalize their banking sectors at any time, without necessarily extending such preferential treatment to the remaining ASEAN Member States on an MFN basis.[46]

---

[46] See Art. 5 of the Protocol to Implement the Sixth Package of Commitments on Financial Services under the ASEAN Framework

4.3.2 *Air Transport Services*

The first three packages of commitments in air transport services were contained in the first, second and third packages of AFAS commitments signed by the ASEAN Economic Ministers. There have been seven additional packages of commitments on air transport signed by ASEAN Transport Ministers as follows:

fourth package, signed on 23 November 2004 in Phnom Penh, Cambodia
fifth package, signed on 8 February 2007 in Bangkok, Thailand
sixth package, signed on 10 December 2009 in Hanoi, Vietnam
seventh package, signed on 16 December 2011 in Phnom Penh, Cambodia
eighth package, signed on 19 December 2013 in Pakse City, Lao PDR
ninth package, signed on 6 November 2015 in Kuala Lumpur, Malaysia
tenth package, signed on 13 October 2017 in Singapore.

In addition to the above packages of commitment in air transport, a number of other important ASEAN agreements on air transport have been signed. These include:

- the ASEAN Memorandum of Understanding on Air Freight Services, signed on 19 September 2002 in Jakarta, Indonesia, and its amending Protocol signed on 8 February 2007 in Bangkok, Thailand;

Agreement on Services and Art. 5 of the Protocol to Implement the Seventh Package of Commitments on Financial Services under the ASEAN Framework Agreement on Services.

- the ASEAN Multilateral Agreement on the Full Liberalization of Air Freight Services, signed on 20 May 2009 in Manila, the Philippines;
- the ASEAN Multilateral Agreement on Air Services, signed on 20 May 2009 in Manila, the Philippines;
- ASEAN Multilateral Agreement on the Full Liberalization of Passenger Air Services, signed on 12 November 2010 in Bandar Seri Begawan, Brunei Darussalam; and
- Implementation Framework of the ASEAN Single Aviation Market (ASAM), adopted on 15 December 2011 in Phnom Penh, Cambodia

4.3.3 Priority Integration Sectors

The ASEAN Economic Ministers identified eleven priority integration sectors in 2003 and a twelfth sector in 2005 that they hoped would serve as a catalyst for overall ASEAN economic integration. Of these, five have a direct connection with trade in services, namely tourism, e-ASEAN, air travel, healthcare and logistics. At the ninth ASEAN Summit, held on 7 October 2003 in Bali, Indonesia, ASEAN Heads of States signed the ASEAN Framework Agreement for the Integration of Priority Sectors, which lists the measures to be implemented, with clear timelines, by Member States in respect of the above priority sectors. Each of the priority integration sectors has a road map that sets out specific sectoral initiatives as well as broader initiatives cutting across all sectors. Under the relevant road maps, substantial liberalization of trade in the four priority service sectors of tourism, e-ASEAN, air travel and healthcare was to be achieved by 2010, while the deadline for the logistics sector, which was identified later than the others as a priority service sector, was set for 2013.

AFAS stands out among the world's leading integration agreements in services as one in which concerted forward movement on the market-opening front is most orchestrated – far more, for instance, than the NAFTA or several other bilateral compacts agreed by the world's leading exporters of services.

e-ASEAN

The e-ASEAN Road map[47] is intended to enable the progressive, expeditious and systematic integration of ASEAN Member States in the digital age through the liberalization of trade in information and communications technology (ICT) products and services. The measures in the e-ASEAN Road map relating to services include horizontal issues across all sectors as well was sector-specific issues such as regulatory standards and capacity building in relation to telecommunications services and measures facilitating the certification and recognition of ICT skills and qualifications. Horizontal measures affecting the supply of services include the development of integrated transport logistics services within ASEAN; acceleration of liberalization of trade in services in the priority services sectors; accelerating the development of MRAs and promoting joint ventures; as well as facilitating the movement of business persons, experts and professionals. Similar horizontal measures are also found in the Road maps for Tourism and for Healthcare.

---

[47] ASEAN Sectoral Integration Protocol for e-ASEAN, Appendix I: Road map for Integration of e-ASEAN Sector.

Despite the identification of e-ASEAN as a priority sector for market opening, there arises the question why Member States have chosen to eschew the incorporation into AFAS of a range of provisions on digital trade now routinely found in the services and investment chapters of a growing number of PTAs, several of which were entered into on a bilateral or plurilateral basis by individual ASEAN Member States (e.g. the Singapore–US Free Trade Agreement or, most recently, the detailed provisions found in the Comprehensive and Progressive Trans Pacific Partnership (CPTPP) agreement). The specific aim of such chapters, which are typically embedded in the cross-border services and investment sections of PTAs, is typically to prohibit recourse to various types of trade impediments on digital transactions, to address a range of data protection, privacy and data flow issues as well as to facilitate the unimpeded remote delivery or consumption of services on a cross-border basis via Modes 1 and 2.

Tourism

The objectives of the Road map for the Integration of the Tourism Sector include the full integration of the Tourism sector across all ASEAN Member Countries, and the strengthening of regional integration efforts through various liberalization, facilitation and promotion measures.[48] The measures relating specifically to services consist of the horizontal measures listed above in relation to e-ASEAN, as well as sector specific human resource development measures such as

[48] ASEAN Sectoral Integration Protocol for Tourism, Appendix I: Road map for Integration of Tourism Sector.

the establishment of minimum competency standards for tourism professionals. Tourism and travel-related services sectors cover hotels and restaurants (including catering); travel agencies and tour operators services and tourist guide services.[49]

Healthcare

The Road map for Integration of the Healthcare Sector aims to strengthen the regionalization of the healthcare sector through selected liberalization and facilitation measures in the area of trade in goods, services and investments, as well as to promote private-sector involvement.[50] The measures relating specifically to services consist of horizontal measures similar to those directed to e-ASEAN and the tourism sector.

Air Travel

The Road map for the Integration of the Air Travel Sector seeks to advance the full liberalization of air transport services in ASEAN with a view to achieving open skies in the ASEAN region. The destination points stated in the Road map are the full liberalization of ASEAN air freight services as well as ASEAN-wide liberalization of scheduled passenger services, with no limitations on fifth freedom traffic rights for the capital city in each ASEAN Member Country.[51]

---

[49] ASEAN Sectoral Integration Protocol for Tourism, Appendix I: Road map for Integration of Tourism Sector, Attachment 1: Coverage of the Tourism Sector.

[50] ASEAN Sectoral Integration Protocol for Healthcare, Appendix I: Road map for integration of Healthcare Sector.

[51] ASEAN Sectoral Integration Protocol for Air Travel, Appendix I: Road map for Integration of Air Travel Sector.

Logistics

The aims stated in the Logistics Road map are to 'create an ASEAN single market by 2015 by strengthening ASEAN economic integration through liberalization and facilitation measures in the area of logistics services' and 'to support the establishment and enhance the competitiveness of an ASEAN production base through creation of an integrated ASEAN logistics environment'.[52] The sectors covered in this initiative are: maritime cargo-handling services; storage and warehousing services; freight transport agency services; other auxiliary services; courier services; packaging services; custom clearing services; maritime transport services (international freight transportation excluding cabotage); air freight services (via the implementation of the ASEAN Multilateral Agreement of the Full Liberalization of Air Freight Services); rail freight services (international rail freight transport services); and road freight transport services (international road freight transport services).

4.4 Mutual Recognition Agreements in Services

AFAS provides for MRAs in services that facilitate trade by mutual recognition of authorization, licensing or certification of professional service suppliers. These enable professional services suppliers who are certified or registered by the relevant authorities in their home country to be mutually

---

[52] ASEAN Sectoral Integration Protocol for the Logistics Services Sector, Appendix I: Road map for Integration of Logistics Services.

recognized by other signatory Member States. MRAs encourage the freer flow of foreign professionals within ASEAN, allowing them the advantage, if they possess mutually recognized qualifications, of being able to work in participating ASEAN countries without having to go through a full requalification process in each jurisdiction.

At the seventh ASEAN Summit in 2001, the ASEAN heads of states mandated the start of negotiations on MRAs to facilitate the flow of professional services under AFAS. Two working groups were tasked by the ASEAN Coordinating Committee on Services Council to negotiate MRAs in business services and healthcare services in 2003 and 2004, respectively. As a result of their work, the ASEAN Economic Ministers have concluded and signed seven services-related MRAs to date:

1. MRA on Engineering Services (Kuala Lumpur, Malaysia, 9 December 2005)
2. MRA on Nursing Services (Cebu, Philippines, 8 December 2006)
3. MRA on Architectural Services (Singapore, 19 November 2007)
4. Framework Arrangement for the Mutual Recognition of Surveying Qualifications (Singapore, 19 November 2007)
5. MRA on Medical Practitioners (Cha-am, Thailand, 26 February 2009)
6. MRA on Dental Practitioners (Cha-am, Thailand, 26 February 2009)
7. MRA on Accountancy Services (Nay Pyi Taw, Myanmar, 13 November 2014).

In addition, an MRA on Tourism Professionals under the ASEAN Tourism Ministers was completed in Bangkok, Thailand on 9 November 2012.

The eight MRAs vary significantly in detail and ambition.[53] The most basic is the agreement relating to surveying qualifications, which is a framework agreement with two aims: (1) to facilitate the negotiations of MRAs in the relevant services between or among ASEAN Member States by providing a structure, framework and basis towards the conclusion of such MRAs; and (2) to exchange information in order to promote the development of the best practices on standards and qualifications in the relevant profession.[54] Accountancy services were initially dealt with under a similar framework agreement, but are now covered by a fully fledged MRA. To date, no ASEAN-wide, bilateral or plurilateral agreement has been established on surveying qualifications. A road map has been developed and is being implemented by ASEAN Members States to promote mobility of ASEAN surveying professionals.[55]

The other ASEAN MRAs relating to trade in professional services are more detailed and tend to pursue broader and largely similar aims that include most or all or the following: (1) to facilitate mobility of the relevant professionals

---

[53] See generally Yoshifumi Fukunaga, 'Assessing the Progress of ASEAN MRAs on Professional Services', ERIA Discussion Paper Series, ERIA-DP-2015-21: www.eria.org/ERIA-DP-2015-21.pdf
[54] ASEAN Framework Arrangement for the Mutual Recognition of Surveying Qualifications, Art. 1.
[55] ASEAN Services Report 2017: The Evolving Landscape (Jakarta: ASEAN Secretariat, August 2017), p. 31.

within ASEAN; (2) to exchange information and enhance cooperation in respect of mutual recognition of the relevant professionals; (3) to promote adoption of best practices on standards and qualifications; and (4) to provide opportunities for capacity building and training of the relevant professionals.

The MRAs for engineers and architects are well developed and contain broadly similar principles leading towards ASEAN-wide certification for qualified professionals. The MRA for accountancy services also operates on broadly similar principles as these two MRAs, although the wording and numbering differ.[56] A central coordinating body has been established under each of these three MRAs (the ASEAN Chartered Professional Engineer Coordinating Committee, the ASEAN Architect Council and the ASEAN Chartered Professional Accountant Coordinating Committee), which have the authority to confer the titles of ASEAN Chartered Professional Engineer, ASEAN Architect or ASEAN Chartered Professional Accountant respectively on professionals who have met the requirements set out in the relevant MRAs.[57] Generally, the professional must meet the

---

[56] The MRA for accountancy services covers accountancy services under Central Product Classification (CPC) 862 of the Provisional CPC of the United Nations, except for signing off of the independent auditor's report and other accountancy services that require domestic licensing in the ASEAN Member States. See ASEAN MRA on Accountancy Services (2014), Art. 3.1.

[57] ASEAN MRA on Engineering Services (2005), Art. 4.3; ASEAN MRA on Architectural Services (2007), Art. 4.3; and ASEAN MRA on Accountancy Services (2014), Art. 7.1.

requirements applicable in his or her country of origin, such as appropriate qualification, professional registration and/or licence, minimum experience, satisfaction of continuing education requirements and absence of professional misconduct.[58]

A Monitoring Committee set up in each participating ASEAN Member Country is tasked with developing and maintaining a register of ASEAN Chartered Professional Engineers, ASEAN Architects or ASEAN Chartered Professional Accountants, certifying their qualifications and experience and monitoring compliance with the requirements of the respective MRAs.[59] Under the MRAs, the authority of the respective central coordinating bodies to confer the titles of ASEAN Chartered Professional Engineer, ASEAN Architect or ASEAN Chartered Professional Accountant can be delegated to the authorized Monitoring Committee in each participating ASEAN Member Country.[60] An ASEAN Chartered Professional Engineer, ASEAN Architect or ASEAN Chartered Professional Accountant may apply to the professional regulatory authority of a host country to be registered and to work as a Registered Foreign

---

[58] ASEAN MRA on Engineering Services (2005), Art. 3.1; ASEAN MRA on Architectural Services (2007), Art. 3.1; and ASEAN MRA on Accountancy Services (2014), Art. 4.1.
[59] ASEAN MRA on Engineering Services (2005), Art. 4.2; ASEAN MRA on Architectural Services (2007), Art. 4.2; and ASEAN MRA on Accountancy Services (2014), Art. 6.
[60] ASEAN MRA on Engineering Services (2005), Art. 4.3.1; ASEAN MRA on Architectural Services (2007), Art. 4.3.1; and ASEAN MRA on Accountancy Services (2014), Art. 7.1.

Professional Engineer, a Registered Foreign Architect or a Registered Foreign Professional Accountant. Engineers who are registered as Registered Foreign Professional Engineer may be allowed to work either independently or in collaboration with designated local Professional Engineers in the host country, while architects or accountants who are Registered Foreign Architects or Registered Foreign Professional Accountants cannot work independently but only in collaboration with licensed Architects or designated Professional Accountants in the host country.[61] Such practice shall, for Registered Foreign Professional Engineers, Registered Foreign Architects and Registered Foreign Professional Accountants, be subject to the domestic laws and regulations of the host country.

The MRAs on engineers and architects each provide that any ASEAN Member Country that wishes to participate in the arrangements as a 'participating ASEAN Member Country' under the respective MRA must notify the ASEAN Secretary General of its intention.[62] All ten ASEAN Member States have officially participated in both the MRAs on engineers and architects. As of October 2015, 1,483 ASEAN Chartered Professional Engineers from nine Member States were registered, and 284 ASEAN Architects from nine

---

[61] ASEAN MRA on Engineering Services (2005), Art. 4.1; ASEAN MRA on Architectural Services (2007), Art. 4.1; and ASEAN MRA on Accountancy Services (2014), Art. 4.3.2.

[62] ASEAN Mutual Recognition Arrangement on Engineering Services (2005), Art. 8; and ASEAN Mutual Recognition Arrangement on Architectural Services (2007), Art. 8.

Member States were also registered.[63] By August 2017, the number registered grew to 2,552 engineers and 417 architects,[64] and all ten Member States were represented.[65] The growing numbers show that both MRAs are off to an encouraging start. It would appear that the MRA on engineers has had more success than that on architects, further evidence of this being that six ASEAN Chartered Professional Engineers were registered as Registered Foreign Professional Engineers as of October 2015, whereas, at the same date, no ASEAN Architects had obtained a registration as a Registered Foreign Architect.[66] Obtaining an ASEAN certification is just the first step towards working in a foreign country. Crucially, the next major milestone will be met when a core of ASEAN Chartered Professional Engineers and ASEAN Architects successfully register in individual ASEAN Host Countries as Registered Foreign Professional Engineers or Registered Foreign Architects with a view to practising their professional skills in these countries. Obstacles include required legislative changes to the rules of professional practice and impediments imposed by domestic immigration law.

The MRA on Accountancy Services is an upgrade from the framework agreement, and is the most recent

[63] See *ASEAN Integration in Services* (Jakarta: ASEAN Secretariat, December 2015), pp. 28–9.
[64] See *ASEAN Services Report 2017: The Evolving Landscape* (Jakarta, ASEAN Secretariat, August 2017), p. 30.
[65] See the websites of the ASEAN Chartered Professional Engineer Coordinating Committee at www.acpecc.net and the ASEAN Architect Council at www.aseanarchitectcouncil.org
[66] See *ASEAN Integration in Services* (Jakarta: ASEAN Secretariat, December 2015), pp. 28–9.

services MRA to have entered into force. It is still in its early stages of implementation. The Monitoring Committees of all ASEAN Member States have been established, and the ASEAN Chartered Professional Accountant Coordinating Committee started its meeting in October 2015. Although broadly similar in structure to the MRAs on architectural services and on engineering services, it differs from them in doing away with the additional step of requiring Member States to notify the ASEAN Secretariat of their participation, so that the agreement automatically applies to all members unless they give notice of their intention to withdraw.

Under the three MRAs relating to healthcare services, i.e. those on nursing services, medical practitioners and dental practitioners, persons who meet the criteria listed in the respective MRAs may apply for registration in a host country to be allowed to practise their professions in accordance with the laws and regulations of the host country concerned. Such criteria include the possession of qualifications that are recognized by the regulatory bodies in the country of origin as well as the host country; possession of a valid licence from the country of origin; completion of a minimum period of practical or professional experience in the country of origin; compliance with any continuing professional development requirements in the country of origin; and certification of good conduct by the regulatory authorities of the country of origin.[67]

Medical and dental professionals additionally have to attest that no investigation or legal proceeding is pending

---

[67] MRA on Medical Practitioners, Art. 3.1; MRA on Dental Practitioners, Art. 3.1; and MRA on Nurses, Art. 3.1.

against them in the country of origin or another country, and that they comply with any other assessment or requirement as may be imposed by them on the regulatory authorities of the host country.[68] The professional regulatory authority for doctors, dentists or nurses of the host country will evaluate the qualifications of foreign applicants; impose requirements for registration; monitor and assess compliance with professional and ethical standards of the host country; and take action in the event of any failure to comply with these standards.[69] A foreign medical practitioner, dental practitioner or nurse who is allowed by the relevant professional regulatory authority to practise in the host country shall be subject to domestic regulations and conditions such as to be bound by the professional and ethical codes in the host country, to be bound by its prevailing laws, to subscribe to any required insurance liability scheme in the host country and to respect its culture and religious practice.[70] The MRAs for medical and dental practitioners provide that the MRA shall not reduce, eliminate or modify the rights, power and authority of each ASEAN Member State and its professional and other relevant authorities to regulate and control medical or dental practitioners and the practice of medicine or dentistry, and that such regulatory power should be exercised reasonably and in good faith without creating any unnecessary barriers to the

---

[68] MRA on Medical Practitioners, Arts. 3.1.6 and 3.1.7; and MRA on Dental Practitioners, Arts. 3.1.6 and 3.1.7.

[69] MRA on Medical Practitioners, Art. 4.1; MRA on Dental Practitioners, Art. 4.1; and MRA on Nurses, Art. 4.1.

[70] MRA on Medical Practitioners, Art. 3.3; MRA on Dental Practitioners, Art. 3.3; and MRA on Nurses, Art. 3.3.

practice of medicine or dentistry.[71] Each of the three healthcare MRAs mandates the setting up of an ASEAN Joint Coordinating Committee for medical practitioners, dental practitioners and nurses respectively to facilitate the implementation of the respective MRAs.[72] Unlike the MRAs for engineers, architects and accountants, by which the ASEAN-wide coordinating body has the power to register the respective professionals as ASEAN practitioners, the registration of foreign nurses, medical practitioners and dental practitioners is to take place on a bilateral rather than an ASEAN-wide basis. According to the AEC Scorecard 2012, the healthcare MRAs were still in various stages of implementation. As the healthcare sector has been identified as a priority integration sector under the AEC Blueprint, which is intended to serve as a catalyst for economic growth in the region, further delays would prove detrimental to this goal and hold back the tangible benefits that may be derived from these agreements. Nevertheless, the example of nursing services shows that a significant number of foreign nurses (including those from ASEAN) are permitted to work in individual ASEAN countries under various domestic regulations, although it is not clear to what extent this is being facilitated by the MRA on nursing services.[73]

---

[71] MRA on Medical Practitioners, Art. 5; and MRA on Dental Practitioners, Art. 5.
[72] MRA on Medical Practitioners, Art. 6; MRA on Dental Practitioners, Art. 6; and MRA on Nurses, Art. 4.2.
[73] Yoshifumi Fukunaga, 'Assessing the Progress of ASEAN MRAs on Professional Services', ERIA Discussion Paper Series, ERIA-DP-2015-21: www.eria.org/ERIA-DP-2015-21.pdf at pp. 18–22.

Under the MRA on Tourism Professionals, such professionals whose qualifications are recognized by other ASEAN Member States may be eligible to work in a host country provided that they possesses a valid tourism competency certificate in a specific tourism job title as specified in the ASEAN Common Competency Standards for Tourism Professionals, issued by the Tourism Professional Certification Board of an ASEAN Member State.[74] Such eligibility to work in a host country will be subject to the prevailing domestic laws and regulations of the host country. A wide range of job titles – 32 in all – are covered under the MRA. These range from hotel-related services such as front office manager, room attendant, baker and waiter, to travel-related services such as travel consultant, ticketing manager and tour manager. A number of the elements necessary for the implementation of the MRA have been completed, such as the ASEAN Common Competency Standards for Tourism Professionals, the Common ASEAN Tourism Curriculum, the Regional Qualifying Framework and Skills Recognition System, the ASEAN Tourism Professionals Monitoring Committee, and the National Tourism Professionals Board and Tourism Professionals Certification Board in respective ASEAN Member States.[75] Also completed are various training toolboxes to build competences for the priority tourism labour divisions, covering common and generic competencies

---

[74] MRA on Tourism Professionals, Art. 3. For details of the mechanisms and requirements instituted by this MRA, see *ASEAN MRA on Tourism Professionals Handbook* (Jakarta: ASEAN Secretariat, 2013).

[75] www.asean.org/news/asean-statement-communiques/item/thailand-signs-mra-on-tourism-professionals

across all six tourism labour divisions and specific competencies of the house-keeping division. The training of ASEAN Master Trainers and Master Assessors for various divisions such as house-keeping, food production, front office, food and beverage services have been successfully concluded. At the Eighteenth Meeting of the ASEAN Tourism Ministers in January 2015, the Tourism Ministers endorsed the final text to establish a regional secretariat for ASEAN tourism professionals hosted by Indonesia in order to provide effective facilitation and monitoring support for the implementation of the MRA.[76] An ASEAN Tourism Professionals Registration System (ATPRS) has been set up to facilitate registration for those possessing ASEAN certificates so as to maintain quality assurance.[77]

In addition to the MRAs discussed above, the AEC Blueprint 2015 also affirmed the aim of identifying and developing MRAs for other professional services by 2012, to be completed by 2015, but there seems to have been no follow-up on this by the end of 2015.

4.5 Movement of Natural Persons

The ASEAN Agreement on the Movement of Natural Persons (MNP Agreement), signed on 19 November 2012, has the objective of enhancing the framework for greater mobility of

---

[76] http://aseantourism.travel/pressrelease/detail/the-sixteenth-meeting-of-asean-tourism-ministers-16th-m-atm-20-january-2013-vientiane-lao-pdr www.asean.org/images/2015/January/jms_matm/JMS-M-ATM-18-Final.pdf</u>

[77] This is available at www.atprs.org/?state=account

natural persons engaged in trade in goods and services, as well as investment. Nevertheless, the ASEAN MNP Agreement only covers all the service sectors and does not cover non-services sectors. The free flow of skilled labour is one of the core elements of the ASEAN single market and production base mandated under the AEC Blueprint 2015. Facilitating the movement of natural persons within ASEAN would enhance trade in services supplied under Mode 4, which would in turn aid the general AFAS aim of eliminating trade barriers in relation to all modes of supply. Mode 4 was the only mode for which no specific targets were set in the AEC Blueprint 2015, apart from the general target of setting the parameters for liberalization by the year 2009. This deadline was missed and the parameters for Mode 4 have still not been set, even with the signing of the MNP Agreement. This, in turn, raises legitimate doubts as to how the MRAs discussed above can be made operational so long as the putative benefits deriving therefrom are in effect nullified or impaired by the inability to ensure the freedom of underlying temporary labour mobility.

As is also the case under the GATS Annex on the Movement of Natural Persons, the ASEAN MNP Agreement applies only to measures affecting the temporary entry or temporary stay of natural persons of a Member State into the territory of another Member State, and not to persons seeking employment, or citizenship or residence on a permanent basis. Although the Agreement specifically mentions 'natural persons' as including business visitors, intra-corporate transferees, and contractual service suppliers, the types of persons covered by the Agreement are not closed and could include such other categories of persons as may be specified in the schedules of commitments of ASEAN Member States (such as trainees).[78] The requirements in the MNP Agreement are largely procedural, providing for Member States to specify in their schedules their commitments relating to the temporary stay of natural persons covered by the agreement and the general conditions and limitations governing those commitments, including the length of stay. The Agreement also sets out requirements for the streamlined and transparent processing of applications and proper publicity of immigration formalities and regulations relating to the temporary entry or stay of natural persons, including the setting up of contact or enquiry points. These requirements enjoy a range of general exceptions which allow, for example, measures necessary for the protection of public morals or the privacy of individuals, or to maintain public order to be enacted by host countries.[79] There are also security exceptions, such as those exempting a Member State from furnishing information which it considers contrary to its essential security interests, or allowing each State to take any action which it considers necessary for the protection of its essential security interests.[80]

The schedule of commitments of ASEAN Member States in the MNP Agreement is annexed to this Agreement. Nothing in the MNP Agreement requires a Member State to make any further substantive commitments to liberalize

---

[78] ASEAN Agreement on the Movement of Natural Persons, Art. 1.
[79] Ibid., Art. 9.
[80] ASEAN Agreement on the Movement of Natural Persons, Art. 10.

Mode 4 than it already has under its existing AFAS commitments. Other than uniformly adding the new information required by the MNP Agreement regarding the conditions and limitations of entry, Member States have made varying degrees of improvements to their existing AFAS 8 Mode 4 commitments. Singapore and Brunei Darussalam, for instance, have generally kept to their existing horizontal commitments in terms of the types of natural persons allowed to supply services and the service sectors to which these commitments apply. They have limited their horizontal commitments in Mode 4 to intra-corporate transferees as already inscribed in their existing AFAS schedules, and make no commitment in relation to the other types of natural persons mentioned in the MNP Agreement.[81] The Philippines and Lao PDR made the greatest improvements over their AFAS 8 schedules, with their MNP schedules allowing for business visitors and intra-corporate transferees, which were not covered in their existing AFAS 8 schedules, and also committing to more service sectors. Under AFAS 8, commitments in respect of intra-corporate transferees had already been made by a majority of the Member States, and by about half of them in respect of business visitors, and commitments of the Philippines and Lao PDR improved the position. In total, Mode 4 sectoral improvement was seen in the MNP schedules of six Member States (the Philippines, Lao PDR, Myanmar,

---

[81] See Singapore – Schedule of Specific Commitments for the Eighth Package of Commitments under ASEAN Framework Agreement on Services; and Malaysia – Schedule of Specific Commitments for the Eighth Package of Commitments under ASEAN Framework Agreement on Services.

Malaysia, Vietnam and Thailand), while (Cambodia and Vietnam) made MNP commitments for the new category of contractual service providers. The MNP Agreement can only be depicted as an encouraging and useful, if modest, start and further liberalization of Mode 4 will need to be carried out over time. The Agreement came into force on 14 June 2016. Upon this event, Mode 4 commitments made previously under AFAS packages (AFAS eighth package and signed by the ASEAN Finance Ministers and the ASEAN Transport Ministers) was superseded by the schedule of commitments of Member States under the MNP Agreement. The ninth AFAS package, which was completed before the coming into force of the MNP Agreement, did not contain Mode 4 commitments. ASEAN Member States are required by the MNP Agreement to enter into discussions within one year of its entry into force, to review their schedules of commitments with a view to achieving further liberalization on the movement of natural persons.

As noted above, the ultimate effectiveness of the MRAs in professional services is closely linked to commitments relating to the movement of natural persons and to the liberalization of Mode 4. Because the MNP Agreement has yet to include parameters for liberalizing Mode 4 trade in services, it is likely to remain of limited effectiveness in encouraging the intra-ASEAN movement of professionals under the MRAs. Indeed, professionals such as engineers, architects, doctors, dentists and nurses who seek employment in a host State might not fall into the categories of persons mentioned in the MNP Agreement. Professionals seeking temporary entry or stay in another ASEAN Member State will fall within the MNP Agreement only if they meet the definition of business visitors, intra-corporate transferees, contractual service suppliers or whatever other category of visitor may be specified by their host state. These definitions contain a range of requirements that anchor the visitor to his home state, which professionals often do not satisfy. Examples include the requirement that the visitor's remuneration and financial support be derived from outside the host state (for business visitors); or that the visitor be employed by a company in another ASEAN country and temporarily transferred to a branch office located in the host country (for intra-corporate transferees); or that he or she be employed by a company in another ASEAN country with no commercial presence in the host state and enter the territory of the host state only to supply a contractual service on behalf of his or her employer (for contract service suppliers).

4.6 ASEAN Qualifications Reference Framework

The ASEAN Qualifications Reference Framework (AQRF) is an initiative started by the ASEAN Economic Ministers in 2014, and subsequently endorsed also by the ASEAN Education Ministers and the ASEAN Labour Ministers, that will aid the mobility of workers and learners within ASEAN. It is a common reference framework that facilitates the comparison of qualifications in education and training sectors across the ASEAN Member States. The AQRF exists in parallel with each country's national qualifications system. Countries can voluntarily reference their national qualifications framework to the ASEAN level framework, where there are eight levels of qualifications based on (a) knowledge and skills and (b) application and responsibility. This will help employers to assess the qualifications of job applicants from other ASEAN countries and enable workers and learners to plan for their own career and education ASEAN-wide.

4.7 Services Liberalization under AFAS

As discussed earlier, AFAS commitments starting from the seventh package were scheduled according to the formula set out in the AEC Blueprint 2015, as updated by subsequent decisions of the ASEAN Economic Ministers. This section traces the development of the commitments under AFAS and explores salient aspects of the seventh, eighth and ninth packages.[82] In the process, a comparison is made between AFAS commitments and the GATS commitments of ASEAN Member States, drawing largely from studies made in relation to the AFAS seventh package.

4.7.1 AFAS Seventh Package

In the Second AEC Scorecard released in March 2012 it was reported that, under the seventh package of commitments, ASEAN Member States committed to at least sixty-five sub-sectors for liberalization, at a level in accordance with the

---

[82] The protocol to implement the tenth package was signed on 29 August 2018 – too late to be analysed in this volume: www.mfa.gov.sg/Overseas-Mission/ASEAN/Press-Statements-Speeches/2018/08/Press_2018-08-291

targets set by the AEC Blueprint 2015. Apart from the fact that it was completed late, with the implementation protocol being signed in 2011 instead of 2009 as targeted, the seventh package can be seen as a success.

AFAS versus GATS Commitments
Several studies have compared the level of services liberalization achieved under AFAS 7 with that achieved under the GATS. This section draws on two such studies. One is the work of the WTO Secretariat, using data available in 2011, which quantified the level of services openness in the GATS and in other PTAs for various WTO Members, and includes an analysis of AFAS 7 commitments (excluding Myanmar, Cambodia and Lao PDR).[83] Another is a 2012 quantitative study made by Ishido and Fukunaga, using the Hoekman Index methodology.[84]

The Hoekman Index ranks among the most commonly used metrics applied to GATS-type commitments in services agreements.[85] Using this method, market access and national treatment commitments for each of the four modes of supply in a given services sector are assigned a value and tabulated into eight cells. A value of 1 is assigned when the relevant sector is

[83] The data is available at: www.wto.org/english/tratop_e/serv_e/dataset_e/dataset_e.htm
[84] Hikari Ishido and Yoshifumi Fukunaga, 'Liberalization of Trade in Services: Toward a Harmonized ASEAN++ FTA', ERIA Policy Brief, No. 2012–02, ERIA, 2012.
[85] B. Hoekman, 'Assessing the General Agreement on Trade in Services' in Will Martin and L. Alan Winters (eds.), The Uruguay Round and the Developing Economies, World Bank Discussion Paper No. 307 (Washington, DC: 1995).

fully liberalized with no restrictions, a value of 0.5 is assigned when there are partial commitments in the sector (bound but with limitations to market access and national treatment), and a value of 0 is assigned when the sector is unbound. The simple average of these values will produce a measure of the degree of liberalization of the sector in question. The dataset can be expanded to work out the average value by selected services sectors or by country. This methodology has been used in a number of interesting and useful calculations – for instance, those by researchers based at the Economic Research Institute for ASEAN and East Asia (ERIA).

In the study made by the WTO Secretariat, a modified version of the Hoekman method was used to construct a dataset measuring the level of restrictiveness of commitments made in a selected number of PTAs compared with the GATS.[86] The WTO method used in constructing the dataset takes each mode of supply and sub-sector under a Member's GATS commitments (as improved by Doha Round services offers) and assigns it a value of 0, 0.5 or 1 using the Hoekman Index as described above. To create a comparative score for each PTA, the WTO method refines the above approach and awards, for instance, a score of 0.75 where a Member who has made a partial commitment in a particular mode and sub-sector under the GATS has made a better commitment (e.g. lower foreign equity limitations than in its GATS

[86] The data and methodology are set out at: www.wto.org/english/tra top_e/serv_e/dataset_e/dataset_e.htm. See also M. Roy 'Services Commitments in Preferential Trade Agreements: An Expanded Dataset', Staff Working Paper ERSD-2011–18, World Trade Organization, 9 December 2011.

Table 4.2 *Level of services liberalization in ASEAN and the GATS*[87]

ASEAN (seventh package)							
	Brunei Darussalam	Indonesia	Malaysia	Philippines	Singapore	Thailand	Vietnam
GATS	7.99	17.26	27.47	16.41	37.59	19.39	34.18
AFAS 7	30.78	41.58	43.39	34.95	42.03	37.86	38.27

Source: WTO website

schedule) in the same sector and mode in an FTA. The index value is obtained by adding up the score for each sub-sector and mode of supply and converting this to a score between 0 and 100.

Table 4.2 was prepared by the WTO Secretariat based on this index, and shows the extent of each country's commitments relating to national treatment and market access for Modes 1 and 3 under AFAS compared with the GATS. It is clear that in all the seven ASEAN countries included in the table, the level of liberalization achieved in AFAS 7 was GATS+ in character. This is evidence, if any were needed, to prove an intuitive point: that of the greater willingness of ASEAN countries to open up their services sectors to selected trade partners rather than on a multilateral basis. This indication takes on even more significance when we note that the data used to compute the GATS index included not just formal GATS commitments but also offers made in the services negotiations under the Doha Development Agenda,

[87] Index Scores for GATS commitments and PTA commitments, by PTA, available online at: www.wto.org/english/tratop_e/serv_e/dataset_e/dataset_e.htm

which already represented an improvement over existing GATS commitments. The difference between the levels of GATS and AFAS commitments varies across the ASEAN countries, with the greatest difference being seen in the commitments of Brunei and the smallest being seen in those of Singapore and Vietnam.

In their study, Ishido and Fukunaga calculated the level of liberalization in ASEAN at the various stages of economic integration the Hoekman Index, as described above. A higher figure indicates a higher level of liberalization. They found that the level of liberalization across ASEAN following the implementation of the AFAS fifth package of commitments did not go beyond the GATS level. This confirms the view taken by earlier studies, such as that by Thanh and Bartlett in 2006, which assessed the first ten years of operation of AFAS in terms of the extent of bound liberalization compared with the GATS and the extent to which services restrictions in ASEAN Member Countries had been removed.[88] The general conclusion of this study, as well as several others done slightly later, was that liberalization under AFAS lacked breadth and depth and did not go much further than the GATS.[89] However, Ishido and Fukunaga demonstrated that, from the seventh package onwards, AFAS was already achieving a GATS+ level of liberalization (see Table 4.3). They showed, further, that AFAS 7 generally produced the highest level of liberalization when compared with

---

[88] See *ASEAN Integration in Services* (Jakarta: ASEAN Secretariat, December 2015), pp. 28–9.

[89] See *ASEAN Services Report 2017: The Evolving Landscape* (Jakarta: ASEAN Secretariat, August 2017), p. 30.

Table 4.3 Services liberalization in AFAS 7 and gains compared with the GATS[90]

AFAS 7	1 Business	2 Communication	3 Construction	4 Distribution	5 Education	6 Environment	7 Finance	8 Health	9 Tourism	10 Recreation	11 Transport
Brunei Dar.	0.38	0.10	0.33	0.00	0.45	0.00	0.33	0.31	0.28	0.11	0.21
Cambodia	0.30	0.30	0.51	0.75	0.45	0.75	0.44	0.19	0.53	0.30	0.20
Indonesia	0.27	0.16	0.53	0.21	0.48	0.42	0.25	0.66	0.61	0.24	0.30
Lao PDR	0.35	0.28	0.75	0.34	0.56	0.56	0.24	0.27	0.42	0.00	0.14
Malaysia	0.50	0.19	0.50	0.43	0.39	0.34	0.28	0.33	0.56	0.23	0.14
Myanmar	0.25	0.35	0.63	0.38	0.48	0.47	0.09	0.50	0.52	0.30	0.13
Philippines	0.42	0.52	0.35	0.28	0.00	0.27	0.45	0.14	0.47	0.30	0.38
Singapore	0.52	0.38	0.75	0.60	0.15	0.25	0.34	0.38	0.66	0.30	0.14
Thailand	0.66	0.20	0.64	0.60	0.58	0.75	0.39	0.31	0.64	0.64	0.24
Vietnam	0.39	0.33	0.56	0.25	0.43	0.50	0.49	0.63	0.52	0.18	0.19
ASEAN	0.41	0.28	0.55	0.38	0.40	0.43	0.33	0.37	0.52	0.26	0.21
Gains compared with GATS commitments											
Brunei Dar.	0.26	0.06	0.33	0.00	0.45	0.00	0.20	0.31	0.28	0.11	0.20
Cambodia	0.01	0.02	0.01	0.05	0.00	0.00	0.09	0.00	0.08	0.15	0.03
Indonesia	0.23	0.06	0.30	0.21	0.48	0.42	0.04	0.66	0.44	0.24	0.28

[90] *Sources:* Ikumo Isono, based on Ishido's (2011) calculation, reproduced from Hikari Ishido and Yoshifumi Fukunaga, 'Liberalization of Trade in Services: Toward a Harmonized ASEAN++ FTA', ERIA Policy Brief, No. 2012–02, ERIA, 2012 at p. 3.

Lao PDR	NA	NA	NA	NA	NA	NA	NA	NA	NA	NA
Malaysia	0.20	0.14	0.41	0.43	0.39	0.34	0.07	0.17	0.34	0.05	0.12
Myanmar	0.25	0.35	0.63	0.38	0.48	0.47	0.09	0.50	0.17	0.30	0.12
Philippines	0.39	0.30	0.35	0.28	0.00	0.27	0.11	0.14	0.11	0.30	0.22
Singapore	0.31	0.23	0.60	0.60	0.15	0.25	0.02	0.38	0.38	0.15	0.10
Thailand	0.44	0.10	0.23	0.50	0.28	0.06	0.19	0.31	0.13	0.50	0.13
Vietnam	0.05	0.06	0.06	0.00	0.23	0.06	0.08	0.38	0.16	0.09	0.08
ASEAN	0.24	0.15	0.32	0.27	0.27	0.21	0.10	0.32	0.23	0.21	0.14

Source: Ishido and Fukunaga (2012)

liberalization[90] under the various ASEAN bilateral PTAs that had been completed by the same point in time – a finding that is further discussed in the next part of this section. In terms of the connection between liberalization and economic advancement, Ishido and Fukunaga found that AFAS 7 produced the highest average GATS+ component in construction and health-related services, but that two of the arguably most pivotal sectors for economic development – finance and transport – did not generate tangible improvements.

The current discussion is based on the snapshot provided by AFAS 7. Any snapshot only shows the liberalization journey at a particular point in time. For instance, studies done in the early stages of AFAS, before the adoption of the AEC Blueprint 2015 in 2007, which stepped up the pace, breadth and depth of services trade liberalization, will naturally reveal an unfavourable result. Even studies done after the AEC Blueprint 2015 was finalized must be treated with care, as the Blueprint provides a moving target. A level of commitment that is gauged to be unsatisfactory at any point before the end of the journey might be cured by the time the journey is completed. With AFAS 7 already achieving GATS+ commitments, it was reasonable to extrapolate that liberalization under the later AFAS packages would progressively pull further and further ahead from the limited achievements of the GATS. Indeed, ever since the AEC Blueprint 2015 was made public, AFAS targets at each stage were set out clearly. There is no question that these cumulative targets go way beyond the GATS. Initially, there may have been some uncertainty as to whether the ASEAN Member States could meet these targets. But with the completion of the final tenth package, there is no doubt that AFAS commitments far surpass those under the GATS.

Ishido has complied data showing the most liberalized sub-sectors for each ASEAN Member State under AFAS 7.[91] These findings are summarized in Table 4.4, which includes the Hoekman Index for the most liberal sub-sectors mentioned, as well as the Hoekman Index for the average level of commitment across all sub-sectors for that particular country. Where more than one sub-sector has the same index number, all these sub-sectors are listed as being the most liberalized. The table reveals that the levels of commitment in the most liberalized sectors for each country were much higher than the average level of liberalization across all sectors in that particular country. Two sectors – 'computer and related services' and 'courier services' – were the most liberalized sectors in half of the ASEAN countries. The telecommunication services sector was a close second, appearing top in four of the ten countries. While most of the countries had a few preferred sectors (some only one sector) that obtained the highest score, Cambodia and Singapore had a more wide-ranging list of most liberalized sectors what shared the same top index number. Ishido also found that the average level of services commitment by all the ASEAN Member Countries in AFAS 7 was 0.33, and that the hotels and restaurants (09A) sub-sector had the highest average commitment level by participating countries with an index factor of 0.68.

---

[91] Hikari Ishido, 'Liberalization of Trade in Services under ASEAN+n: A Mapping Exercise', ERIA Discussion Paper 2011-02, ERIA, 2011.

Table 4.4 Most liberalized sub-sectors for each ASEAN Member State under AFAS 7

Country	Most liberalized sub-sectors	Hoekman Index	All sub-sectors comparative average
Brunei Dar.	Computer and related services	0.69	0.18
Cambodia	Computer and related services, courier services, telecommunications services, commission agents' Services, Wholesale Trade Services, Retailing services, franchising, higher education services, adult education, other education services, sewage services, refuse disposal services, sanitation and similar services, other environmental services, travel agencies and tour operators services, tourist guides services, and road transport services	0.75	0.36
Indonesia	Telecommunication services	0.79	0.36
Lao PDR	Courier services	0.88	0.33
Malaysia	Computer and related services, and travel agencies and tour operators services	0.75	0.31
Myanmar	Computer and related services, courier services, social services and hotels and restaurants	0.75	0.33
Philippines	Courier services	0.94	0.29

Singapore	Research and development services, audio-visual services, general construction work for building, general construction work for civil engineering, installation and assembly work, building completion and finishing work, commission agents' services, wholesale trade services, retailing services, franchising, adult education, tourist guides services, entertainment services, libraries, archives, museums and other cultural services.	0.75	0.36
Thailand	Computer and related services, sewage services, hotels and restaurants, other health-related and social services	0.75	0.36
Vietnam	Courier services, telecommunication services, franchising, hotels and restaurants, travel agencies and tour operators services	0.75	0.33

Source: Author's compilation based on data in Ishido (2011)

4.7.2 AFAS Eighth Package

AFAS 8 was signed in December 2013. The number of sectors targeted by the AEC Blueprint 2015 for this package was eighty. Most of the ASEAN Member States scheduled more than the targeted eighty sectors, with Thailand opening up 104 sub-sectors. Only Brunei and Myanmar scheduled fewer than eighty, with a total of seventy-nine sub-sectors each. The substantive improvements produced by the eighth package of commitments compared with the seventh package varied across different countries. Certain members – such as Myanmar, Malaysia, Brunei Darussalam, Lao PDR, Cambodia and Thailand – scheduled new sectors that had not been opened in any of their previous trade agreements. This can be noted by the opening of Modes 1 and 2, as required by the AEC Blueprint. Other members – such as Singapore, Vietnam and Indonesia – focused on raising foreign equity limits for Mode 3, and scheduled very few new sectors. The list below reports the new sub-sectors scheduled by each member according to the mode of supply. The numbers in parenthesis indicate the mode of supply that was the object of further liberalization. It should be noted that, with regard to Mode 3, the list does not differentiate between a simple increase in the permissible equity limit and the full liberalization of investment in the sector.

Brunei Darussalam
Business Services: Research and development services (3); Other business services -translation, packaging, advertising, poll, marketing, management consulting, technical testing and scientific services, building, photographic, packaging,

printing, publishing, duplicating, translation, design, mailing list compilation (3); **Communication Services:** Courier services (1-2-3); Telecommunication services: voice telephone (1-2-3); packed switched data transmission (3); paging services (1-2-3); trunked radio services (1-2-3); video text (1-2-3); **Environmental Services:** refuse disposal and other environmental services (1-2-3); **Health-related Services:** pharmaceutical services (1-2-3); **Tourism and Travel-related Services:** hotel lodging, restaurants, and other youth tourism services (3); theme parks (3); **Transport Services:** maritime transport (1-2-3); internal waterways transport (1-2-3); space transport (3); rail transport (3) – except freight transportation (1-2-3); Services auxiliary to all modes of transport – maritime cargo, maritime freight forwarding, storage and warehousing services (3).

Cambodia

Transport Services: Maritime transport services – international maritime transport (3); rental of maritime vessels with crew (3); maintenance and repair of vessels for maritime transport, pushing and towing services, supporting services for maritime transport (1-2-3); Internal waterways transport (1-2-3); Rail transport services (1-2-3).

Indonesia[92]

Business Services: Computer-related services (3); Research and development services (3); Rental and leasing services

---

[92] Indonesia did not schedule any new sector. All improvements in Mode 3 consist of increased foreign equity caps and non-discrimination obligations.

without operators (3); Other business services (3); Telecommunication services – public local telephone services (1–2–3); dedicated network services (1–2–3); electronic data interchange (3); enhanced data services (3); online database services (3); voicemail (3); electronic mail (3); videotext (3); **Distribution Service:** distribution and direct selling (3); **Educational Services:** Secondary education (3); Higher education (3); Other education services (3); **Environmental Services:** Sewage services (3); cleaning services (3); environmental protection services (3); **Health-related and Social Services:** specialized clinic and veterinary healthcare services (3); social services (3); motel (3); meal services (3); hotel operators (3); **Transport Services:** Maintenance and repair of vessels (3).

Lao PDR

Business Services: Other business services – technical testing and analysis services (1–2–3); postal services (2); **Communication Services:** Telecommunication services – voice telephone and telex services (3); voice mail, online information database retrieval, and enhanced value added facsimile services (3); electronic data interchange and online information processing (1–2–3); data transmission (1–2–3); telecom consulting (1–2–3); **Health-related and Social Services:** private hospital services (3); **Tourism and Travel-related Services:** hotel services (3); travel agencies (3); **Transport Services:** rail transport (1–2–3–4); supporting services, rental of vessels and freight transportation for road transport (1–2–3–4).

Malaysia

Malaysia has increased to a minimum of 51 percent the equity limits on foreign investment in almost all services sectors (few exceptions apply); In the telecoms, health, tourism and travel sectors has increased the equity limit to 70 percent in all sub-sectors scheduled. It has opened the following sectors, which were not committed under AFAS 7: **Business Services:** Architectural services – other architectural services covering preparation for promotional material (1-2-3); Research and development services -research and development services on pharmacy (3); Other business services – services incidental to energy distribution (1-2-3); executive search (1-2-3); alarm monitoring services (1-2-3); repair and maintenance of equipment (1-2-3); printing and publishing (1-2-3); **Communication Services:** courier services (1-2-3); Telecommunication services – interconnection and integrated telecom services (1-2-3); Audio-visual services – motion picture projection (1-2-3); sound recording (1-2-3); **Distribution Services:** wholesale and retail trade (1-2-3); **Environmental Services:** refuse disposal (1-2-3); **Health-related and Social Services:** pharmacy services (1-2-3); Social services – vocational services for handicapped (1-2-3); **Transport Services:** rail transport services (1-2-3); private services provided by car parks, and maintenance and repair services for car transport (1-2-3).

Myanmar
Business Services: Research and development services (1-2); Other business services – packaging services (1-2-3); Rental/leasing services without operators – rental of cargo vessels (1-2-3-4); **Transport Services** – Maritime transport (3-4) – rental, maintenance and repair of vessels (1-2-3-4); classification societies (3-4); Services auxiliary to all modes

of transport – ship broking services (1–2-3–4); **Communication Services:** Postal services (1–2-3–4); Telecommunication services – facsimile, private leased circuit services, and data transmission services (1–2-3–4); telecom equipment maintenance services (1–2-3–4); **Educational Services**: Primary and secondary education services (1–2-3–4); **Recreational, Cultural and Sporting Services**: News agency (1–2).

Philippines[93]
Business Services: Professional services – bookkeeping (3); industrial engineering (1–2-3); Computer and related services – data processing/data base/others (3); Research and development services – Research and development/R and D in economics/Interdisciplinary R and D in ICT (3); Real estate services – residential property management (3); rental leasing services (3); Other business services – market research (3); project management (3); maintenance and repair of equipment (3); window cleaning (3); **Communication Services:** Audio-visual (3); **Health-related and Social Services:** veterinary (3); **Distribution Services:** wholesale trade/retailing/franchising/petroleum retail (3); **Environmental Services:** cleaning services of gases (3); refuse disposal (3); **Tourism and Travel-related Services:** travel agency (3); **Recreational, Cultural and Sporting Services:** recreational services (3); **Transport Services:** parking services (3); packing and crating

---

[93] The new AFAS 8 commitments for the Philippines were essentially limited at increasing the foreign equity limits from 49 per cent to 51 percent for Mode 3 trade. Apart from Industrial Engineering Services, no new sub-sector was opened.

and unpacking and de-crating services (3); **Other Services Not Included Elsewhere:** religious services (3).

Singapore

Business Services: Professional services: integrated engineering services (3); Computer related services – maintenance and repair services of computers (1-2-3); Rental/leasing services without operators – rental and leasing of studio recording equipment; **Health-related and Social Services:** deliveries and related services, nursing services, physiotherapists, and para-medical personnel (3); private hospital services (1-2); ambulance services (3); laboratories licensed under the Private Hospital and Medical Clinics Act (3); **Tourism and Travel-related Services:** beverage serving services (3); other tourism services (3); **Transport Services:** maintenance and repair of vessels (3); vessels salvage and re-floating (3).

Thailand

Business Services: Professional services – Legal advisory services (1-2-3); integrated engineering services, and engineering advisory services (1-2-3); weather forecasting (1-2-3); Computer and related services – Hardware and software consulting services (1-2-3); Research and development services – research and development services for science and languages (1-2-3); Other business services – investigation and security (1-2-3); fair and exhibition (1-2-3); **Real Estate Services:** On a fee or contract basis – residential condominium management (1-2-3); **Rental/Leasing Services without Operator:** leasing of transport equipment (1-2-3); **Communication Services:** Telecommunication services – telegraph, telex and facsimile (1-2-3); code and protocol conversion (1-2-3); communication equipment maintenance (1-2-3); **Environmental Services:** marine environmental protection services (1-2-3); **Health-related Services:** residential health facilities, day care, diagnostic imaging services (1-2-3); **Tourism and Travel-related Services:** travel agency (without operator) (3); **Transport Services:** space transport (1-2-3).

Vietnam
Business Services: <u>Rental and leasing services without operator</u> (3); <u>Other business services</u> – packaging services (3); printing and publishing (3); <u>Professional services</u> – medical and dental services, nursing services, and hospital services (3); <u>Health-related and social services</u> (3) – Other human health services (1-2-3-4); <u>Tourism and travel-related services</u> – Hotel lodging services (3); **Transport Services:** Rental of maritime vessels with crew (3); maintenance and repair of vessels (3); maintenance and repair of vessels for passenger transport (1-2-3); rail transport services (3); maintenance and repair of transport equipment (1-2-3).

Box 4.1 Methodological Limitations

A quantitative analysis of services commitments that chiefly relies on counting commitments across sectors and modes suffers from a number of methodological limitations and may not be fully indicative of the level of services liberalization in a particular country. Dee (2013) points out that this method gives equal weight to each service sector and mode of supply although, in

Box 4.1 (cont.)

reality, some modes of supply are far more important than others for any given service. For instance, Mode 1 trade (i.e. cross-border supply) is important for air and maritime transport whereas Mode 2 (consumption abroad) will be less significant for such services. Furthermore, some sectors will be more economically significant than others within ASEAN, and the liberalization of these sectors will correspondingly have more impact on ASEAN-wide economic development. A quantitative analysis of the type on offer in the studies reviewed also does not indicate how far services commitments might lag behind *actual* regulatory practices, and might thus overstate the positive effect of the commitments.[94] It also does not differentiate between various types of limitations.

4.7.3 AFAS Ninth Package

The AFAS ninth package, signed in November 2015, saw a mixture of the opening of new sub-sectors, as well as the improvement of commitments in existing sub-sectors,

---

[94] Philippa Dee, 'Does AFAS have bite? Comparing Commitments with Actual Practice', Working Paper drawn from 'Services Liberalization: Impact and Way Forward', paper presented for the ASEAN Economic Community Mid-Term Review, ERIA, Jakarta, January 2013, available at: https://crawford.anu.edu.au/pdf/staff/phillippa_dee/2013/does-afas-have-bite.pdf

although in a few countries, notably the Philippines and Lao PDR, the greater focus was to improve existing commitments for Mode 3 rather than the scheduling of new sub-sectors. No additional commitments were made for Mode 4 under the ninth AFAS package as it had been decided that liberalization on the movement of natural persons after the eighth AFAS package would instead take place under the Agreement for the Movement of Natural Persons. Under the AEC Blueprint 2015, 104 sub-sectors were targeted for liberalization under AFAS 9. Thailand's commitments exceeded this number, but the other nine ASEAN countries fell below the target. Table 4.5 summarizes the number of sub-sectors covered in AFAS 7–9, classified according to W/120.

As was done for AFAS 8, the following lists summarize the new sub-sectors scheduled by each member, according to the mode of supply. The numbers in parenthesis indicate the mode of supply that was the object of further liberalization. The sub-sectors in this list may not correspond exactly to the W/120 classification, as some countries, such as the Philippines, have deviated from this classification. Further, even where the W/120 classification has been followed, some countries have made commitments at a greater level of detail than is reflected under a particular CPC heading. As stated earlier, it should be noted that, with regard to Mode 3, the list does not differentiate between a simple increase in the permissible equity limit and the full liberalization of investment in the sector.

Brunei Darussalam
Business Services: Professional services – Legal services (1-2-3), Architectural services (3), Urban planning and landscape

architectural services (3), Veterinary services (1–2–3), Other business services – Services incidental to energy distribution (1–2–3), Packaging services (3), Convention services (1–2–3).

Communication Services: Courier services (3) – Telecommunication services – Private leased circuit services (1–2–3).

Distribution Services: Franchising (1–2–3)

Educational Services: Primary education services (for international schools) (3), Secondary education services (for international schools) (3), Higher education (1–2–3), Adult education (max duration three months) (3), Adult education (services for skill centre only) (3), Foreign language training centre (3).

Environmental Services: Sewage services (1–2–3), Sanitation and similar services (1–2–3).

Healthcare Services: Social services (1–2–3).

Tourism and Travel-related Services: Travel agencies and tour operators services (1–2–3).

Recreational, Cultural and Sporting Services: News agency services (1–2–3), Sports events promotion/organization, facility operation services (1–2–3), Library, archive services (1–2–3).

Cambodia

Healthcare Services: Specialized medical services, specialized dental services (3), Hospital services (3) – Ambulance services (1–2–3), Nursing services (1–2–3).

Transport Services: Rail transport services – Maintenance and repair of rail transport equipment (1-2-3), Supporting services for rail transport services (1-2-3), Pipeline transport services – Transport of fuels, other goods (1, 3), Storage and warehousing services (1,3), Cargo handling, freight transport agency, Other services (1-3).

Indonesia

Business Services: Professional services – Engineering (3), Integrated engineering services (3), Research and development – Research on experimental development on linguistic and languages (3), Rental and leasing services without operator – Others: rental services for video tapes (2-3), Other business services – Investigation and security, photographic, printing, publishing, other: telephone answering (2-3), Packaging (3).

Environmental Services: Sanitation and similar services (1-2-3).

Healthcare Services: Nursing services (3), Other human health services (3).

Recreational, Cultural and Sporting Services: Other entertainment (1-2), Libraries, archives, museums – Jewellery museums (2-3).

Transport Services: Internal waterways transport – Passenger, freight transportation (3), Pushing and towing (3), Rail transport service – Freight transportation, pushing and towing (3), Road transport services – Passenger by man- or-animal-drawn vehicles (1-2-3), Freight transportation by man- or-animal-drawn vehicles (1-2-3), Parking services (1-2-3), Pipeline transport –

Transportation of petroleum and natural gas (1–2–3), Services auxiliary to all modes of transport – Maritime cargo-handling services (3).

Lao PDR

Business Services: Professional services – Legal services (1–2-3), Accounting, auditing and bookkeeping (3), Taxation consulting (3), Architectural (3), Engineering (3), Integrated engineering (3), Urban planning and landscape architectural (3), Computer and related services (3), Research and development services (3), Rental/leasing services without operators (3), Other business services – Advertising, marketing research, management consulting, Technical testing and analysis (3), Building-cleaning services (3), Photographic (3), Specialty design (1–2-3).

Communication Services: Postal services (1), Telecommunication services – Voice-telephone (3) Code and protocol conversion (1–2-3), Radio and television services (3).

Construction and Related Engineering Services: Construction work for buildings, civil engineering, assembly and erection of prefabricated constructions, installation, building completion and finishing, pre-erection work, special trade, rental services related to equipment for construction (3).

Distribution Services: Commission agents' services, Franchising (3)

Education Services: Secondary education – General secondary education, technical and vocational training, Higher education, adult education, other education – short-term foreign language training (3).

Environment Services: <u>Sewage, refuse disposal, sanitation,</u> Cleaning of exhaust gases, noise abatement, nature and landscape protection (3).

Health-related and Social Services: <u>Hospital services</u> – General and specialized medical services (3), Private hospital services.

Tourism and Travel-related Services: <u>Hotels and restaurants</u> – Hotel lodging, meal serving, beverage serving services (3). <u>Travel agencies and tour operations</u> – Others: Tourism consulting (3).

Transport Services: <u>Maritime transport services</u> – Passenger and freight transportation, rental of vessels with crew, pushing and towing, maintenance and repair of vessels, vessels salvage and re-floating (3), <u>Internal waterway transport</u> – Passenger and freight transportation, rental of vessels with crew, maintenance and repair of vessels, <u>Rail transport services</u> – Passenger and freight transportation, pushing and towing services, maintenance and repair of rail transport equipment, supporting services for rail transport (3), <u>Road transport services</u> – Maintenance and repair of road transport equipment (3), <u>Services auxiliary to all modes of transport</u> – Storage and warehousing (3), Freight agency, maritime cargo handling, other auxiliary services (1–2)

Malaysia

Business Services: <u>Professional services</u> – Accounting, auditing and bookkeeping (3), Taxation (3), Urban planning (1-2-3), Other professional services: Geographical indication agent (2–3), <u>Real estate services</u> – Renting/leasing services involving own or leased residential property (1-2-3), <u>Rental/</u>

leasing services without operator – Rental of cargo vessels without crew for international shipping (3).

Environmental Services: Protection of ambient air climate (3)

Healthcare Services: Veterinary services (3).

Transport Services: Maritime transport service – International maritime transportation services (3), Rail transport services – Maintenance and repair of rail transport equipment (3), Passenger transportation (1-2-3), freight transportation (1-2-3), pushing or towing services (1-2-3), Road transport services – Freight transportation, covering carriers (3), Services auxiliary to all modes of transport – Maritime freight forwarding services (3).

Myanmar

Business Services: Professional services – Accounting, auditing and bookkeeping (3), Architectural services (3), Engineering services (3), Integrated engineering services (3), Landscape architectural services (3), Computer and related services – Consultancy services, Software implementation, Data processing and others (3), Real estate services (1-2-3), Rental/leasing services without operator – Rental and leasing of studio recording equipment (3), Other business services – Advertising (3), Technical and analysis services (1-2-3), Services incidental to energy manufacturing (3), Building-cleaning services (1-2-3), Photographic services (1-2-3), Printing and publishing (3), Translation and interpretation (3)

Communication Services: Postal services (3), Courier services (3), Telecommunication services – Facsimile, enhanced/value-added facsimile, packet-switched data, circuit-switched data transmission and private leased circuit services (3), Telex services (3), Telegraph services (3), Electronic mail (3), Voice mail (3), On-line information and data base retrieval (3), Electronic data interchange (3), Code and protocol conversion (3), On-line information and/or data processing (3), Public telephone services (3), Mobile telephone service (3), Paging services(3), Private leased circuit services (3), Packet-switched and Circuit-switched data transmission services (3), Telecommunication equipment maintenance services (3), Audio visual services – Motion picture and video tape production and distribution (3), Motion picture projection (3), Sound recording (1–2–3), Cinema theatre services (3).

Construction and Engineering Related Services: (3)
Distribution Services: Commission agent services (3), Wholesale trade in services (3), Retailing services (3).

Education Services: Primary education, secondary education, higher education, adult education, other education services (3).

Environmental Services: Sewage services (3), Refuse disposal service (3), Others: Noise abatement, Environmental consultancy, cleaning of exhaust gases (1–2–3).

Healthcare Services: Medical and dental – General medical, Specialized medical, dental, veterinary, deliveries and related, nursing, physiotherapist and paramedical personnel, hospital, ambulance, laboratory, residential health facilities, other human health (3).

Tourism and Travel-related Services: <u>Hotels and restaurants</u> – Hotel and other lodging (3), Motel lodging (3), <u>Sporting and other recreational services</u> – Sporting event promotion, organization (1-2-3).

Transport Services: <u>Maritime transport services</u> – International passenger transport, International freight transport (3), Rental of cargo vessels with crew (3), Maintenance and repair of vessels (3), Pushing and towing (1-2-3), <u>Supporting services for maritime transport</u> – Vessel salvage and refloating services, Port and waterway operation (1-2-3), Navigation aid (1-2-3), <u>Road transport services</u> – Passenger, freight transportation (1-2-3), <u>Pipeline transport</u> – Transportation of fuels (1-2-3), <u>Services auxiliary to all modes of transport</u> – Maritime cargo handling, storage and warehouse, Maritime freight forwarding, ship broking (3).

Singapore

Business Services: <u>Professional services</u> – International commercial arbitration (1-2-3), Accounting and auditing (1-3), Book-keeping services (1-2-3), Architectural services (3), Engineering services (3), <u>Real estate services</u> – Rental or leasing services (1-2-3), <u>Rental/leasing services without operators</u> – Leasing or rental concerning private cars, goods transport vehicles and other land transport equipment (1-2-3), Leasing or rental relating to other machinery and equipment without operator (3), <u>Other business services</u> – Transport distribution incidental to distribution of piped gas (2-3), Retail of electricity (2-3), Geological, geophysical and other scientific prospecting (2-3)

Communication Services: Telecommunication services – Value-added network services (1–3).

Education Services: Primary education, General secondary and higher secondary education, Post-secondary technical and vocational, other higher education services (1-2-3)

Environmental Services: Refuse disposal services – Refuse collection services except hazardous waste and except landfill services (1-2-3).

Health-related and Social Services: Medical services, specialized medical services (3), Hospital services (1–3), Ambulance services (3), Laboratories licensed (1–3).

Tourism and Travel-related Services: Hotel lodging services (1).

Recreational, Cultural and Sporting Services: Sports and recreational services except gambling (2–3).

Transport Services: Maritime transport services – Rental of vessels with crew (1-2-3), Maintenance and repair of vessels (3), Vessels salvage and re-floating services (3), Rail Transport – Pushing and towing, Maintenance and repair of urban and suburban rail transport (2–3), Road transport – Maintenance and repair services, and parts of motor vehicles, Parking services (2–3).

Other Services Not Included Elsewhere: Washing, cleaning and dyeing, Hairdressing, Funeral cremation and undertaking (1-2-3).

Philippines

Business Services: Professional services – All sub-sectors (4), Book-keeping services, except tax returns (3), Architectural services (3), Industrial engineering (3), Research and development services – R and D services on agricultural sciences, on economics, Interdisciplinary R and D on infocomms technology (3), Real estate services – Renting or leasing services involving own or leased residential property, Residential property management services on contract/fee basis (3), Rental/leasing services without operators – Relating to ships (3), Relating to other machinery and equipment except construction (3), Leasing or rental services concerning TV, radios etc. (3), Other business services – Market research services, General management consulting services except legal, Other management consulting services (3), Project management services other than construction (3), Testing and analysis services of physical properties, Technical inspection services (3), Services incidental to energy distribution (3), Maintenance and repair of equipment (3), Window cleaning services (3), Portrait photography services (3), Printing, publishing (3), Other: Translation and interpretation for private meetings/conferences (3).

Communication Services: Postal services – Domestic, international mail, money order services (3) Telecommunication services – Voice telephone, packet-switched data transmission, Circuit-switched data transmission, telex, telegraph, facsimile, private leased circuit, other services (3), Value-added services (3), Other telecommunication services (1–2-3), Audio-visual services – Production services for animated cartoons (3),

Motion picture projection in private screening rooms (3), Sound recording (3), Other: Colour correction (1-2-3).

Distribution Services: Wholesale trade services – For fur articles (3), Retailing services – Wholesaling of snowmobiles (3), Franchising services (3).

Education Services: Higher education services (2-3) – Post-secondary technical and vocational institutes by religious groups (2-3), Adult education services – Educational institutions by religious groups (2-3), Other education services – educational institutions by religious groups (2-3).

Environmental Services: Sewerage services (3), Refuse disposal services (3), Sanitation and similar services (1-2-3).

Health-related and Social Services: Veterinary medicine (3), Social services – Welfare services to elderly/handicapped (1-2-3) – Welfare services to elderly/handicapped (1-2-3), Other services – Ambulance services ancillary to private hospitals (1-2-3).

Tourism and Travel-related Services: Hotels and restaurants – Hotel, resort, pension houses, tourists inns (3), Meal serving services (3), Beverage serving services (3) Other services – Hotel management services for all hotel categories (1-2-3).

Recreational, Cultural and Sporting Services: Entertainment services – Others: Certified ballroom dance (3), Singer group and band entertainment (3), News agency – Supply services of news pictures (3), Libraries, archives, museums – Private museum Services (3), Sporting – Sport event organization (3).

Transport Services: Maritime transport services – Maritime cargo freight services (1-2-3), Maintenance and repair of vessels (3), Pushing and towing (3), Supporting services for maritime transport (3), Port and waterway operation, Maritime agency (3), Other Supporting services for water transport (3), Vessel and salvage refloating services (1-2-3). Rail transport services – Passenger and freight transportation, Supporting services (3), Road transport services – Routine cleaning and maintenance services (2-3), Passenger and freight transportation, rental of commercial vehicles with operator, supporting services for road transport services (3), Pipeline transport (3), Services auxiliary to all modes of transport – Cargo handling services at Subic Bay Freeport Zone (2-3), Storage and warehouse services at Subic Bay Freeport Zone (2-3), Freight transport agency (3), Domestic freight forwarding by sea (3), Other: Packing and crating and unpacking and de-crating (3).

Other Services Not Included Elsewhere: Services related to supply of energy – Oil terminals/depot, oil refinery (3), Oil and gas, geothermal, coal exploration and development (3). Services related to power generation – Construction of power plants under BOT scheme (3), Religious services (3).

Thailand

Business Services: Professional services – Legal: Legal advisory for drafting international commercial law documents (3), Taxation: Individual tax preparation and planning for employees of own company (1-2-3), Book-keeping services (3), Architectural advisory and pre-design services (3), Rental/leasing services without operators – Relating to ships: Leasing or rental services concerning non-Thai flag vessels without operator (3), Other business services – Supply services of industrial workers (1-2-3).

Communication Services: Courier services – Bicycle courier services for food delivery (1-2-3), Telecommunication services – Dedicated network services, on-line information and data base retrieval (3), On-line information and/or data processing services provided over public telecommunications (3), Audio-visual services – Motion picture: Video projection services (1-2-3), Other: Colour correction services (3).

Transport Services: Maritime transport services – Passenger transportation: international sea cruises (3), Freight transportation: Transoceanic water transport (3), Rental of non-Thai flag vessels with crew (1-2-3), Maintenance and repair of vessels exceeding 100,000 DWT (3) Towing and pushing on transoceanic waters (1-2-3), Supporting services: Vessels salvage and re-floating (3), Road transport service – Maintenance and repair: Car valeting services (1-2-3), Supporting services: Parking services (1-2-3), Services auxiliary to all transport modes – Maritime cargo handling services in private-owned port (1-2-3), Storage and warehousing services of frozen/refrigerated goods (1-2-3), Ship brokerage services (1-2-3), Other: Freight brokerage service (1-2-3).

Vietnam

Business Services: Research and development services – R and D services on social sciences and humanities,

Interdisciplinary R and D Services (1-2-3), <u>Real estate services</u> – (Residential and non-residential property management services) (1-2-3), <u>Rental/leasing services without operator</u> – Leasing or rental services for furniture and other household appliances (1-2-3), Relating to ships (1-2-3), <u>Other business services</u> – Building-cleaning services (1-2-3), Packaging services (3)

Communication Services: <u>Courier services</u> (3), <u>Telecommunication services</u> – Value-added services (3).

Educational Services: <u>Primary education</u> (1-2-3).

Tourism and Travel-related Services: <u>Others</u> – Tourist theme parks (3).

Transport Services: <u>Maritime transport services</u> – Freight transportation less cabotage (3), Rental of vessels with crew (3), Maintenance and repair of vessels (3), <u>Rail transport services</u> – Freight transportation (3), Pushing and towing services (1-2-3), Supporting services for trail transport services (1-2-3), <u>Road transport services</u> – Freight transportation (3), Maintenance and repair of road transport equipment (1-2-3), <u>Services auxiliary to all modes of transport</u> – Rail handling services (1-2-3), Storage and warehouse services (3), Freight transport agency services (1).

Other Services Not Included Elsewhere: Laundry collection services (1-2-3), Dry cleaning services (1-2-3), Pressing service (1-2-3).

4.8 Assessment of Liberalization of Trade in Services under AFAS

4.8.1 AFAS, GATS and AEC Blueprint 2015

The level of ambition for the liberalization of trade in services was spelled out in the AEC Blueprint 2015 and the degree of services commitments expected under AFAS was clearly stated therein. This is summarized in Table 4.5. Upon attainment of the aims stated in the Blueprint, the level of commitments under AFAS should cover all 128 sub-sectors negotiated under the ASEAN Economic Ministers. The remaining sub-sectors, largely in financial services and air transport services, were also subject to liberalization plans under the 2015 Blueprint, although the latter were not couched in the same terms through reference to pre-set formulas comprising numbers of sectors and modes of supply. The overall sectoral coverage under AFAS upon attainment of the AEC thus aimed at being substantial.

The comparison of commitments under each progressive AFAS package with those scheduled by AMS under the GATS is relatively straightforward. As the foregoing discussion has shown, levels of commitment in the seventh package of AFAS commitments already surpassed the (admittedly low and precaution-laden) levels attained under the GATS at the end of the Uruguay Round. The gap between the GATS and AFAS sectoral commitments has widened with every new AFAS Package.

How does services trade liberalization under AFAS measure up against the targets set by the AEC Blueprint 2015 as subsequently updated? Although the updates to the AEC targets have not always been clearly publicized or explained, a helpful summary in tabular form has been provided by the ASEAN Secretariat, and this information is summarized in Table 4.5.

Progress in implementing the AEC commitments and measures taken at the regional and national levels to this end were initially tracked by ASEAN's self-monitoring system: the AEC Scorecard. Two Scorecards were produced, in 2010 and 2012, to review progress in Phase 1 (2008–9) and Phase 2 (2010–11), respectively. Under the 2012 Scorecard, it was found that ASEAN had completed 67.5 percent (187 out of 277) of the total AEC measures due for Phases 1 and 2 combined. After this, the focus was more on the overall implementation of the AEC Blueprint 2015 and, according to the ASEAN Secretariat, reports on implementation 'have become more thematic'.[96] There were clearly challenges to achieving the targets in the AEC Blueprint 2015 in relation to the free flow of services, at least within the time limits set by the Blueprint, so tough progress was being made. The ERIA Mid-Term Review of the AEC Blueprint 2015 in 2012 had recommended that such key measures should include those relating to liberalizing trade in services.[97] The decision of the ASEAN Economic Ministers in 2012 that the AEC 2015 target date would be set at 31 December 2015[98] gave more time to

[96] *AEC 2105 Progress and Achievements* (Jakarta: ASEAN Secretariat, 2015), p. 8.
[97] See Mid-Term Review of the Implementation of the AEC Blueprint: Executive Summary, ERIA, October 2012.
[98] See www.asean.org/news/asean-secretariat-news/item/aec-2015-remains-on-track-and-top-priority

Table 4.5 *Summary of selected targets set by AEC Blueprint 2015*[95]

	Seventh package	Eighth package	New ninth package	New tenth package
Completion target	AEM 2009	AEM 2011	AEM 2013	AEM 2015
Scheduled sub-sectors	65	80	104	128
Mode 1	None	None (For all 80 sub-sectors)	None (For all 104 sub-sectors)	None (For all 128 sub-sectors)
Mode 2	None	None (For all 80 sub-sectors)	None (For all 104 sub-sectors)	None (For all 128 sub-sectors)
Mode 3 Foreign equity limitation	29 PIS: 51%	29 PIS: 70%	29 PIS: 70%	29 PIS: 70%
	9 LOG: 49%	9 LOG: 51%	9 LOG: 51–70%	9 LOG: 70%
	27 Other: 49%	42 Other: 51%	66 Other: 51%	90 Other:51–70%
Mode 3 MA limitations	29 PIS: Max 2 limitations	29 PIS: No limitation	29 PIS: No limitation	29 PIS: No limitation

[95] See *ASEAN Integration Report 2015* (Jakarta: ASEAN Secretariat, 2015) at p 29. See also Dionisius Norjoko, *AEC Blueprint Implementation Performance and Challenges: Services Liberalisation*. ERIA Discussion Paper Series, May 2015, p. 5.

(including horizontal)	9 LOG : max 3 limitations 27 Other: max 3 limitations	9 LOG : max 2 limitations 16 Other: max 3 limitations 16 Other: max 2 limitations	9 LOG : No limitation 26 Other: max 2 limitations 26 Other: max 1 limitation	9 LOG : No limitation 90 Other: No limitation
Mode 3NT (including horizontal)	NA	Max 4 limitations/sub-sector	Max 3 limitations/sub-sector	Max 1 limitation/sub-sector
Mode 4 15% flexibility	NA NA	To be agreed 15%*(80*3)= 36 modes Max 60% (22 Sub-sectors) in 1 mode	To be agreed 15%*(104*3)= 47 modes Max 55% (26 Sub-sectors) in 1 Mode	To be agreed 15%*(128*3)= 58 modes Max 50% (29 Sub-sectors) in 1 mode

Source: ASEAN Secretariat
KEY: PIS = Priority Integration Sectors
LOG = Logistics

fulfil the AEC 2015 commitments, but at the time of the establishment of the AEC, the tenth services package under AFAS had not been completed.

A few studies have included an analysis of selected key service sectors in ASEAN Member Countries and identified problems and suggested improvements.[99] Details of findings for specific sectors will not be reproduced here, but the most important general problem is that, despite the level of services liberalization committed 'on paper' under AFAS, there are problems of implementation 'on the ground' in almost all the ASEAN countries. Some of the barriers preventing meaningful services liberalization could be seen as structural in character, such as those linked to corruption, a lack of regulatory transparency, and the presence of state-owned enterprises in strategic sectors, as well as underlying macroeconomic problems.[100] This confirms the early findings

---

[99] USITC, 'ASEAN: Regional Trends in Economic Integration, Export Competitiveness, and Inbound Investment for Selected Industries', Publication No. 4176, USITC; Malcolm Bosworth, Ray Trewin, Adam McCarty, Gregore Lopez and Jane Drake-Brockman, 'Services Diagnostic and Needs Assessment Study', ASEAN-Australia Development Cooperation Program Phase II, 2011; Ben Shepherd and Gloria Pasadilla, 'Services as the Engine of Growth for ASEAN, the People Republic of China and India', ADBI Working Paper 349, Asian Development Bank Institute, 2012; Philippa Dee, 'Does AFAS have bite? Comparing Commitments with Actual Practice', working paper drawn from 'Services Liberalization: Impact and Way Forward', a paper presented for the ASEAN Economic Community Mid Term Review, ERIA, Jakarta, January 2013, available at: https://crawford.anu.edu.au/pdf/staff/phillippa_dee/2013/does-afas-have-bite.pdf

[100] Malcolm Bosworth, Ray Trewin, Adam McCarty, Gregore Lopez and Jane Drake-Brockman, 'Services Diagnostic and Needs Assessment

of Thanh and Bartlett, who found that the disparity of commitments and economic development across Member Countries had impaired regulatory harmonization, especially for Modes 3 and 4, and that AFAS transparency and predictability had been 'severely hindered by the low level of governance in the region'.[101]

Other obstacles to services liberalization include domestic rules such as those that continue to restrict intra-ASEAN foreign equity ownership in certain industries.[102] The problem of implementation was also highlighted in the 2012 AEC Scorecard as a challenge that might prevent the meeting of the 2015 deadline unless efforts at both country and regional levels were intensified to ensure that implementation gaps were addressed. In particular, the Scorecard found that enhanced implementation of AEC initiatives was needed at country level. It also found a need to address the legislative and regulatory limitations that impede the implementation of

Study', ASEAN-Australia Development Cooperation Program Phase II, 2011.

[101] V. T. Thanh and P. Bartlett (2006), 'Ten years of the ASEAN Framework Agreement in Services (AFAS): An Assessment', REPSF Project 05/004, Jakarta, Regional Economic Policy Support Facility, ASEAN Australia Development Cooperation Program, ASEAN Secretariat.

[102] A study by USITC (2010) expressed concern about the foreign ownership restrictions in Thailand, the Philippines and Indonesia in the logistics sector. The study observed that Thailand, for example, prohibited majority foreign ownership of domestic transportation activities, including those that were part of an international shipment. Another example provided by the study was that of Indonesia, where the law allows only Indonesians to invest in logistics services, leaving foreigners to enter the market only through joint ventures with local partners.

Table 4.6 *Number of sub-sectors committed in AFAS Packages 7, 8 and 9*[103]

	AFAS Package		
	seventh	eighth	ninth
AEC 2015 Target	65	80	104
Brunei	65	79	92
Cambodia	74	87	94
Indonesia	83	86	97
Lao PDR	74	89	92
Malaysia	81	96	101
Myanmar	66	79	90
Philippines	95	98	99
Singapore	78	84	101
Thailand	93	104	108
Vietnam	84	88	99

intra- and extra-ASEAN commitments.[104] These concerns are likely to have contributed in no small part to the limited success of AFAS at the end of 2015.

The number of sub-sectors committed by each ASEAN Member State in AFAS 7, 8 and 9, compared with the targets set by the AEC Blueprint 2015 is shown in Table 4.6. Although all ASEAN Member States committed at least the AEC 2015 number of sixty-five targeted sub-sectors in AFAS 7, the picture was different for AFAS 8 and more obviously so in AFAS 9. In AFAS 8, Brunei and Myanmar failed to commit the minimum targeted eighty sub-sectors. The AEC 2015 target for

[103] See *ASEAN Integration Report 2015* (Jakarta: ASEAN Secretariat, 2015), pp. 29–30.
[104] AEC Scorecard 2012, pp. 17–18.

AFAS 9 was 104 sub-sectors, but this was met only by Thailand, which surpassed the target by committing 108 sub-sectors. The other nine ASEAN Member States fell short of 104 sub-sectors, with Brunei committing the lowest number of ninety sub-sectors in AFAS 9. This is evidence of the operation of the 15 percent flexibility rule. The same observation was made by Narjoko, who, after a detailed analysis of AFAS 7 and AFAS 8, found that AFAS 8 did not make significant progress in terms of liberalization rate as compared with AFAS 7.[105] He suggested that one possible reason for the ASEAN Member States agreeing to signing AFAS 8 despite this slow progress was that the Member States decided to utilize the 15 percent flexibility rule allowed by the AFAS modality. The 15 percent flexibility rule is summarized in Table 4.5. Each Member State can have 15 percent of its mode-sector combinations defined as sensitive sectors so that these are not required to meet the AFAS target of liberalization. Taking the summary of the 15 percent rule for AFAS 8 shown in Table 4.5, it can be articulated in this way: the target number of sectors in AFAS 8 is 80. Taken over Modes 1, 2 and 3, this gives 240 mode–sector combinations, 15 percent of which is thirty-six. This means that up to thirty-six mode–sector combinations do not have to meet the AFAS 8 target of liberalization. From the table, the additional rule for AFAS 8 is that not more than 60 percent of these sensitive mode–sector combinations (i.e. twenty-two sub-sectors) are allowed in one mode.

[105] Dionisius Narjoko, 'AEC Blueprint Implementation Performance and Challenges: Service Liberalization', ERIA Discussion Paper Series, May 2015, p. 11.

The 15 percent flexibility rule enables trade restrictions in selected sub-sectors and modes to be retained even post-AEC. While such departures from full liberalization inevitably water down trade and investment liberalization within ASEAN, its political economy realism raises the likelihood of a successful attainment of AEC aims. Even with such flexibility, given the diversity of realities on offer within ASEAN, and as delays in completing the ninth and tenth packages revealed, it became increasingly difficult for ASEAN Member States to conclude each successive AFAS package, as increasingly sensitive sub-sectors had to be listed.

It bears noting that the breadth of sectoral coverage mandated under the AEC Blueprint 2015 was not matched by a similar depth in the required commitments in terms of modes of supply. While the requirements for Modes 1 and 2 were strict, requiring that all restrictions be removed except for those which are retained for *bona fide* regulatory reasons, the requirements for Mode 3 were initially confined to minimum foreign equity participation, while no controls were mandated for Mode 4. In relation to Mode 3, the maximum required commitment upon the attainment of the AEC is a minimum foreign (ASEAN) participation target that falls short of 100 percent, being fixed at 70 percent. This arguably runs counter to the AEC's stated aims. Meanwhile, the updated AEC 2015 requirement in relation to Mode 3 calls for the progressive removal of all other Mode 3 market access limitations by the AFAS tenth package – a challenging aim that may be one of the reasons for the delay in completing AFAS 10. The liberalization of services supplied under Mode 4 is clearly the most problematic. This has received, at most, a slight boost from the signing of the ASEAN Framework Agreement for the Movement of Natural Persons.

The eight MRAs in professional services are important achievements under the AEC Blueprint 2015. How far these would actually facilitate the movement of professionals depends on proper management of the challenges, both external and internal, to the MRAs themselves. Being registered as a foreign professional under a particular MRA will depend on being able to satisfy various requirements, some of which may be onerous and opaque. For example, medical and dental professionals who already meet the stringent requirements to practise in a host country in terms of education, years of professional practice, continuing professional development exposure and good conduct, additionally have to comply with any other assessment or requirement that may be imposed by the regulatory authorities of the host country. Even where a professional is sufficiently qualified to meet the criteria for achieving recognition for his or her qualifications under a particular MRA, he or she may still not be able to work in another ASEAN country unless the general rules and regulations of the host country allow this. For instance, immigration rules regarding the grant of work permits, as well as the statutory requirements for the practice of the relevant professional practice, might need to be created or modified in order to facilitate the entry of ASEAN foreign professionals into ASEAN host countries under the respective MRAs. To this end, Mode 4 commitments directed towards the relevant professional services are required to complement the provisions of the respective MRAs. To date, such an alignment has yet to occur.

4.8.2 Looking to the Future

Even when the services targets under the AEC Blueprint 2015 have been met, there remains much room for improvement. Limitations to the coverage of AFAS have been mentioned earlier. Under the Bandar Seri Begawan Declaration adopted at the 23rd ASEAN Summit on 9 October 2013, the ASEAN Leaders committed to developing the ASEAN Community's Post-2015 Vision. Building on this, the ASEAN Economic Ministers reiterated that the pursuit of expanding and deepening market integration would need to continue beyond 2015 in order to sustain regional economic development and resilience, and enhance ASEAN's role in East Asia and the global economy. A new AEC Blueprint 2025 was unveiled in 2015,[106] wherein it was confirmed that services integration in the region would take place under a new agreement, ATISA, for which discussions started in 2013, and concluded in November 2018 at the 17th AEC Council Meeting.[107] Under the AEC Blueprint 2025, existing flexibilities, limitations and carve-outs would be reviewed; mechanisms to attract foreign direct investments in the services sectors would be enhanced, and alternative approaches to the liberalization of services would be explored. Among the initiatives to be considered are the establishment of possible disciplines on domestic regulations and the development of sectoral annexes. This next phase of services liberalization and integration in

---

[106] ASEAN Secretariat, *ASEAN 2025: Forging Ahead Together* (Jakarta: November 2015).

[107] See www.mti.gov.sg/-/media/MTI/Newsroom/Press-Releases/2018/11/17th-AECC/Media-Release-17th-AECC-12-Nov-2018.pdf

ASEAN is to be welcomed. If ASEAN's experience with AFAS is any indication, the journey ahead will not be easy but, with continued collective political will, the prospects for sustained progress remain favourable, given the diversity of political, developmental and institutional capacities present within ASEAN.

4.9 Services Liberalization in ASEAN+ and ASEAN Member States' PTAs

4.9.1 ASEAN+ Services PTAs

ASEAN as a group has been actively engaged in the negotiation of PTAs[110] and assorted comprehensive economic partnership (CEP) agreements with an increasing number of strategic partners. Five such agreements are in force with six key partners: Australia, China, India, Japan, Korea and New Zealand. These agreements envisage the liberalization of trade in goods and services, together with investment liberalization, as important objectives, but progress on these different aspects of liberalization has varied. Liberalization of trade in goods has been successfully completed across the five agreements, but achieving similar success in the services component of these agreements has proven more challenging, and, at the time of writing, the services components of one of these five agreements has yet to be completed. In November 2017, ASEAN signed a sixth preferential trade agreement, with Hong Kong, covering both goods and services, with the aim that it should come into force by January 2019.

These six agreements are as follows:

(i) The Trade in Services Agreement of the Framework Agreement on Comprehensive Economic Cooperation between ASEAN and the People's Republic of China (ACFTA), signed on 14 January 2007 in Cebu, the Philippines, entered into force on 1 July 2007.[108]

(ii) The Trade in Services Agreement under the Framework Agreement on Comprehensive Economic Cooperation among the Governments of the Member Countries of ASEAN and the Republic of Korea (AKFTA), signed on 21 November 2007 in Singapore, entered into force on 1 May 2009.[109]

(iii) The Agreement Establishing the ASEAN–Australia–New Zealand Free Trade Area (AANZFTA), signed on 27 February 2009 in Cha-Am, Thailand, entered into force on various dates for different ASEAN Members, from 1 January 2010 to 10 January 2012.[110] (This was the

---

[108] In November 2002, China and ASEAN signed their first Framework Agreement on Comprehensive Economic Cooperation, which was limited to trade in goods. Three subsequent packages of commitments for services have been agreed upon, with the Protocol for the Third Package of commitments being signed in November 2015.

[109] Negotiations for the ASEAN–Korea Free Trade Agreement (AKFTA) began in 2005, and the trade in goods chapter of the AKFTA entered into force in June 2007.

[110] The AANZFTA agreement is the first comprehensive free trade agreement that ASEAN has signed with a Dialogue Partner with initial commitments in all three pillars of goods, services and investments. Negotiations began in 2005. The Agreement was signed in February 2009 and entered into force on 1 January 2010 for (and among) the following countries: Australia, Brunei, Malaysia, Myanmar, New

first comprehensive free trade agreement signed by ASEAN with a Dialogue Partner that contained initial commitments in all three pillars of goods, services and investments.)

(iv) The Framework Agreement on Comprehensive Economic Cooperation between the Republic of India and ASEAN (AIFTA) originally covered only trade in goods.[111] Negotiations between ASEAN and India for an agreement covering services and investment were concluded in December 2012. The resulting agreement was signed by all ASEAN Member States and India by January 2015 and entered into force on 1 July 2015.

(v) The ASEAN–Japan Comprehensive Economic Partnership (AJCEP) Agreement was signed in 2008, and substantial conclusion of the negotiations on its Services and Investment Chapters was announced in December 2013.[112] It had initially been hoped that this

Zealand, Singapore, the Philippines and Vietnam. It entered into force for Thailand on 12 March 2010; for Lao PDR and Cambodia on 1 and 4 January 2011, respectively; and for Indonesia on 10 January 2012: www.asean.fta.govt.nz/what-is-the-asean-fta/

[111] Negotiations for an ASEAN–India Trade in Goods Agreement began in 2003; the Agreement was signed in August 2009 and came into force in January 2010. See Overview ASEAN–India Dialogue Relations, available at: http://asean.org/wp-content/uploads/images/2015/November/asean-india/Overview%20ASEAN-India%20Dialogue%20Relations%20-%20November%202015.pdf

[112] This was done at the ASEAN–Japan Commemorative Summit in Tokyo, Japan, on 14 December 2013: www.pmo.gov.sg/content/pmosite/media centre/pressreleases/2013/December/asean-japan-commemorative-summit-in-tokyo-japan-on-14-december-.html Negotiations for the ASEAN–Japan CEP Agreement began in 2005. The agreement relating

agreement would be signed as early as in 2014,[113] but as of November 2017, final negotiations were still ongoing.
(vi) The ASEAN–Hong Kong, China, Free Trade Agreement was signed on 12 November 2017 in Pasay City, the Philippines, covering both goods and services. To complement this, the ASEAN–Hong Kong, China Investment Agreement was signed on the same day. The two Agreements are expected to enter into force by 1 January 2019.

The Regional Comprehensive Economic Partnership and Other Negotiations

By far the most ambitious ASEAN FTA will be the Regional Comprehensive Economic Partnership (RCEP), a sixteen-party (ASEAN+6) preferential trade agreement that was launched on 20 November 2012 at the twenty-first ASEAN Summit and Related Summits in Phnom Penh, Cambodia,[114] between the ten ASEAN Member States and ASEAN's PTA partners Australia, China, India, Korea, Japan and New Zealand. Alongside the recently completed Comprehensive and Progressive Trans-Pacific Partnership (CPTPP) agreement, which associates four ASEAN Member States (Brunei Darussalam, Malaysia, Singapore and Vietnam) and the

to goods was signed in April 2008 and came into force at different times in relation to various signatories, between December 2008 and November 2009.

[113] The 20th ASEAN Economic Ministers (AEM) Retreat, 26–27 February 2014, Singapore, Joint Media Statement.
[114] See details at: www.asean.org/news/asean-secretariat-news/item/asean-and-fta-partners-launch-the-world-s-biggest-regional-free-trade-deal

Continental Free Trade Area (CFTA) linking fifty-four African economies, RCEP stands out among the new generation of so-called 'mega regional' groupings. RCEP involves sixteen countries that account for almost half of the world's population, close to a third of world output, and just under 30 percent of global trade.[115] Such numbers would make it the world's largest regional trading arrangement should it be successfully concluded.

Negotiations among RCEP Members began in May 2013, with an initial target date of end-2015 for their conclusion, which has since been extended without setting a new formal end date. Under the Guiding Principles and Objectives for Negotiating the RCEP, which were adopted by Economic Ministers in August 2012 and endorsed at the twenty-first ASEAN Summit in November 2012, the agreement will cover trade in goods and services as well as investment, and will feature an accession clause allowing other countries to join as long as they agree to comply with the grouping's rules and guidelines The Joint Statement of the First Meeting of the Negotiation Committee on 10 May 2013 highlighted that RCEP would bring significant improvements over the existing ASEAN+1 FTAs by featuring broader and deeper commitments while at the same time recognizing the individual and diverse circumstances of the participating countries. The Agreement will include provisions to facilitate trade and investment and to enhance transparency in trade and investment relations between the participating countries, as well as

---

[115] Joint Leaders' Statement on the Negotiations for the RCEP, 14 November 2017, Manila, the Philippines.

to facilitate the participating countries' engagement in global and regional supply chains. It will also include appropriate forms of flexibility, including provision for special and differential treatment, plus additional flexibility for the least-developed ASEAN Member States, consistent with the existing ASEAN+1 FTAs, in order to take account of differing levels of economic development among participating countries. In addition to work related to trade in goods, trade in services and investment; work also being done in other areas such as intellectual property, competition, economic and technical cooperation, and dispute settlement.[116] As of August 2018, twenty-three rounds of RCEP negotiations[117] and six Ministerial Meetings had been completed.[118]

At the RCEP Summit on 14 November 2017 in Manila, the Philippines, the Joint Leaders' Statement included a current outline of the RCEP Agreement showing its distinct features.[119] This indicated that the Trade in Services Chapter of RCEP would build on the services commitments in the GATS and the ASEAN+1 FTAs with no *a priori* exclusion of any sector or mode of supply. There would be separate Annexes under the Trade in Services Chapter of the RCEP to cover Financial

[116] Joint Media Statement of the 20th ASEAN Economic Ministers Retreat, 26–27 February 2014, Singapore.
[117] See https://dfat.gov.au/trade/agreements/negotiations/rcep/news/Pages/twenty-third-round-of-negotiations-17-27-july-2018-bangkok-thailand.aspx
[118] See https://asean.org/joint-media-statement-sixth-regional-comprehensive-economic-partnership-rcep-ministerial-meeting/
[119] See Joint Leaders' Statement on the Negotiations for the RCEP, 14 November 2017, Manila, the Philippines, available at: http://asean.org/storage/2017/11/RCEP-Summit_Leaders-Joint-Statement-FINAL1.pdf

Services and Telecommunication Services. The Financial Services Annex would support enhanced rules on financial regulation while providing enough regulatory space to guard against risks in instability of the financial system. The Telecommunications Services Annex would provide a framework of rules, and affirm the rights of Participating Countries to regulate while maintaining a reasonable and non-discriminatory telecommunications environment. The outline also showed that there would be a separate chapter on the movement of natural persons, and that discussions were ongoing regarding the structure and relationship between the commitments in this and the trade in services chapter. At the Sixth RCEP Ministerial Meeting on 30–31 August 2018, the Ministers adopted a Package of Year-End Deliverables developed by the Trade Negotiating Committee and expressed the hope that the Package could be completed by the end of 2018, which would mark the conclusion of the RCEP negotiations. The Ministers highlighted 'the significance of establishing the world's largest free trade area among 16 diverse participating countries under RCEP amidst escalating trade frictions' and reaffirmed their commitment to see RCEP through to its conclusion notwithstanding rising uncertainties in the global trade environment.[120]

In 2007, ASEAN began talks with the EU towards a bloc to bloc preferential trade agreement, but negotiations encountered protracted difficulties and were suspended in

---

[120] See Joint Media Statement of the Sixth RCEP Ministerial Meeting, 30–31 August 2018, para. 5: http://asean.org/wp-content/uploads/2018/08/RCEP-MM-6-JMS_FINAL.pdf

2009, after which the EU decided to pursue bilateral PTAs with a select number of individual ASEAN Member States.[121] These bilateral agreements are seen by the EU as building blocks towards a regional ASEAN–EU FTA upon resumption of negotiations in the future.[122] In March 2017, the EU and ASEAN indicated that they would try to revive plans for an FTA between them.[123] A working group representing both parties was formed to explore this possibility and held its first meeting in October 2017.[124] At the annual ASEAN Economic Ministers–EU Trade Commissioner Consultations in March 2018, it was stressed that ASEAN and the EU would work to get to the final stages for approving such an initiative.[125]

---

[121] Two main issues were reportedly the differing levels of economic development in ASEAN, which made negotiations difficult, and the slow pace of democratic reforms and poor human rights record of Myanmar. See interview with EU Trade Commissioner Karel De Gucht in *The Jakarta Post*, 7 May 2011, available at: www.thejakartapost.com/news/2011/05/07/eu-negotiate-fta-with-all-asean-countries-except-myanmar.html. With the rapid and far-reaching reforms that have taken place in Myanmar since then, the way may be paved for EU and ASEAN to return to the negotiating table in the not-too-distant future.

[122] This was stated by the EU Trade Commissioner at the 12th ASEAN Economic Ministers-EU Trade Commissioner Consultations on 8 March 2013 at Ha Noi. See: http://asean.org/?static_post=overview-of-asean-eu-dialogue-relations

[123] 'EU and ASEAN agree to put free trade pact back on agenda', *Reuters*, 10 March, 2017. See: www.reuters.com/article/us-eu-asean/eu-and-asean-agree-to-put-free-trade-pact-back-on-agenda-idUSKBN16H0S7

[124] 'ASEAN revives FTA talks with Europe', 2 October 2017, *Philippine Daily Enquirer*. See http://business.inquirer.net/237819/asean-revives-fta-talks-europe

[125] https://english.vov.vn/politics/aseaneu-fta-expected-to-be-approved-by-yearend-369670.vov

It bears noting that no ASEAN Member State took part in the now suspended Geneva-based negotiations towards a plurilateral Trade in Services Agreement (TiSA) among the so-called 'Really Good Friends of Services' grouping of WTO Members. While the Government of Singapore had been associated to the discussions that preceded the launch of TiSA, it subsequently chose not to partake in the start of formal negotiations.[126]

4.9.2 Services PTAs of Individual ASEAN Member States

In addition to the ASEAN-wide agreements depicted above, ASEAN Member States have also been actively engaged in the pursuit and conclusion of a dense and growing network of bilateral and plurilateral PTAs with third countries, most of which include provisions and liberalization commitments on trade in services. The liberalization process under these agreements is an ongoing one and the situation is in constant flux, with a continuum consisting of agreements that are in force; those that have been signed but are not yet in force; those that have been concluded but are not yet signed or ratified; those which are still under negotiation; and those in various stages of being considered for negotiation.

The bilateral and plurilateral agreements liberalizing trade in services between individual ASEAN Member States

---

[126] For a fuller discussion of TISA and its aims, see Pierre Sauvé (2013), 'A Plurilateral Agenda for Services? Assessing the Case for a Trade in Services Agreement', *NCCR Working Paper 2013/29* (May) (Bern: World Trade Institute), available at: www.wti.org/nccr-trade

and third countries are summarized below. It should be noted that some ASEAN Member States have PTAs in force that only cover trade in goods which are not reflected in the summary. Examples include the Malaysia–Chile FTA and the Thailand–Peru FTA. Also left out are the substantial number of potential PTAs between ASEAN Member States and third countries or other regional groupings that are in the process of being negotiated or under consideration which are widely expected to cover trade in services.

Brunei Darussalam[127]

1. Brunei–Japan Economic Partnership Agreement (BJEPA), signed by Brunei Darussalam on 18 June 2007 and entered into force for Brunei Darussalam on 31 July 2008.
2. Trans Pacific Strategic Economic Partnership Agreement involving Brunei Darussalam, Chile, New Zealand and Singapore ('TPSEP, also commonly referred to as P4), signed on 2 August 2005 and entered into force on 12 July 2006.
3. CPTPP, signed 8 March 2018, and not in force as at August 2018.

Indonesia[128]

1. Agreement Between Japan and the Republic of Indonesia for an Economic Partnership (IJEPA), signed on 20 August 2007 and entered into force on 1 July 2008.

---

[127] www.mofat.gov.bn/SitePages/Brunei%20Darussalam's%20FTA%20Policy.aspx

[128] See website of the Indonesian Ministry of Commerce at www.kemendag.go.id/en/perdagangan-kita/agreements; and website of Japan's

Malaysia[129]

1. Malaysia–Japan Economic Partnership Agreement (MJEPA), signed on 13 December 2005 and entered into force on 13 July 2006.
2. Malaysia–Pakistan Closer Economic Partnership Agreement (MPCEPA), established on 8 November 2007 and entered into force on 1 January 2008.
3. Malaysia–New Zealand FTA (MNZFTA), signed on 26 October 2009 and entered into force on 1 August 2010.
4. Malaysia–India Comprehensive Economic Cooperation Agreement (MICECA), established on 24 September 2010 and came into force on 1 July 2011.
5. Malaysia–Australia Free Trade Agreement (MAFTA), signed on 22 May 2012 and entered into force on 1 January 2013.
6. CPTPP, signed 8 March 2018, and not in force as at August 2018.

Ministry of Foreign Affairs at www.mofa.go.jp/policy/economy/fta/indonesia.html. In February 2012, Indonesia signed a PTA with Pakistan that came into effect in January 2013, providing market access for certain products at preferential tariff rates, which is hoped to provide the foundation for a comprehensive FTA: www.nation.com.pk/pakistan-news-newspaper-daily-english-online/business/17-Feb-2013/pak-indonesia-pta-to-begin-new-era

[129] See website of the Malaysian Ministry for International Trade and Industry at: http://fta.miti.gov.my/index.php/pages/view/4. Malaysia has FTAs with Chile and with Turkey, covering trade in goods only.

Philippines[130]

1. Japan–Philippine Economic Partnership Agreement (JPEPA), signed on 9 September 2006 and entered into force on 11 December 2008.[131]
2. European Free Trade Association–Philippine Free Trade Agreement (EFTA) signed on 28 April 2016, not in force as of November 2017.[132]

Singapore[133]

1. Agreement between New Zealand and Singapore on a Closer Economic Partnership (ANZSCEP), signed on 14 November 2000 and entered into force on 1 January 2001.
2. Agreement between Japan and the Republic of Singapore for a New-Age Economic Partnership Agreement (JSEPA), signed on 13 January 2002 and entered into force on 30 November 2002.[134]

---

[130] See website of the Philippines Department of Trade and Industry at: www.dti.gov.ph/15-main-content/dummy-article/682-free-trade-agreements#

[131] www.mofa.go.jp/announce/announce/2008/11/1185418_1070.html and www.mofa.go.jp/policy/economy/fta/philippines.html

[132] The EFTA countries comprise Switzerland, Iceland, Liechtenstein and Norway.

[133] See www.fta.gov.sg/. Singapore is also party to the Agreement between Singapore and the Separate Customs Territory of Taiwan, Penghu, Kinmen and Matsu on Economic Partnership (ASTEP), which covers trade in goods, services, and investments. See www.iesingapore.gov.sg/Trade-From-Singapore/ASTEP/Overview-of-ASTEP. This agreement was signed on 7 November 2013 and came into force on 19 April 2014: http://aric.adb.org/fta/singapore-taipei_china_fta#

[134] This agreement was reviewed and revised in 2007.

3. European Free Trade Association (EFTA)–Singapore Free Trade Agreement (ESFTA), signed on 26 June 2002 and entered into force on 1 January 2003.[135]
4. Singapore–Australia Free Trade Agreement (SAFTA), signed on 17 February 2003 and entered into force on 28 July 2003.[136]
5. US–Singapore Free Trade Agreement (USSFTA), signed on 6 May 2003 and entered into force on 1 January 2004.
6. India–Singapore Comprehensive Economic Cooperation Agreement (CECA), signed on 29 June 2005 and entered into force on 1 August 2005.
7. Singapore–Jordan Free Trade Agreement (SJFTA), signed on 16May 2004 and entered into force on 22August 2005.
8. Korea–Singapore Free Trade Agreement (KSFTA), signed on 4 August 2005 and entered into force on 2 March 2006.
9. Trans-Pacific Strategic Economic Partnership Agreement (Trans-Pacific SEP, also known as Pacific-4 or P4), signed on 18 July 2005 and entered into force on 28 May 2006.[137] Brunei Darussalam, Chile and New Zealand are Singapore's partners in this agreement. Prior to Brunei Darussalam's participation as a party to the negotiations,

---

[135] The EFTA countries comprise Switzerland, Iceland, Liechtenstein and Norway.
[136] The second review of this agreement was implemented on 2 September 2011.
[137] The Trans-Pacific SEP came into force on 28 May 2006 for Singapore and New Zealand, on 12 July 2006 for Brunei and on 8 November 2006 for Chile.

the Trans-Pacific SEP was known as the Pacific-Three or P3 FTA.
10. Panama–Singapore Free Trade Agreement (PSFTA), signed on 1 March 2006 and entered into force on 24 July 2006.
11. China–Singapore Free Trade Agreement (CSFTA), signed on 23 October 2008 and entered into force on 1 January 2009.
12. Peru–Singapore Free Trade Agreement (PeSFTA), signed on 29 May 2008 and entered into force on 1 August 2009.
13. Singapore–Costa Rica Free Trade Agreement (SCRFTA), signed on April 2010 and entered into force 1 July 2013.
14. Gulf Cooperation Council Singapore Free Trade Agreement (GSFTA), signed on 15 December 2008 and entered into force 1 September 2013.[138]
15. The European Union–Singapore Free Trade Agreement (EUSAFTA) was signed on 20 September 2013 (Goods and Services Agreement) and 22 May 2015 (Investment Protections Chapter), not in force as of November 2017.[139]

---

[138] The Gulf Cooperation Council (GCC) countries comprise Bahrain, Kuwait, Oman, Qatar, Saudi Arabia and the United Arab Emirates.

[139] The ratification of this agreement has been delayed because of the EU's decision to seek the opinion of the European Court of Justice (ECJ) to clarify the EU's competence to sign and ratify the agreement with Singapore. In May 2017, the ECJ ruled that the EUSFTA, in its current form, could not be concluded by the EU alone but needed the agreement of each EU member country, The EU did not have exclusive competence in the respect of two areas of the Agreement: the field of non-direct foreign investment ('portfolio' investments made without any intention to influence the management and control of an undertaking) and the regime governing dispute settlement between investors and states.

16. The Turkey–Singapore Free Trade Agreement (TRSFTA) was signed on 14 November 2015 and entered into force on 1 October 2017.
17. CPTPP, signed 8 March 2018, and not in force as at August 2018.

Thailand[140]

1. Thailand–Australia Closer Free Trade Agreement (TAFTA) was signed on 5 July 2004 and entered into force on 1 January 2005.
2. Agreement Between Japan and the Kingdom of Thailand for an Economic Partnership (JTEPA) was signed on 3 April 2007 and entered into force on 1 November 2007.
3. The Free Agreement between Chile and Thailand was signed on 4 October 2013 and entered into force on 5 November 2015.

---

[140] See www.thaifta.com/engfta/?language=en-US. The Thailand–Peru FTA does not have a services chapter, while the services chapter under Thailand's FTA with New Zealand has not yet been concluded. See www.thaifta.com/engfta/Home/FTAbyCountry/tabid/53/ctl/detail/id/65/mid/480/usemastercontainer/true/Default.aspx. Thailand is also in negotiations with India to establish an FTA that includes goods and services. See www.thaifta.com/engfta/Home/FTAbyCountry/tabid/53/ctl/detail/id/83/mid/480/usemastercontainer/true/Default.aspx. Further, Thailand is a member of the seven-country Bay of Bengal Initiative for Multi-Sectoral Technical and Economic Cooperation (BIMSTEC) group. In addition to Thailand, BIMSTEC includes fellow ASEAN Member State Myanmar, and five other countries: Bangladesh, Bhutan, India, Nepal and Sri Lanka. BIMSTEC signed a Framework Agreement in 2004 to establish a free trade area covering trade in goods, services and investment, beginning with an agreement on trade in goods that is under negotiation: www.thaifta.com/english/eng_bim.html

Vietnam[141]

1. Agreement between Japan and the Socialist Republic of Viet Nam for an Economic Partnership (VJEP) was signed on 25 December 2008 and entered into force on 1 October 2009.[142]
2. The Vietnam–Korea Free Trade Agreement (VKFTA) was signed on 5 May 2015 and came into effect on 20 December 2015.
3. The Free Trade Agreement between Vietnam and the Eurasian Economic Union (VN–EAEU FTA) was signed on 29 May 2015 and came into effect on 5 October 2016.[143]
4. The Free Trade Agreement between the European Union and Vietnam (EVFTA) was signed on 2 December 2015, and is not yet in force as of November 2017.
5. CPTPP, signed 8 March 2018, and not in force as at August 2018.

---

[141] See http://wtocenter.vn/fta. Vietnam also has an FTA with Chile, which covers only trade in goods: Agreement between the United States of America and the Socialist Republic of Vietnam on Trade Relations, which was signed on 13 July 2000 and came into force on 10 December 2001. See www.usvtc.org/trade/bta/. This agreement seems to have faded into the background and does not appear in the FTA sections of the website of the Vietnamese Ministry of Industry and Trade nor on that of the Office of the US Trade Representative.

[142] www.mofa.go.jp/policy/economy/fta/vietnam.html

[143] The Member States of the Eurasian Economic Union are the Republic of Armenia, the Republic of Belarus, the Republic of Kazakhstan, the Kyrgyz Republic and the Russian Federation. Chapter 8 of the VN–EAEU FTA, covering trade in services, investment and movement of natural persons, applies only between Vietnam and the Russian Federation.

Cambodia, Lao PDR and Myanmar

Lao PDR is a participant in the 2011 Framework Agreement on the Promotion and Liberalization of Trade in Services Among Asia-Pacific Trade Agreement (APTA) Participating States.[144] Other APTA participating states are Bangladesh, China, India, Korea and Sri Lanka. This framework agreement provides generally for participating states to strengthen and enhance existing cooperation efforts in service sectors, to gradually reduce existing discriminatory measures and market access limitations among participating states, and to refrain from introducing new or more discriminatory measures and market access limitations. It also provides for the participating states to enter into negotiations for specific commitments that are beyond each of their individual GATS schedule. Lao PDR signed a bilateral trade agreement with the United States on 18 September 2003, which was upgraded to a Trade and Investment Framework Agreement on 17 February 2016. Cambodia and Myanmar do not currently have services agreements in force with third countries outside ASEAN. Myanmar has signed two framework agreements: one with the Bay of Bengal Initiative for Multi-Sectorial Technical and Economic Cooperation (BIMSTEC) to establish a free trade area covering trade in goods, services and investment, beginning with an agreement on trade in goods which is under

---

[144] See www.unescap.org/apta. The Asia-Pacific Trade Agreement (APTA) was signed in 1975 as an initiative of ESCAP (the Economic and Social Commission for Asia and the Pacific). Previously named the Bangkok Agreement, it is the oldest PTA among developing countries in the Asia-Pacific. It provides for trade liberalization measures and economic integration, with the aim of promoting economic development.

negotiation, and another with the USA on 21 May 2013. A trade and investment framework agreement also exists between Cambodia and the USA, signed on 14 July 2006.

4.10 Patterns of Commitment in ASEAN+ PTAs and Bilateral Agreements

Table 4.7 shows the ASEAN+ agreements and the bilateral and plurilateral agreements which relate to trade in services, as mentioned earlier in this volume. The focus of the table is on services agreements that are in force, but the services agreement between ASEAN Member States and Japan that is still being negotiated at the time of writing is also included for the sake of comparison. Some observations may be made from the pattern of commitments in ASEAN+ PTAs and bilateral agreements of ASEAN Member States.

It is clear that ASEAN collectively and individual ASEAN Member States subscribe to a policy of entering into PTAs as a means of achieving strategic advantages and economic advancement over and above their membership of the GATS and AFAS. All ten ASEAN Member States are members of the ASEAN+ PTAs and each has individually bought into the collective approach advocated by such groupings.

All but two of the newest (and least economically advantaged) members (Myanmar and Cambodia) have also entered into bilateral and/or plurilateral services PTAs with non-ASEAN countries. The absence of bilateral services agreements by these lower-income ASEAN countries is unlikely to be the result of a lack of interest in services trade on the part of the two countries, and it is likely just a matter of time

Table 4.7 Selected services agreements involving ASEAN Member States and third countries

		PTA PARTNERS												
		Australia	New Zealand	China	India	Korea	Japan	HongKong	Chile	Peru	USA	Canada	Mexico
ASEAN MEMBER STATES	Brunei Darussalam	A1 CPTPP (RCEP)	A1 P4 CPTPP (RCEP)	A2 (RCEP)	A3 (RCEP)	A4 (RCEP)	A5 n X1 CPTPP (RCEP)	A6	P4 CPTPP	CPTPP		CPTPP	CPTPP
	Cambodia	A1 (RCEP)	A1 (RCEP)	A2 (RCEP)	A3 (RCEP)	A4 (RCEP)	A5 n (RCEP)	A6					
	Indonesia	A1 (RCEP)	A1 (RCEP)	A2 (RCEP)	A3 (RCEP)	A4 (RCEP)	A5 n X2 (RCEP)	A6					
	Lao PDR	A1 (RCEP)	A1 (RCEP)	A2 (RCEP) APTA	A3 (RCEP) APTA	A4 (RCEP) APTA	A5 n (RCEP)	A6					
	Malaysia	A 1 X3 CPTPP (RCEP)	A1 X4 CPTPP (RCEP)	A2 (RCEP)	A3 X5 (RCEP)	A4 (RCEP)	A5 n X6 CPTPP (RCEP)	A6	CPTPP	CPTPP		CPTPP	CPTPP
	Myanmar	A1 (RCEP)	A1 (RCEP)	A2 (RCEP)	A3 (RCEP)	A4 (RCEP)	A5 n (RCEP)	A6					

Table 4.7 (cont.)

	\multicolumn{11}{c}{PTA PARTNERS}
	Australia	New Zealand	China	India	Korea	Japan	HongKong	Chile	Peru	USA	Canada	Mexico
Philippines	A1 (RCEP)	A1 (RCEP)	A2 (RCEP)	A3 (RCEP)	A4 (RCEP)	A5 n X7 (RCEP)	A6					
Singapore	A1 X8 CPTPP (RCEP)	A1 X9 P4 CPTPP (RCEP)	A2 X10 (RCEP)	A3 X11 (RCEP)	A4 X12 (RCEP)	A5 n X13 CPTPP (RCEP)	A6	P4 CPTPP	X14 CPTPP	X15	CPTPP	CPTPP
Thailand	A1 X16 (RCEP)	A1 (RCEP)	A2 (RCEP)	A3 (RCEP)	A4 (RCEP)	A5 n X17 (RCEP)	A6	X18				
Vietnam	A1 CPTPP (RCEP)	A1 CPTPP (RCEP)	A2 (RCEP)	A3 (RCEP)	A4 (RCEP)	A5 n X20 CPTPP (RCEP)	A6	CPTPP	CPTPP		CPTPP	CPTPP

A1 to A4 and A6: ASEAN+1 or ASEAN+2 agreement covering goods and services is in force
A5 n: ASEAN+1 PTA, services agreement under negotiation
X1 to X20: PTA signed with goods and services agreement between an individual ASEAN Member State and a non-ASEAN country which are in force as of August 2018.
P4 (Trans-Pacific Strategic Economic Partnership) is in force. P4 Members = Brunei Darussalam, Chile, New Zealand and Singapore
APTA: Members are Lao PDR, China, India, Korea, Bangladesh, Sri Lanka and Mongolia (finalised but not ratified).
CPTPP: Signed but not yet in force as of August 2018.
(RCEP): Negotiations ongoing as at August 2018. RCEP Members = ASEAN, Australia, New Zealand, China, India, Japan and Korea

before all ten ASEAN Member States are parties to their own bilateral services PTAs. This is illustrated by the example of Lao PDR, also a lower-income country, which has entered into the Framework Agreement on the Promotion and Liberalization of Trade in Services Among Participating States of the Asia-Pacific Trade Agreement (APTA). Although this agreement was couched in general terms at its inception, participating countries have agreed to start negotiating specific commitments that are improvements on their GATS commitments.

Singapore was the first ASEAN Member State actively to pursue bilateral PTAs, concluding its first such agreement with New Zealand in 2000. Singapore remains the most active in this regard. As of November 2017, Singapore had fifteen services agreements in force, two signed but not yet in force, and a number of others under negotiation. This is entirely in keeping with Singapore's open trading policy and its comparative advantage as a leading services hub. The fact that Singapore applies an almost zero tariff rate in goods trade had also led to its potential PTA partners, particularly those from developed countries, to pressure Singapore in scheduling a high level of services commitments in order to reap the highest possible benefits from the resulting trade and investment activity.

In the mid-2000s, other ASEAN Member States joined in the PTA frenzy, with Thailand and Brunei Darussalam signing their first agreements in 2004, followed by Malaysia in 2005. As an indication of the hectic pace of PTA activity in ASEAN and globally, Singapore, the first mover, had already signed nine FTAs by this time. Although the global financial crisis beginning in 2007 may have heightened awareness of the vital importance of diversified economic partnerships and markets, this would seem to have merely led to the reinforcement of an already clear policy stance among ASEAN Member States of anchoring their development strategies in stable trade and investment liberalization initiatives.

Studying the services agreements entered into in the ASEAN region also gives some insight into the PTA activity of non-ASEAN countries. Most notable is Japan, which has been relentlessly pursuing a policy aimed at promoting high-level economic partnerships with major trading powers in its resolve to 'open up the country' and 'pioneer a new future'.[145] In addition to Japan's PTA with ASEAN as a group (currently covering goods only, with ongoing negotiations on a services and investment chapter), it has concluded bilateral services agreements with seven out of the ten ASEAN countries, i.e. all but Cambodia, Lao PDR and Myanmar. Australia and New Zealand together have a services agreement with ASEAN as a group, and each has bilateral services agreements with several individual ASEAN Member States. Australia and New Zealand are also members of a plurilateral agreement that includes four ASEAN states, the CPTPP.[146] These agreements reflect a generally positive attitude towards trade agreements as instruments of pro-competitive good governance. Such

---

[145] www.mofa.go.jp/policy/economy/fta/index.html

[146] The precursor to the CPTPP was the P4 Agreement, which included two ASEAN Member States (Brunei and Singapore) as well as New Zealand and Chile.

activism must also be seen in the context of high and (value-chain-infused) rising trade and investment volumes and other economic links between Japan, Australia and Zealand, on the one hand, and the individual ASEAN countries on the other.

The history and pattern of services agreements as discussed in the previous section and summarized in Table 4.7 show that the general approach is for non-ASEAN countries interested in trading with ASEAN countries to start off by pursuing bilateral PTAs with individual ASEAN Member States concurrently or as a precursor to a wider ASEAN+ agreement. Examples are Australia, New Zealand and Japan. An exception is Hong Kong, which has a PTA with ASEAN as a whole but none with individual Member Countries. This PTA is the most recent ASEAN+ Agreement to be signed, and is not yet in force. In certain instances, non-ASEAN countries have continued to work towards bilateral PTAs with individual ASEAN Member States even after an ASEAN+ Agreement had been concluded. An example is Korea, which signed a PTA with Vietnam in 2015, some years after its agreement with ASEAN came into force in 2009.

This history of success augurs well for the likelihood of an eventual ASEAN–EU FTA, if the process applies equally on a larger scale in relation to the EU grouping as it did in the case of individual non-ASEAN countries. As noted earlier, the process of trade liberalization between the EU and the ASEAN region began with the aim of reaching an EU–ASEAN PTA, but talks were suspended in 2009 and the EU then pursued a strategy of negotiating bilateral PTAs with individual countries in ASEAN. Negotiations of agreements with Singapore and Vietnam have been concluded, with both agreements awaiting signature and ratification. Negotiations are ongoing with Thailand,[147] the Philippines, Myanmar and Indonesia and are at different stages of progress.[148] Negotiations were also proceeding with Malaysia, but have since been suspended at the request of the ASEAN partner. In 2016, a stocktaking exercise was initiated to assess the prospect of resuming EU–ASEAN negotiations. Both sides are currently assessing whether there is enough common ground to re-launch the negotiations in due course. The EU's position is that it considers bilateral FTAs with ASEAN Member States to be building blocks towards an EU–ASEAN agreement, which remains the ultimate aim of the EU.[149]

The ability of a small plurilateral agreement to grow into a much larger one is illustrated by the transformation of the four-member Trans-Pacific Strategic Partnership (or P4 agreement), which was the foundation for a would-be twelve-member Trans Pacific Partnership (TPP) which has now been replaced by an eleven-member CPTPP. The process of incremental growth began with the early history of P4. The initial

---

[147] In February 2013 the EU Council endorsed the launch of negotiations on an FTA with Thailand. The talks were officially launched in March 2013 and four rounds took place, with the last one being held in April 2014. Since the military takeover in Thailand in May 2014, no further FTA rounds have been scheduled.

[148] See http://ec.europa.eu/trade/policy/countries-and-regions/negotiations-and-agreements/ and http://trade.ec.europa.eu/doclib/docs/2006/december/tradoc_118238.pdf

[149] See www.asean.org/asean/external-relations/european-union/item/overview-of-asean-eu-dialogue-relations and http://ec.europa.eu/trade/creating-opportunities/bilateral-relations/regions/asean/

negotiations were launched in 2002 by Chile, Singapore and New Zealand at the Asia-Pacific Economic Cooperation (APEC) Leaders' Summit. Brunei Darussalam was first an observer and joined as a 'founding member' only later, at the fifth negotiating round in 2005. The aim of P4 was to provide a high-quality vehicle for economic integration in the Asia-Pacific Region. It was designed so that other countries could later come on board. The preamble to P4 affirms the Parties' commitment to APEC goals and principles, to the promotion of common frameworks within the Asia-Pacific Region and to encouraging accession to the agreement by other economies. Eight other countries joined the P4 group to form the TPP, which was signed in February 2016 and provoked controversy with its wide-ranging coverage. The TPP has since been replaced by the CPTPP, as is discussed in section 4.13.

It is obvious from the above discussion and the summary in Table 4.7 that there is coexistence and overlap of bilateral, plurilateral and regional agreements involving ASEAN Member States. This is particularly prevalent in the case of Singapore, Brunei Darussalam and New Zealand. For example, between Singapore and New Zealand, parties can potentially choose from the Singapore–New Zealand FTA, the P4 and the ASEAN–New Zealand FTA. For trade between Brunei Darussalam and Singapore, the choice is between AFAS, all the five existing ASEAN+ Agreements, and the P4. If the CPTPP and the RCEP are factored into the equation, the choice would be even greater, as Brunei, Singapore and New Zealand are also members of these two groupings.

If and when the RCEP and the CPTPP are both in force, the potential overlap of various agreements involving ASEAN countries will also have significant effects outside ASEAN. For example, if Japan and Australia have a trade dispute, they could potentially use the RCEP as well as the CPTPP, in addition to their bilateral FTA,[150] against each other. And if a dispute involves Australia and New Zealand, in addition to potentially using the RCEP and the CPTPP, the two countries could also use the AANZFTA, in addition to their bilateral FTA.[151] Further, a side effect of the RCEP (from the ASEAN point of view) is that it would also bring together countries that do not yet have bilateral trade agreements with each other, such as India and China; India and Australia; and China and New Zealand.

However, as the discussion later in this chapter demonstrates, parties by no means grant similar access and commitments to the same counterparts over different agreements. Such overlaps are messy and confusing for the trading community, and particularly business users, complicating attempts at identifying the best arrangements, specific preferences and optimal market access paths available to them.

To date, governments have shown little proclivity to rationalize such rule-making overlaps. This would appear suggestive of the fact that governments in the region are subject to limited pressures from the user (business)

---

[150] Japan–Australia Economic Partnership Agreement: www.mofa.go.jp/policy/economy/fta/australia.html
[151] NZ–Australia Closer Economic Relations Agreement: www.mfat.govt.nz/en/trade/free-trade-agreements/free-trade-agreements-in-force/nz-australia-closer-economic-relations-cer/

community to perform such rationalization and exploit possible scale economies. In turn, this may reflect the oft-remarked concern over the limited traction preferential agreements appear to exert, with generally low preference utilization rates, particularly in goods trade.[152]

Nevertheless, the above trends suggest, despite the potential confusion stemming from treaty overlap, that countries consider that benefits can be gained from entering into additional agreements with the same partner country or countries even where they are already bound by existing agreements. This lends weight to the idea that bilateral and plurilateral PTAs can be building blocks for larger scale agreements. As mentioned above, the CPTPP is one such example of treaty expansion, being an extension of the P4. The proposal to establish a sixteen-member RCEP involving all ten ASEAN Member States and their six existing PTA partners (China, India, Japan, Korea, Australia and New Zealand), has clearly taken root in the scale and learning economies achieved under the ASEAN+ PTAs (i.e. ACFTA, AJCEP, AKFTA and AANZFTA). Taken on a larger scale, one could extrapolate from these developments that the expansion of PTA networks globally might represent a WTO-compatible route towards the incipient multilateralization of regional (preferential) advances in services trade.

---

[152] See M. Kawai and G. Wignaraja (eds.), *Asia's Free Trade Agreements: How Is Business Responding?* (London and Tokyo: Edward Elgar and Asian Development Bank Institute, 2011), available at: www.adbi.org/files/2011.01.31.book.asia.free.trade.agreements.pdf

4.11 Commitments and Rule-Making under ASEAN+ Agreements

4.11.1 Commitments

With the proliferation of PTAs involving ASEAN as a group and ASEAN Member States individually, an important question arises in respect of the level of liberalization that has been achieved under such agreements. How do the commitments in each agreement compare with those in other agreements, and what are the implications of these findings?

Various quantitative methods have been devised to measure the level of services liberalization in the GATS and other agreements. None is perfect, but they are nevertheless useful as a general indication of the level of services liberalization a country or regional grouping has committed to for broad brush comparative purposes across agreements and time. The Hoekman Index is one of the most commonly used metrics applied to GATS-type commitments in services agreements. As discussed earlier, a modified version of the Hoekman method has also been used by the WTO Secretariat to construct a dataset measuring the level of restrictiveness of commitments made in a selected number of PTAs compared with the GATS.[153] The WTO Secretariat highlighted that the methodology does not attempt to assess the quality of commitments nor to determine the level of trade restrictiveness.

---

[153] The data and methodology are set out at: www.wto.org/english/tratop_e/serv_e/dataset_e/dataset_e.htm. See also M. Roy, 'Services Commitments in Preferential Trade Agreements: An Expanded Dataset', Staff Working Paper ERSD-2011-18, World Trade Organization, 9 December 2011.

Nevertheless, by comparing how much further (or otherwise) commitments in two or more PTAs go beyond the GATS, it would seem possible to extrapolate the relative restrictiveness of the agreements considered *vis a vis* each other.

The remainder of this section will compare the commitments made largely under AFAS 7 (some data for AFAS 5 is also included) and three ASEAN+ FTAs, i.e. those with China, Korea and Australia–New Zealand. The analysis will rely on a qualitative assessment of the services commitments made by participants in the relevant agreements as well as the quantitative data prepared by ERIA and the WTO Secretariat mentioned above. The completion of later AFAs packages does not generally affect the observations made in this section, and attention will be drawn to the instances where it may do so.

It might seem intuitive that an important rationale for signing more agreements involving the same partners would be to achieve better and deeper liberalization commitments and novel rules in services trade, at least compared with those of the GATS, whose rules and commitments are common to all WTO Members. However, it is not uncommon to find agreements that contain negative preferences, also referred to as agreements that are GATS-minus. These could arise for various reasons, for instance as an attempt to retract overly generous or ambiguously framed commitments in the GATS schedules or for non-economic reasons, though their legality under the GATS may be called in question and it could be argued that the GATS still applies despite the GATS-minus commitments in an FTA. Adlung and Morison offer some examples of GATS-minus commitments in the ASEAN context, for instance the first package of commitments under the ASEAN–China Agreement on Trade in Services (ACFTA), in which the overall sectoral scope of China's commitments was more than halved compared with its WTO accession commitments under the GATS. Similarly, the number of sub-sectors scheduled by Indonesia was lower than that it had offered under the GATS.[154] Further, a significant number of ASEAN countries did not include some of their GATS commitments in the first package of ACFTA commitments.[155] Nevertheless, it has been observed that such limited liberalization can still be meaningful in light of the fact that services negotiation under the ACFTA is intended to be progressive, and subsequent packages could provide substantial GATS-plus liberalization[156] Fukunaga and Ishido compared the first package of commitments under the ACFTA with the second package using the Hoekman Index and found that ASEAN (on average) and China made more

---

[154] Rudolf Adlung and Peter Morrison, 'Less than the GATS: "Negative Preferences" in Regional Services Agreements', *Journal of International Economic Law*, 13(4) (2010), 1103–43 at 1135. See also Rudolf Adlung and Sébastien Miroudot, 'Poison in the Wine? Tracing GATS-Minus Commitments in Regional Trade Agreements', Staff Working Paper ERSD-2012-04, World Trade Organization, 2012, which identifies the Japan–Philippines Economic Partnership Agreement and the Japan–Thailand Economic Partnership Agreement as having a GATS-minus level of liberalization.

[155] Yoshifumi Fukunaga and Hikari Ishido, 'Assessing the Profess of Services Liberalization in the ASEAN–China Free Trade Area (ACFTA)', ERIA Discussion Paper Series, ERIA-DP-2013=07, May 2013, p. 7.

[156] Ibid., p. 1.

commitments in the ACFTA second package than in their respective GATS commitments.[157] With the third and subsequent packages under ACFTA, more improvements may be expected in future.

In a study in 2012, Ishido and Fukunaga at ERIA used the Hoekman Index to compare the average overall level of services liberalization of ASEAN Members in AFAS 5, AFAS 7 and the three ASEAN+ FTAS with China, Korea and Australia–New Zealand. Their findings are shown in Table 4.8.[158] These results should be approached with the caveat that they do not take into account the qualitative differences in the various types of limitations that might exist in different sectors, and that the average value of a country's commitments could mask vastly different commitment levels across sectors. Table 4.8 shows that, almost across the board, the level of commitments made by each ASEAN Member State in the ASEAN–China FTA (first package) and the ASEAN–Korean FTA, was at around the same level or less than that they made under AFAS 5. Exceptions are Singapore and Korea that had marginally higher commitments under AKFTA than under AFAS 5. This general lack of improvement in AKFTA over AFAS 5 is not surprising if one considers that ASEAN

---

[157] Ibid., p. 12.
[158] Hikari Ishido and Yoshifumi Fukunaga, 'Liberalization of Trade in Services: Toward a Harmonized ASEAN++ FTA', ERIA Policy Brief, No. 2012-02, ERIA, 2012. In Table 4.8, a higher number indicates a higher level of liberalization. This can be contrasted with another way in which the Hoekman Index is sometimes used, which is to deduct the resulting figure from 1, i.e. (1−x), where a higher figure would indicate a higher level of restrictiveness.

Table 4.8 *Services liberalization in ASEAN services agreements and ASEAN+ FTAs*[159]

	AFAS (5)	AFAS (7)	AANZFTA	ACFTA	AKFTA
Brunei Darussalam	0.17	0.23	0.18	0.05	0.08
Cambodia	0.40	0.41	0.51	0.38	0.38
Indonesia	0.18	0.36	0.29	0.09	0.18
Lao PDR	0.09	0.34	0.24	0.02	0.07
Malaysia	0.22	0.34	0.31	0.11	0.20
Myanmar	0.20	0.36	0.26	0.04	0.06
Philippines	0.22	0.33	0.26	0.11	0.17
Singapore	0.28	0.39	0.44	0.30	0.33
Thailand	0.30	0.50	0.36	0.25	n.a.
Vietnam	0.31	0.38	0.46	0.34	0.32
ASEAN average	0.24	0.36	0.33	0.17	0.20
Australia			0.52		
New Zealand			0.51		
China				0.28	
Korea					0.31

Source: Ishido and Fukunaga (2012)

Member States might justifiably want to keep their best commitments within the ASEAN bloc rather than extend them to third-country trading partners. However, such sentiment might not always prevail, as can be shown by the commitments made in the ASEAN–Australia–New Zealand FTA, where the average level of liberalization was extended beyond

---

[159] Reproduced from Hikari Ishido and Yoshifumi Fukunaga, 'Liberalization of Trade in Services: Toward a Harmonized ASEAN++ FTA', ERIA Policy Brief, No. 2012-02, ERIA, 2012 at p. 2.

AFAS 5 for all ASEAN countries. Part of the reason for this greater liberalization might have been the fact that by the time of the negotiation of the AANZFTA, ASEAN was already moving towards a higher internal level of liberalization under the sixth and seventh packages of AFAS commitments, which would have gone beyond commitment levels of AFAS 5 and the ASEAN FTAs. Nevertheless, Ishido and Fukunaga observed that based on their calculations, in three cases – Vietnam, Cambodia and Singapore – the overall level of liberalization agreed under the AAZNFTA went even beyond AFAS 7.

The above shows that ASEAN+ PTAs have in some instances moved ahead and produced higher average levels of liberalization than that obtaining between ASEAN Member States within AFAS at a similar point in time. The absolute level of commitments under AFAs has been subject to iterative change since this study was done as later packages of commitments have been offered under AFAS involving progressively greater commitments than before.

The WTO Secretariat has analysed the services PTAs entered into by a select list of countries, including seven of the ASEAN Member States (See Table 4.9).[160] Cambodia, Lao PDR and Myanmar were not included in the study owing to data limitations. The results show that the overall average level of liberalization achieved under the ASEAN–China FTA (first package) and the ASEAN–Korea FTA hardly improved on what the protagonists put on the table in their

---

[160] The data is available at: www.wto.org/english/tratop_e/serv_e/dataset_e/dataset_e.htm

Table 4.9 *Level of liberalization in ASEAN services agreements compared with the GATS*[161]

	Br. D	IND	MSA	PHP	SNG	TH	VN	China	RoK	Aust.	NZ
GATS	7.99	17.26	27.47	16.41	37.59	19.39	34.18	39.29	48.81	57.06	54.42
AFAS 7	30.78	41.58	43.39	34.95	42.03	37.86	38.27	-	-	-	-
ASEAN–CHINA (first package)	9.18	17.52	28.66	18.75	42.37	20.32	34.18	39.97	-	-	-
ASEAN–KOREA	9.52	23.43	33.89	21.47	40.31	19.69	34.18	-	49.70	-	-
ASEAN–AU/NZ	10.2	22.3	32.36	21.47	40.31	19.69	34.35	-	-	57.06	55.44

Source: Author's compilation based on WTO Secretariat 2011

[161] The WTO Index includes GATS services offers made in the Doha Round until 1 March 2010.

Doha Round offers and revised offers under the GATS, which were taken into account in constructing the table. The comparison with the original GATS commitments is not shown in the WTO dataset. It confirms the results of the Ishido and Fukunaga study that, in overall terms, the average level of intra-ASEAN commitments in AFAS 7 is much higher than under any of the ASEAN+ services agreements.

As an indication of the non-exact nature of quantitative studies in this area, the WTO Secretariat's analysis reached a stronger conclusion on the above point than the Ishido and Fukunaga study did. The latter had found that Singapore and Vietnam showed overall levels of liberalization in AANZFA that went beyond AFAS 7, while the former suggested that AFAS 7 commitments were higher than AANZFTA commitments for all seven ASEAN Members analysed, including Singapore and Vietnam.[162]

Although the eighth and ninth packages of AFAS commitments have not been publicly analysed in quantitative terms by ERIA or the WTO Secretariat, the analysis earlier in the chapter has shown that these packages achieved substantial progressive liberalization compared with AFAS 7. One can therefore extrapolate that the level of services openness committed by ASEAN Members in these packages has far surpassed that found in any ASEAN+ services agreements.

---

[162] One of the reasons for the disparity between the WTO position and the analysis of Ishido-Fukunaga might be that the WTO methodology distinguishes between different levels of restrictiveness, with an intermediate score of 0.75 for better partial commitments than under the GATS, whereas partial commitments are awarded standard score of 0.5 under the Hoekman Index.

It is possible to look behind the general levels of commitments in AFAS and ASEAN+ agreements in order to analyse the sectoral patterns of liberalization by using the helpful quantitative work based on the Hoekman Index produced by ERIA. A study by Ishido and Fukunaga (2012) groups commitments at the level of eleven sectors based on W/120.[163] Another study by Ishido (2011) provides more detail by providing data at the level of fifty-five sub-sectors.[164] The data produced in these studies facilitate a comparison of AFAS commitments with those in the ASEAN+ PTAs with China, Korea and Australia–New Zealand across different sectors, and also identification of the sectors and sub-sectors with the greatest levels of liberalization under AFAS and each of these ASEAN+ agreements.

The picture regarding overall levels of commitment in AFAS 7 and the ASEAN+ FTAs is supplemented by sectoral data in the Ishido and Fukunaga (2012) study. Annex 4.1 contains three tables created by the present authors using data from this study. The information shows that there were a number of specific sectors in which ASEAN Member States made better commitments under the ASEAN+ Agreements than under AFAS 7. These improvements were in disparate sectors and vary across the various ASEAN Member States so it is difficult to discern any overall pattern.

---

[163] Hikari Ishido and Yoshifumi Fukunaga, 'Liberalization of Trade in Services: Toward a Harmonized ASEAN++ FTA', ERIA Policy Brief, No. 2012-02, ERIA, 2012.

[164] Hikari Ishido, 'Liberalization of Trade in Services under ASEAN+n: A Mapping Exercise', ERIA Discussion Paper 2011-02, ERIA, 2011.

In the ASEAN–China FTA (first package), Singapore's commitments in the education, finance, recreation and transport sectors and Thailand's commitments in the finance and health sectors were slightly better than their AFAS commitments. In the ASEAN–Korea FTA, Singapore's commitments were marginally better in the financial sector and Vietnam's commitments were better in the construction, distribution and recreation sectors. In the ASEAN–Australia–New Zealand FTA, the improvements in sectoral commitments over AFAS 7 were even greater, with each ASEAN Member State making better commitments in various sectors, ranging from a minimum of two sectors in the case of Myanmar, Lao PDR and Thailand, to nine sectors in the case of Vietnam and Cambodia. Looking at the data from a sectoral point of view, there were improved commitments in all eleven sectors from various ASEAN Member States. This is a significant contrast to the picture when looking at the relative overall commitments in AFAS 7 and the AANZFTA, where AFAS 7 generally saw higher overall levels of commitments.

Ishido's work (2011) shows the sub-sectors (at the fifty-five sub-sector level) with the greatest levels of commitment under AFAS 7 and each of the ASEAN+ agreements under discussion in this section. His findings regarding the most liberalized sub-sectors in each agreement is reproduced below for comparison purposes.[165] The most liberalized sectors (based on the Hoekman Index) for each country are listed. Where more than one sector has the same index number, all of these sectors are listed as being the most liberalized.

[165] Ibid.

AFAS 7

The sub-sectors with the greatest level of liberalization under AFAS 7 were discussed in the preceding section. The list is reproduced here for ease of comparison:

Brunei Darussalam: Computer and Related Services (Hoekman Index 0.69, average level of commitment 0.18).

Cambodia: Computer and Related Services, Courier Services, Telecommunication Services, Commission Agents' Services, Wholesale Trade Services, Retailing Services, Franchising, Higher Education Services, Adult Education, Other Education Services, Sewage Services, Refuse Disposal Services, Sanitation and Similar Services, Other Environmental Services, Travel Agencies and Tour Operators Services, Tourist Guides Services, and Road Transport Services (Hoekman Index 0.75, average level of commitment 0.36).

Indonesia: Telecommunication Services (Hoekman Index 0.79, average level of commitment 0.36).

Lao PDR: Courier Services (Hoekman Index 0.88, average level of commitment 0.33).

Malaysia: Computer and Related Services, and Travel Agencies and Tour Operators Services (Hoekman Index 0.75, average level of commitment 0.31).

Myanmar: Computer and Related Services, Courier Services, Social Services and Hotels and Restaurants (Hoekman Index 0.75, average level of commitment 0.33).

Philippines: Courier Services (Hoekman Index 0.94, average level of commitment 0.29).

Singapore: Research and Development Services, Audio-visual Services, General Construction Work for Building, General Construction work for Civil Engineering, Installation and Assembly Work, Building Completion and Finishing Work, Commission Agents' Services, Wholesale Trade Services, Retailing Services, Franchising, Adult Education, Tourist Guides Services, Entertainment Services, Libraries, archives, museums and other cultural services.

Thailand: Computer and Related Services, Sewage Services, Hotels and Restaurants, Other Health Related and Social Services (Hoekman Index 0.75, average level of commitment 0.36).

Vietnam: Courier Services, Telecommunication Services, Franchising, Hotels and Restaurants, Travel Agencies and Tour Operators Services (Hoekman Index 0.75, average level of commitment 0.33).

ASEAN–China Free Trade Agreement (First Package)

The most liberalized sectors per ASEAN Member in the ACFTA are as follows:

Brunei Darussalam: Road Transport Services (Hoekman Index 0.75, average level of commitment 0.2)

Cambodia: Computer and Related Services, Courier Services, Commission Agents' Services, Wholesale Trade

Services, Retailing Services, Franchising, Other Distribution Services, Higher Education Services, Adult Education, Other Education Services, Sewage Services, Refuse Disposal Services, Sanitation and Similar Services, Other Environmental Services, Hospital Services, Travel Agencies and Tour Operators Services, Tourist Guides Services, Entertainment (Hoekman Index 0.75, average level of commitment 0.36).

Indonesia: Hotels and Restaurants (Hoekman Index 0.63, average level of commitment 0.4).

Lao PDR: All Insurance and Insurance-related Services (Hoekman Index 0.50, average level of commitment 0.02).

Malaysia: Telecommunication Services, Banking and Other Financial Services (Hoekman Index 0.69, average level of commitment 0.06).

Myanmar: Audio-visual Services (Hoekman Index 0.44, average level of commitment 0.02).

Philippines: Travel Agencies and Tour Operators Service (Hoekman Index 1.0, average level of commitment 0.04).

Singapore: Franchising, Adult Education, Other Education Services, Travel Agencies and Tour Operators Services, Tourist Guides Services, Entertainment Services, Libraries, archives, museums and other cultural services (Hoekman Index 0.75, average level of commitment 0.23).

Thailand: Tourist Guides Services (Hoekman Index 0.81, average level of commitment 0.06).

Vietnam: Computer and Related Services, Courier Services, Franchising, All Insurance and Insurance-related Services, Hotels and Restaurants, Travel Agencies and Tour Operators Services (Hoekman Index 0.75, average level of commitment 0.33).[166]

In November 2011, the second package of Specific Commitments under the ACFTA was signed, and this entered into force on 1 January 2012. ASEAN members agreed to commitments in tourism, air and maritime transportation, as well as business and construction services which went beyond their GATS commitments and those made under the first ACFTA package.[167]

ASEAN-Korea Free Trade Agreement
The following is a summary of the most liberalized sectors by individual ASEAN Members under the AKFTA:

Brunei Darussalam: Hospital Services (Hoekman Index 0.75, average level of commitment 0.08).

Cambodia: Computer and Related Services, Courier Services, Commission Agents' Services, Wholesale Trade Services, Retailing Services, Franchising, Other Distribution Services, Higher Education Services, Adult Education, Other

---

[166] Based on Hikari Ishido, 'Liberalization of Trade in Services under ASEAN+n: A Mapping Exercise', ERIA Discussion Paper 2011-02, ERIA, 2011.

[167] Jeffrey J. Schott, Minsoo Lee, and Julia Muir, 'Prospects for Services Trade Negotiations', PIIE Working Paper 12-17, Peterson Institute for International Economics, 2012.

Education Services, Sewage Services, Refuse Disposal Services, Sanitation and Similar Services, Other Environmental Services, Travel Agencies and Tour Operators Services, Tourist Guides Services, Entertainment Services, Road Transport Services (Hoekman Index 0.75, average level of commitment 0.36).

Indonesia: Hotels and Restaurants (Hoekman Index 0.69, average level of commitment 0.18).

Lao PDR: General Construction work for Civil Engineering, Installation and Assembly Work, Secondary Education Services (Hoekman Index 0.56, average level of commitment 0.07).

Malaysia: Hotels and Restaurants, Other Tourism and Travel Related Services (Hoekman Index 0.69, average level of commitment 0.19).

Myanmar: General Construction work for Civil Engineering (Hoekman Index 0.63, average level of commitment 0.03).

Philippines: Travel Agencies and Tour Operators Services (Hoekman Index 1.0, average level of commitment 0.16).

Singapore: General Construction Work for Building, General Construction work for Civil Engineering, Installation and Assembly Work, Building Completion and Finishing Work, Other Construction and Related Engineering Services, Commission Agents' Services, Wholesale Trade Services, Franchising, Adult Education, Tourist Guides Services, Entertainment Services (Hoekman Index 0.75, average level of commitment 0.31).

Vietnam: Computer and Related Services, Courier Services, Telecommunication Services, Franchising, All Insurance and Insurance-related Services, Hotels and Restaurants, Travel Agencies and Tour Operators Services (Hoekman Index 0.75, average level of commitment 0.31).[168]

ASEAN–Australia–New Zealand Free Trade Agreement

The following is a summary of the most liberalized sectors per ASEAN Member in the AANZFTA:

Brunei Darussalam: Computer and Related Services (Hoekman Index 0.75, average level of commitment 0.07).

Cambodia: Computer and Related Services (Hoekman Index 1.0, average level of commitment 0.38).

Indonesia: Hospital Services, Hotels and Restaurants (Hoekman Index 0.63, average level of commitment 0.16).

Lao PDR: Computer and Related Services (Hoekman Index 0.80, average level of commitment 0.12).

Malaysia: Computer and Related Services (Hoekman Index 0.80, average level of commitment 0.16).

Myanmar: Computer and Related Services (Hoekman Index 0.88, average level of commitment 0.11).

Philippines: Travel Agencies and Tour Operators Services (Hoekman Index 0.75, average level of commitment 0.11).

---

[168] Hikari Ishido, 'Liberalization of Trade in Services under ASEAN+n: A Mapping Exercise', ERIA Discussion Paper 2011-02, ERIA, 2011.

Singapore: Computer and Related Services (Hoekman Index 1.0, average level of commitment 0.32).

Thailand: Computer and Related Services (Hoekman Index 1.0, average level of commitment 0.22).

Vietnam: Courier Services, Telecommunication Services. Franchising, All Insurance and Insurance-related Services, Hotels and Restaurants, Travel Agencies and Tour Operators Services (Hoekman Index 0.75, average level of commitment 0.32).[169]

4.11.2 Comparing Commitments in AFAS 7 and ASEAN+ Services Agreements

AFAS as the Main Driver of Services Liberalization
The analysis put forward earlier in this chapter showed that the overall level of services liberalization was on average higher in AFAS 7 than in the three ASEAN+ FTAs (see Table 4.6). A sectoral analysis of the commitments of each ASEAN Member State using data produced by Ishido and Fukunaga (2012) shows that this is also generally true of individual sectors at the eleven-sector level. In other words, the average ASEAN level of commitment in each of the individual eleven sectors was generally higher in AFAS than in the ASEAN+ FTAs.

Looking at commitments from the point of view of each ASEAN Member State across services sectors at the eleven-sector level, the commitments under AFAS 7 were greater than under individual FTAs in the majority of sectors.

[169] Ibid.

This would appear to suggest quite unambiguously that AFAS is clearly the main driver of services liberalization for ASEAN Member States taken as a group. Taken overall, the internal (intra-ASEAN) preferences offered by ASEAN Member States to each other surpass those they have been willing to offer to non-ASEAN partners.

Comparing Overall and Sectoral Liberalization

The above observation that commitments undertaken by ASEAN Member States in AFAS 7 are more liberal than in the three ASEAN+ FTAs holds almost completely for commitments in individual service sectors under the ACFTA and the AKFTA at the eleven-sector level as surveyed by Ishido and Fukunaga (see Annex 4.1). The few instances in which AFAS+ commitments were scheduled by Singapore, Thailand and Vietnam were mentioned earlier. In contrast, and as discussed earlier, under the AANZFTA, every ASEAN Member State was willing to commit to a higher level of liberalization in selected individual sectors as compared with their commitments in corresponding sectors under AFAS 7. The example of AANZFTA shows that the relative level of commitments in AFAS as compared with ASEAN+ FTAs can be markedly different at the sectoral level compared with the level of the particular services agreement as a whole. In specific sectors, ASEAN Member States have been willing to commit to higher levels of liberalization in ASEAN+ FTAS than under AFAS.

Differing Commitments across Different Agreements

An analysis of the earlier summary identifying the sub-sectors (at the fifty-five sub-sector level) that were most liberalized for each ASEAN Member State under AFAS and ASEAN+ PTAs shows that there are certain sub-sectors that each Member State may be more willing to commit than others – for instance, travel agencies and tour operators in the case of the Philippines; computer services in the case of Brunei Darussalam; and hotels and restaurants in the case of Indonesia. However, it also shows that the total number of sub-sectors that each member is willing to commit, the level of its commitments, as well as the specific sub-sectors in which it decides to offer its best commitments vary across agreements.

The commitments found in any one agreement, and their breadth and depth relative to the commitments in other agreements will depend on many complex factors. These include the relationship between the partners, the pattern of trade between them, the market opening requests made and the concessions granted. It is likely that there are few hard and fast rules, suggesting that most commitments are ultimately subject to negotiation. There will be potential for greater liberalization in new and existing services agreements, where each Party may aim to obtain commitments in particular sectors which are at least as favourable as those made by its partner in the same sectors across the latter's various agreements.

4.11.3 *Rule-Making*

Although the ASEAN+ services agreements aim to reduce discrimination in trade in services and increase market access beyond the GATS level, the same criticism can be made of these agreements as of AFAS generally: that they have tended to follow the traditional GATS disciplines and have not tackled important disciplines targeted at services trade, such as government procurement, domestic regulation or subsidies.[170] One feature present in the AKFTA that was absent in AFAS until recently is an additional chapter on the movement of natural persons (MNP) which facilitates the movement of business people engaged in trade and investment in the ASEAN region by requiring streamlined and transparent procedures for immigration applications and processes for the temporary entry and stay of specific categories of business people. As discussed earlier in this chapter, an Agreement on the Movement of Natural Persons was signed by ASEAN Member States in November 2012 and came into force in June 2016.

4.12 Services Agreements of Individual ASEAN Member States

In addition to AFAS and ASEAN+ services agreements, individual ASEAN Member States have entered into many agreements governing the liberalization of trade in services with non-ASEAN countries, as identified earlier in this chapter and summarized in Table 4.7. It is beyond the aim of this

---

[170] In the context of the ACFTA, see Jeffrey J. Schott, Minsoo Lee and Julia Muir, 'Prospects for Services Trade Negotiations', PIIE Working Paper 12–17, Peterson Institute for International Economics, 2012. See also Aaditya Mattoo and Pierre Sauvé, 'The Preferential Liberalization of Services Trade', NCCR Trade Regulation Working Paper No. 2010/13, May 2010.

study to examine the myriad of services agreements entered into by individual ASEAN Members States in order to draw commonalities or conclusions from them. The following discussion highlights a number of features of selected services agreements that may have wider implications for the overall process of services liberalization of ASEAN countries and in the ASEAN region more broadly.

4.12.1 Liberalization under AFAS versus Bilateral Agreements

The WTO Secretariat's dataset of market access commitments in various PTAs discussed above includes data on AFAS 7, the three ASEAN+ FTAs covering services and nineteen PTAs entered into by individual ASEAN countries excluding Myanmar, Lao PDR and Cambodia, showing the improvements of each agreement over prevailing GATS commitments. It was pointed out earlier in this section that AFAS 7 was generally more liberal than practically all the ASEAN+ PTAs. The leading position of AFAS 7 is reinforced when the commitments of individual Member States in AFAS 7 are compared with their relevant commitments under individual PTAs included in the WTO Secretariat's study. As Table 4.10 shows, all Member States but one committed to higher levels of liberalization under AFAS 7 than they did in their individual PTAs with third countries. The only exception was Singapore, which scheduled higher market access commitments in its individual PTAs than it did in AFAS 7. Singapore's market access commitments under the US–Singapore FTA were the deepest among its various PTAs

Table 4.10 *Level of services liberalization of ASEAN Members in selected trade agreements*

LEVEL OF SERVICES LIBERALIZATION OF ASEAN MEMBERS

	Brunei Daruss.	Indonesia	Malaysia	Philippines	Singapore	Thailand	Vietnam
AFAS 7	30.78	41.58	43.39	34.95	42.03	37.86	38.27
GATS	7.99	17.26	27.47	16.41	37.59	19.39	34.18
ASEAN–Korea	9.52	23.43	33.89	21.47	40.31	19.69	34.18
ASEAN–China	9.18	17.52	28.66	18.75	42.37	20.32	34.18
ASEAN–AU/NZ	10.2	22.3	32.36	21.47	40.31	19.69	34.35
NZ	-	-	unavailable	-	55.55	-	-
Japan	11.73	unavailable	29.08	27.68	59.62	20.37	34.18
Aus	-	-	unavailable	-	68.32	23.26	-
Korea	-	-	-	-	70.98	-	-
India	-	-	unavailable	-	56.04	-	-
Pakistan	-	-	31.57	-	44.07	-	-
Peru	-	-	-	-	55.36	-	-
Panama	-	-	-	-	62.94	-	-
USA	-	-	-	-	75.72	-	-
China	-	-	-	-	44.07	-	-
EFTA	-	-	-	-	61.19	-	-

Source: Author's compilation based on WTO Secretariat Index of Services PTAs

and significantly above its commitments in AFAS 7. The position of Singapore will be further explored below, but this is not an aberration that otherwise displaces ASEAN's dominance as the leading forum for services liberalization among its Member States, especially when we consider that the analysis made in the WTO Secretariat's study used AFAS 7 outcomes that were still three packages short of the ultimate aim agreed under the AEC Blueprint 2015.

4.12.2 Services Agreements of Individual ASEAN Member States with the Same Third-Country Partner

Japan has individual services agreements with seven of the ten ASEAN countries and offers a useful case study in comparative regional dynamics. Table 4.11, showing data as analysed by the WTO Secretariat, indicates that Japan has similar levels of liberalization in its bilateral agreements with Brunei Darussalam, Malaysia, Philippines and Thailand, representing a noticeable improvement over its GATS commitments. Japan's commitments in its bilateral agreements with Singapore and Vietnam are at an intermediate level between its commitments towards other ASEAN Member States and its GATS commitments, representing a small improvement over its GATS commitments. Taken as a whole, Japan's market access commitments in bilateral agreements with individual ASEAN Member States are moderately liberal, ranging from 55 to 63 percent openness. While this narrow band of variation across Japan's agreements with seven countries might suggest that harmonization of services commitments

Table 4.11 *Level of services liberalization of selected non-ASEAN partners*

		LEVEL OF SERVICES LIBERALIZATION OF SELECTED NON-ASEAN PARTNERS						
	GATS	ASEAN–AU/NZ	Brunei Daruss.	Indonesia	Malaysia	Philippines	Singapore	Thailand	Vietnam
Japan	52.89	-	62.84	unavailable	62.84	62.59	58.50	62.33	54.51
Aus	57.06	57.06	-	-	unavailable	-	79.51	58.16	-
USA	55.44	-	-	-	-	-	66.58	-	-

Source: Author's compilation based on WTO Secretariat Index of Services PTAs

at an ASEAN-wide level would be relatively easy, this has not been the case, as the services chapter of the ASEAN-Japan FTA still under negotiation has lagged behind the goods chapter, which has been in force since 2008.

It is interesting to note that reciprocity may not be reflected at the general level of market access commitments. For instance, of all the ASEAN countries, Singapore has shown by far the highest level of commitments in its bilateral agreement with Japan compared with the commitments of other ASEAN Member States (see Table 4.10). At the same time, Japan's own commitments to Singapore fall a little below their general level towards other ASEAN Member States (see Table 4.11). The general picture depicted above is likely to make more sense when supplemented with a more detailed study of Japan's sectoral commitments across its bilateral agreements.

Australia, which has bilateral services agreements with three ASEAN Member States, is the next most frequent third-country bilateral agreement partner of ASEAN Member States after Japan. While a WTO Secretariat computation for the level of liberalization in Australia's agreement with Malaysia does not seem to be available, the existing analysis for Singapore and Thailand show that Australia has a significantly higher level of commitments in relation to Singapore compared with Thailand (see Table 4.11). This is unlike the relatively uniform levels of commitments made by Japan across its various bilateral agreements. Nevertheless, there is some measure of consistency in Australia's position: the commitments in its PTA with Thailand are roughly equivalent to those scheduled under both the GATS and the

ASEAN–Australia–New Zealand FTA. Australia's relatively favourable market access commitments to Singapore compared with Thailand is more than matched by Singapore's commitments in the Singapore–Australia FTA, which far surpass those made by Thailand in the Thailand–Australia FTA.

Singapore's commitments in the Singapore–Australia FTA are also significantly more liberal than its commitments in AFAS 7 or in the ASEAN–Australia–New Zealand FTA. Thailand, too, has made more liberal commitments in its bilateral FTA with Australia than in the ASEAN–Australia–New Zealand FTA, though not by a significant margin, but its commitments in AFAS 7 are still higher than in the bilateral agreement.

4.12.3 AFAS+ Features of Bilateral PTAs of ASEAN Member States with Third Countries

It is apparent from the foregoing discussion that ASEAN Member States have sometimes been prepared, in their bilateral agreements with third countries, to make improvements over their position in AFAS and ASEAN+ PTAs. At one extreme is Singapore, which, judged on the WTO Secretariat's measure of general levels of market access alone, appears to have consistently given its bilateral PTA partners higher levels of access than under AFAS 7 or ASEAN+ PTAs. This is likely to have changed as successive packages of additional and improved commitments have been implemented under AFAS. Detailed studies have not been done of AFAS 8 and AFAS 9, but there might conceivably be at least one agreement under which Singapore's commitments could be more liberal than its commitments under even the AEC. This is the US-Singapore FTA, in which the preferences granted by Singapore are extremely generous. More modestly, a bilateral agreement that reveals interesting AFAs+ features without being overwhelmingly more liberal than AFAS 7 package is the New Zealand-Malaysia FTA.

Singapore-United States Free Trade Agreement
When the US-Singapore FTA (USSFTA) came into effect relatively early in January 2004, it was by far the most advanced Singaporean trade agreement, and also one of the most forward-looking bilateral free trade agreements ever negotiated. The USSFTA covers trade in goods, rules of origin, customs administration, technical barriers to trade, trade remedies, cross border trade in services, financial services, temporary entry, telecommunications, e-commerce, investment, competition, government procurement, intellectual property protection, transparency, general provisions, labour, environment, and dispute settlement. It encompasses provisions that are often not part of conventional bilateral trade agreements, such as intellectual property rights, investment, government procurement, labour and environment. Its scope of protection and its market access coverage go well beyond what Singapore has committed to under the GATS and in all other bilateral PTAS and also in its AFAS 7 and 8 commitments.

Service suppliers from both sides are assured of fair and non-discriminatory treatment and market access unless specifically exempted in writing – the so-called 'negative list' approach. Regulatory authorities are bound to high standards of openness and transparency, including consultations with interested parties, advance notice, reasonable comment period, and publication of regulations.

For professional services, Singapore reduced board of director requirements for architectural and engineering firms and phased out capital ownership requirements for land surveying services. Both sides engaged in consultations to develop mutually acceptable standards and criteria for licensing and certification of professional service providers, especially with regard to architects and engineers. In legal services, typically one of the most protected sectors in any country, and definitely a hitherto closely guarded one in Singapore, Singapore has opened its market significantly, although restrictions remain with regard to criminal law, family law, and domestic matters. US law firms can provide legal services in these restricted areas only through a joint venture with a Singapore law firm. However, US and other foreign lawyers can act as legal counsel in arbitration proceedings set in Singapore without being linked to a Singapore attorney. Finally, the Singapore Bar recognizes law degrees from Harvard, Columbia, the University of Michigan and New York University.[171]

Singapore also gave US banks better access to Singapore's retail banking sector, and it increased US participation in the securities, investment management, and insurance industries. It committed to removing existing quotas on

---

[171] See, e.g., Chee Yoke Heong, 'A Review of The US–Singapore Free Trade Agreement', mimeo, 2010.

Qualifying Full Bank (QFB) and Wholesale Bank licences for US banks within one and a half and three years respectively of the FTA's entry into force; to removing restrictions on customer service locations for QFBs two years after the entry into force of the USSFTA; and allowing Singapore-incorporated US QFBs to negotiate with local banks for access into their ATM networks on commercial terms two and a half years after the agreement's entry into force.

Under the USSFTA, telecommunications service suppliers from both sides have access to their respective public telecommunications networks, including submarine cable landing stations, with transparent and effective enforcement by the telecommunications regulators. Robust competition safeguards exist to protect against discriminatory and anti-competitive behaviour by incumbent suppliers in areas such as interconnection, co-location, access to rights of way and resale. Both sides also promised to work towards the implementation of a comprehensive arrangement for the mutual recognition of conformity assessment for telecommunications equipment. Both sides also committed to the non-discriminatory treatment of digital products and the permanent duty-free status of products delivered electronically. This marked the first time that such commitments were enshrined in an international trade agreement.

In the area of government procurement, both Singapore and the United States committed to allowing market access by service suppliers of the other Party unless specifically reserved, i.e., using the so-called 'negative list' approach. Commitments apply to all procurement contracts for goods and services worth more than US$56,190 and for

AGREEMENTS OF INDIVIDUAL ASEAN MEMBER STATES

construction procurement contracts worth more than US $6,481,000.[172]

New Zealand–Malaysia Free Trade Agreement
The New Zealand–Malaysia FTA improves on AFAS in various ways. For example, it is a positive list agreement but contains a novel provision whereby Malaysia agreed to renegotiate its services commitments with New Zealand if it concludes a negative list agreement with another country in the future. In terms of market access, compared with AFAS 7 and AFAS 8, Malaysia opened to New Zealand the following sectors, which had not been committed yet in the context of AFAS: human resource management (Modes 1–2–3); public relations services (Modes 1–2–3); consulting services related to agriculture (Modes 1–2–3); technical testing and analysis services (Modes 1–2–3); services incidental to manufacturing (Modes 1–2–3); data and message transmission services (Modes 1–2–3); voice telephone services (Modes 1–2–3); telex and telegraph services (Modes 1–2–3); and cleaning services of exhaust gases (Modes 1–2–3).

The willingness shown by Singapore and Malaysia to grant AFAS+ features to third-party partners in bilateral agreements is a factor that must be considered as a side bar to the observation made earlier that AFAS is the most important vehicle of services liberalization in the ASEAN region. A country like Singapore has long been a proponent of free

[172] Government of Singapore, 'Info-kit on United States-Singapore Free Trade Agreement', available at: www.fta.gov.sg/fta_ussfta.asp?hl=13

trade, an attitude seen most clearly in regard to goods trade. Trade in services, on both the import and export sides, is very important to Singapore, despite the fact that Singapore's GATS commitments, like those of many WTO Members, were relatively conservative and laden with regulatory precaution. Singapore obviously has much greater capacity for services liberalization than it has shown in the GATS or the earlier AFAS packages, and a willingness to make correspondingly liberal commitments, but only for the right partners with a view to reaping economic and strategic gains. A country like Malaysia may not be as active as Singapore in its bilateral PTA relationships, but it has special partners, such as New Zealand, with whom it has historically shared strong official business and personal ties, and with whom it is willing to share certain special benefits.

When other ASEAN Member States as a whole are ready to make deeper and broader commitments in services, the pockets of potential special preferences, now reserved by ASEAN Member States for a limited number of bilateral partners, could prove important anchors around which higher levels of ASEAN-wide liberalization could be built.

4.13 Comprehensive and Progressive Agreement for Trans-Pacific Partnership

By far the most ambitious third-party negotiations involving individual ASEAN Members have been those on a proposed Trans-Pacific Partnership (TPP), linking twelve major trading nations: Australia, Brunei Darussalam, Canada, Chile, Japan, Malaysia, Mexico, New Zealand, Peru, Singapore, the USA and Vietnam. The TPP initially grew out of the Trans-Pacific Strategic Economic Partnership (TPSEP or Pacific-4 (P4)) that had linked Singapore, Brunei Darussalam, Chile and New Zealand. The expansion gained momentum after the United States indicated its interest in joining the P4 in September 2008, and the TPP process subsequently saw several important trading powers join the talks – notably Australia, Canada, Japan and Mexico. The agreement was negotiated as a single undertaking covering all key trade and investment-related areas. The TPP was signed by the twelve member countries in 2016. However, the incoming US administration of President Donald J. Trump signalled the decision of the United States Government to withdraw from the agreement upon taking office in January 2017.[173] Following the US withdrawal, negotiations resumed among the remaining eleven participating countries, leading to the January 2018 conclusion and March 2018 signing of the CPTPP, which currently awaits ratification among signatory governments.

The CPTPP is widely considered to represent a 'frontier' PTA, featuring a number of novel provisions in areas of trade governance not addressed (or not addressed in similar depth) in earlier agreements in areas such as labour standards, digital governance, the promotion of small and medium-sized enterprises, gender-related considerations, regulatory coherence, as well as enforceable disciplines on the potentially anti-competitive conduct of state-owned enterprises.

[173] https://ustr.gov/sites/default/files/files/Press/Releases/1-30-17%20USTR%20Letter%20to%20TPP%20Depositary.pdf

The transition from the TPP to the CPTPP saw the suspension of a number of sensitive provisions – twenty-three in all, mostly in the areas of investment rule-making and trade-related intellectual property protection. The CPTPP's far-reaching provisions and commitments on services trade and investment mirrored those agreed earlier in the TPP chapters on cross-border supply of services, investment, digital trade, government procurement, the mobility of service providers and state-owned enterprises, all of which will shape the future contours of services markets and the nature and extent of market contestability in signatories' economies.[174]

Not surprisingly, the TPP/CPTPP negotiations have elicited considerable interest among ASEAN Member States, not least because of the fact that four AMS – Brunei Darussalam, Malaysia, Singapore and Vietnam – embraced the ambitious talks, stoking concerns about the reality of individual ASEAN Member States agreeing to AFAS+ commitments, as well as in regard to the possible agreement's articulation with both AFAS and RCEP.

4.14 Most Favoured Nation Clauses

With such a range of intersecting agreements with different provisions and commitments, MFN clauses have a potentially

---

[174] For a comprehensive survey of the treatment of services in the TPP/CPTPP, see Batshur Gootiz and Aaditya Mattoo, 'Services in the Trans-Pacific Partnership: What Would Be Lost?', Policy Research Working Paper, No. 7964, Washington, DC: The World Bank (February 2017), available at: http://documents.worldbank.org/curated/en/512711486497950394/pdf/WPS7964.pdf

significant effect on ASEAN services trade. A widely drafted MFN clause in a particular PTA could require a Member State to accord other members of that PTA treatment that is at least as favourable as that provided to its counterparts under any other PTA. For instance, it has been seen that individual ASEAN Member States have been willing to grant better treatment to their counterparts in bilateral FTAs than to other ASEAN Member States under AFAS (at least up to AFAS 8) or ASEAN+ FTAs. The most telling recent example of such conduct arises from AFAS+ rules and commitments agreed by four AMS under the CPTPP. A robust MFN clause that is binding on all ASEAN Member States would improve the position of an ASEAN Member State that wishes to enjoy the treatment that another ASEAN Member State is granting to non-ASEAN partners under bilateral or plurilateral PTAs. In a wider context, it is important to consider whether the MFN provisions in AFAS, ASEAN+ agreements and the bilateral agreements of ASEAN countries might facilitate greater liberalization and uniformity across different agreements to which they are parties.

Article II.1 of the GATS provides that 'With respect to any measure covered by this Agreement, each Member shall accord immediately and unconditionally to services and service suppliers of any other Member treatment no less favourable than that it accords to like services and service suppliers of any other country.' Such a provision is a wide one, and if a WTO Member gives service suppliers of a particular country a benefit in relation to a measure affecting trade in services, it must extend the same benefit to other WTO Members. However, the potential breadth of the GATS MFN clause is seriously whittled down by the exception in Article V, which allows discriminatory treatment to be provided under economic integration agreements that satisfy the criteria set out in that article. As some countries can be legitimately given better treatment than others under the GATS MFN regime coupled with its provisions for economic integration agreements, this may not be the best model to ensure that the benefits found in one PTA are extended to members of other PTAs.

AFAS does not have an MFN clause, but Article IV, which provides for the negotiation of specific commitments, states that ASEAN Member States shall enter into negotiations on measures affecting trade in specific service sectors which shall be directed towards achieving commitments which are beyond those inscribed in each Member State's schedule of specific commitments under the GATS and 'for which Member States shall accord preferential treatment to one another on an MFN basis'. This mention of MFN is the closest that AFAS gets to an MFN clause. It is a very limited provision as it is inward rather than outward looking. AFAS members are only required to accord each other MFN treatment in respect of the commitments achieved under AFAS. This provision says nothing about AFAS Member States giving each other MFN treatment compared with treatment that is given to non-AFAS parties under another PTA. The result is that AFAS Member States cannot complain if better treatment is given to non-Member States outside of AFAS. This is clearly problematic given ASEAN's stated aims of deepening community-wide ties and promote broad economic and regulatory convergence.

With the GATS and AFAS being of limited significance in relation to MFN obligations as far as ASEAN Member States are concerned, the spotlight turns to the ASEAN+ agreements on services. As all ASEAN Member States are parties to the ASEAN+ agreements, a strong MFN clause in an ASEAN+ agreement would have a very similar effect among the ASEAN Member States as if the clause had been found in AFAS itself. The services agreements that ASEAN has with China and with Korea do not have MFN provisions and are thus not helpful in this regard. The situation is a little better in ASEAN's agreement with Australia and New Zealand, which contains a lighter version of MFN treatment which does not require MFN treatment to be extended but merely allows the Parties to request consultations to discuss the possibility of obtaining treatment on an MFN basis in specific circumstances.

Article 7.1 of Chapter 8 of the AANZFTA provides that 'if, after this Agreement enters into force, a Party enters into any agreement on trade in services with a non-Party in which it provides treatment to services or service suppliers of that non-Party more favourable than it accords to like services or service suppliers of other Parties under this Agreement, any other Party may request consultations to discuss the possibility of extending, under this Agreement, treatment no less favourable than that provided under the agreement with the non-Party.' The duties of the requested Party are not onerous. It only has to enter into consultations with the requesting Party, without any specifically mandated outcome, but merely bearing in mind the overall balance of benefits. The ambit of this possibility of consultation is intended to be narrow, as can be seen from this enigmatic provision in Article 7.2, which states that 'No Party shall be obliged to apply Paragraph 1 with respect to treatment provided under any bilateral or plurilateral agreement between an individual ASEAN Member State, or individual ASEAN Member States, and non-Parties or Australia or New Zealand'. This provision would appear to rule out the application of Article 7.1 MFN consultation obligation in many instances, except perhaps in situations involving bilateral or plurilateral agreements between Australia and/ or New Zealand and non-ASEAN parties, and between ASEAN parties *inter se*.

The MFN clauses in the bilateral and plurilateral agreements of individual ASEAN Member States vary widely. At one end of the scale, there are agreements with no MFN clauses at all. Examples are the Singapore–Australia FTA and the Singapore–Japan FTA. The bilateral agreement between Japan and Singapore presents an exceptional situation, as the other six bilateral agreements between Japan and individual ASEAN Member States all contain some form of MFN clause. These clauses vary in content and provide useful illustrations of some of the different types of MFN clauses in use in PTAs. For instance, the Japan–Thailand FTA[175] provides that if a party enters into any agreement on trade in services with a non-party, it shall consider a request by the other party for the incorporation of treatment no less favourable than that provided under the former agreement.

Other agreements, such as the Japan–Philippines[176] and Japan–Indonesia[177] FTAs, provide that, subject to any MFN

---

[175] Art. 79.   [176] Art. 76.   [177] Art. 82.

exceptions allowed in the annexes or schedules, each party should accord to services and service suppliers of the other party treatment no less favourable than that it accords to like services and service suppliers of any non-party. In the respective bilateral agreements with Malaysia, Brunei Darussalam and Vietnam,[178] this provision is supplemented by a provision that a party that enters into an agreement with a third state with respect to sectors or activities that are subject to MFN exemptions shall upon the request of the other party, consider according to services and service suppliers of the other party treatment no less favourable than that it accords to like services and service suppliers of that third state pursuant to such an agreement.

A variant of the provisions discussed above can be found in the FTA between Singapore and the member countries of the European Free Trade Area (EFTA) – (Switzerland, Liechtenstein, Norway and Iceland), which contains an MFN clause but provides that treatment granted under other agreements concluded by one of the parties with a non-Party which have been notified under Article V of the GATS shall not be subject to the MFN requirement.[179] This effectively means that more favourable treatment granted under other qualifying PTAs will not translate into a liberalizing effect on the obligations under the ESFTA.

The most effective MFN clause from the point of view of facilitating greater liberalization and uniformity across different agreements would be one which creates a

---

[178] Japan–Malaysia FTA, Art. 101; Japan–Brunei FTA, Art. 79; Japan–Vietnam FTA, Art. 63.
[179] Art. 23.2.

straightforward requirement for MFN treatment without exceptions. The US–Singapore FTA contains such a clause, providing that 'Each Party shall accord to service suppliers of the other Party treatment no less favourable than that it accords, in like circumstances, to service suppliers of a non-Party',[180] but this is less far reaching than it appears as the obligation is subject to the exceptions listed in the Annexes 8A and 8B. Articles 9.5 (Investment) and 10.4 (Cross-border trade in services) of the CPTPP feature what is perhaps the clearest language directed at ensuring that signatories of the agreement enjoy the benefits of any trade and investment liberalization agreed with non-parties. However, these are subject to the exceptions listed in the Annexes to the CPTPP. The supremacy of ASEAN is ensured, as the four ASEAN Member States that are also members of the CPTPP (Brunei, Malaysia, Singapore and Vietnam) have each reserved the right in their respective Annexes to adopt or maintain any measure that accords differential treatment to ASEAN Member States under any ASEAN agreement open to participation by any ASEAN Member State, in force or signed after the date of entry into force of the CPTPP.[181] As the CPTPP provisions apply solely to the eleven signatories, four of which are ASEAN Member States, they afford no automatic gateway for other AMS to enjoy the AFAS+ levels of access granted under the CPTPP.[182] Looking ahead, it will be

---

[180] Art. 8.4.
[181] CPTPP, Annex II (Brunei, Malaysia, Singapore and Vietnam).
[182] Article 9.5 in the Investment chapter reads as follows: '1. Each Party shall accord to investors of another Party treatment no less favorable than that it accords, in like circumstances, to investors of any other Party or

important for ASEAN Member States to ensure that ATISA features an MFN clause aimed at ensuring that any AFAS+ commitments agreed by individual member states are fully and unconditionally shared with the entire regional grouping.

4.15 Tentative Conclusions

There has been constant and continuing PTA activity on trade in services involving ASEAN and ASEAN Member States, as can be seen from the many agreements concluded in recent years and the still large number of agreements

> of any non-Party with respect to the establishment, acquisition, expansion, management, conduct, operation, and sale or other disposition of investments in its territory. 2. Each Party shall accord to covered investments treatment no less favorable than that it accords, in like circumstances, to investments in its territory of investors of any other Party or of any non-Party with respect to the establishment, acquisition, expansion, management, conduct, operation, and sale or other disposition of investments'. Article 9.5.3 clarifies that the MFN privileges arising from the CPTPP Investment chapter relate solely to the chapter's substantive provisions and not its procedural ones relating to investor-state dispute settlement. It reads as follows: 'For greater certainty, the treatment referred to in this Article does not encompass international dispute resolution procedures or mechanisms, such as those included in Section B (Investor–State Dispute Settlement). The above provisions are germane to understanding the relationship between the CPTPP and the ASEAN Comprehensive Investment Agreement (ACIA).' Meanwhile, Art. 10.4 (Most-Favoured Nation Treatment) of the CPTPP chapter on Cross-Border Trade in Services reads as follows: 'Each Party shall accord to services and service suppliers of another Party treatment no less favorable than that it accords, in like circumstances, to services and service suppliers of any other Party or a non-Party.'

currently being negotiated and considered. The RCEP, currently with sixteen members, would add significantly to the existing stock of ASEAN+ PTAs, just as the CPTPP added significant substantive and commercial value to the plurilateral agreements of individual ASEAN Member States. Add to this the bilateral PTAs currently being negotiated or considered by ASEAN and individual ASEAN Member States, and the complex web of PTAs will become even more intricate and harder to navigate in the future. The best-case scenario for achieving the greatest liberalization of trade in services in favour of ASEAN Members collectively would be for the various services agreements involving one or more ASEAN partners to serve as building blocks leading to a unified agreement for all ASEAN Member States featuring the best commitments and most developed provisions. The RCEP is a step towards this end, but parallel (and differing) developments under the CPTPP and in ongoing negotiations with the EU suggest that ASEAN Member States have separate and co-existing collective and individual aspirations. Judging from the reservations made by the four ASEAN Member States in their CPTPP MFN reservations, the best preferences are intended to be reserved for ASEAN as a group. Little is yet known about the RCEP commitments to be made by the sixteen members (all ten ASEAN Member States and all their six ASEAN+ FTA partners), and it remains to be seen whether ASEAN Member States would be willing to give to their ASEAN+ FTA partners the same level of commitments that they give each other, but this seems unlikely, at least at the outset.

Annex 4.1 Hoekman Index of Services Liberalization in AFAS and ASEAN FTAs per Sector/Member

The table shows the level of liberalization committed by each Member in AFAS and in each ASEAN+ FTA across eleven services sectors. The final results are based on the Hoekman Index methodology. (The higher the figure, the more liberal the country's service trade commitments are.) The shaded parts highlight a sector that has been liberalized beyond AFAS 7. The table uses data from Ishido and Fukinaga (2012)

1. *ASEAN–China Free Trade Agreement*

ASEAN–China FTA			Commu.	Constr.	Distrib.	Education	Environ.	Finance	Health	Tourism	Recreation	Transport
Brunei Daruss	AFAS 7	0.38	0.10	0.33	0.00	0.45	0.00	0.33	0.21	0.28	0.11	0.21
	ACFTA	012	0.05	0.00	0.00	0.00	0.00	0.13	0.00	0.02	0.00	0.14
Cambodia	AFAS 7	0.30	0.30	0.51	0.75	0.45	0.75	0.44	0.19	0.53	0.30	0.20
	ACFTA	0.29	0.28	0.50	0.75	0.45	0.75	0.43	0.19	0.45	0.15	0.17
Indonesia	AFAS 7	0.27	0.16	0.53	0.21	0.48	0.42	0.25	0.66	0.61	0.24	0.30
	ACFTA	0.05	0.10	0.40	0.00	0.00	0.00	0.21	0.00	0.33	0.00	0.03
Lao PDR	AFAS 7	0.35	0.28	0.75	0.34	0.56	0.56	0.24	0.27	0.42	0.00	0.14
	ACFTA	0.05	0.00	0.00	0.00	0.00	0.00	0.23	0.00	0.00	0.00	0.00
Malaysia	AFAS 7	0.50	0.19	0.50	0.43	0.39	0.34	0.28	0.33	0.56	0.23	0.14
	ACFTA	0.34	0.05	0.09	0.00	0.01	0.00	0.22	0.16	0.27	0.18	0.04
Myanmar	AFAS 7	0.25	0.35	0.63	0.38	0.48	0.47	0.09	0.50	0.52	0.30	0.13
	ACFTA	0.00	0.00	0.00	0.00	0.00	0.00	0.00	0.00	0.34	0.00	0.07
Philippines	AFAS 7	0.42	0.52	0.35	0.28	0.00	0.27	0.45	0.14	0.47	0.30	0.38
	ACFTA	0.06	0.23	0.00	0.00	0.00	0.11	0.34	0.00	0.44	0.00	0.16
Singapore	AFAS 7	0.52	0.38	0.75	0.60	0.15	0.25	0.34	0.38	0.66	0.30	0.14
	ACFTA	0.40	0.14	0.15	0.45	0.30	0.25	0.39	0.25	0.53	0.40	0.15
Thailand	AFAS 7	0.66	0.20	0.64	0.60	0.58	0.75	0.39	0.31	0.64	0.64	0.24
	ACFTA	0.35	0.33	0.50	0.45	0.31	0.44	0.57	0.34	0.38	0.16	0.18
Vietnam	AFAS 7	0.39	0.33	0.56	0.25	0.43	0.50	0.49	0.63	0.52	0.18	0.19
	ACFTA	0.35	0.33	0.21	0.18	0.15	0.22	0.27	0.09	0.33	0.10	0.10

2. *ASEAN–Korea Free Trade Agreement*

ASEAN-Korea FTA		Business	Comm.	Constr.	Distrib.	Education	Environ.	Finance	Health	Tourism	Recreation	Transport
Brunei	AFAS 7	0.38	0.10	0.33	0.00	0.45	0.00	0.33	0.21	0.28	0.11	0.21
Daruss	AKFTA	0.12	0.06	0.31	0.00	0.00	0.00	0.13	0.19	0.11	0.00	0.06
Cambodia	AFAS 7	0.30	0.30	0.51	0.75	0.45	0.75	0.44	0.19	0.53	0.30	0.20
	AKFTA	0.29	0.30	0.50	0.75	0.45	0.75	0.43	0.19	0.45	0.15	0.17
Indonesia	AFAS 7	0.27	0.16	0.53	0.21	0.48	0.42	0.25	0.66	0.61	0.24	0.30
	AKFTA	0.19	0.13	0.50	0.00	0.46	0.00	0.24	0.16	0.34	0.00	0.04
Lao PDR	AFAS 7	0.35	0.28	0.75	0.34	0.56	0.56	0.24	0.27	0.42	0.00	0.14
	AKFTA	0.02	0.00	0.41	0.00	0.20	0.06	0.01	0.13	0.00	0.00	0.00
Malaysia	AFAS 7	0.50	0.19	0.50	0.43	0.39	0.34	0.28	0.33	0.56	0.23	0.14
	AKFTA	0.34	0.15	0.44	0.18	0.04	0.00	0.24	0.16	0.52	0.20	0.09
Myanmar	AFAS 7	0.25	0.35	0.63	0.38	0.48	0.47	0.09	0.50	0.52	0.30	0.13
	AKFTA	0.03	0.04	0.13	0.00	0.00	0.00	0.00	0.00	0.34	0.00	0.09
Philippines	AFAS 7	0.42	0.52	0.35	0.28	0.00	0.27	0.45	0.14	0.47	0.30	0.38
	AKFTA	0.19	0.40	0.11	0.00	0.00	0.11	0.44	0.00	0.42	0.00	0.25
Singapore	AFAS 7	0.52	0.38	0.75	0.60	0.15	0.25	0.34	0.38	0.66	0.30	0.14
	AKFTA	0.44	0.33	0.75	0.45	0.15	0.25	0.38	0.25	0.47	0.30	0.06
Thailand	AFAS 7	0.66	0.20	0.64	0.60	0.58	0.75	0.39	0.31	0.64	0.64	0.24
	AKFTA	NA	NA	NA	NA	NA	NA	NA	NA	NA	NA	NA
Vietnam	AFAS 7	0.39	0.33	0.56	0.25	0.43	0.50	0.49	0.63	0.52	0.18	0.19
	AKFTA	0.34	0.33	0.75	0.45	0.15	0.25	0.38	0.25	0.47	0.30	0.06

3. ASEAN–Australia/New Zealand Free Trade Agreement

ASEAN–Aus/NZ FTA		Business	Comm.	Constr.	Distrib.	Education	Environ.	Finance	Health	Tourism	Recreation	Transport
Brunei Daruss	AFAS 7	0.38	0.10	0.33	0.00	0.45	0.00	0.33	0.21	0.28	0.11	0.21
	FTA	0.27	0.18	0.38	0.13	0.13	0.13	0.26	0.13	0.13	0.13	0.15
Cambodia	AFAS 7	0.30	0.30	0.51	0.75	0.45	0.75	0.44	0.19	0.53	0.30	0.20
	FTA	0.42	0.43	0.63	0.88	0.58	0.88	0.56	0.31	0.58	0.28	0.29
Indonesia	AFAS 7	0.27	0.16	0.53	0.21	0.48	0.42	0.25	0.66	0.61	0.24	0.30
	FTA	0.27	0.23	0.63	0.13	0.58	0.13	0.35	0.28	0.44	0.13	0.15
Lao PDR	AFAS 7	0.35	0.28	0.75	0.34	0.56	0.56	0.24	0.27	0.42	0.00	0.14
	FTA	0.24	0.15	0.40	0.13	0.33	0.59	0.23	0.13	0.42	0.13	0.12
Malaysia	AFAS 7	0.50	0.19	0.50	0.43	0.39	0.34	0.28	0.33	0.56	0.23	0.14
	FTA	0.47	0.29	0.56	0.13	0.38	0.13	0.40	0.28	0.47	0.30	0.15
Myanmar	AFAS 7	0.25	0.35	0.63	0.38	0.48	0.47	0.09	0.50	0.52	0.30	0.13
	FTA	0.28	0.14	0.63	0.13	0.48	0.13	0.13	0.13	0.45	0.13	0.22
Philippines	AFAS 7	0.42	0.52	0.35	0.28	0.00	0.27	0.45	0.14	0.47	0.30	0.38
	FTA	0.20	0.37	0.20	0.13	0.25	0.23	0.50	0.13	0.50	0.13	0.32
Singapore	AFAS 7	0.52	0.38	0.75	0.60	0.15	0.25	0.34	0.38	0.66	0.30	0.14
	FTA	0.61	0.34	0.88	0.43	0.28	0.38	0.49	0.38	0.66	0.40	0.19
Thailand	AFAS 7	0.66	0.20	0.64	0.60	0.58	0.75	0.39	0.31	0.64	0.64	0.24
	FTA	0.37	0.24	0.46	0.23	0.58	0.69	0.35	0.13	0.58	0.24	0.26
Vietnam	AFAS 7	0.39	0.33	0.56	0.25	0.43	0.50	0.49	0.63	0.52	0.18	0.19
	FTA	0.47	0.45	0.63	0.58	0.45	0.56	0.70	0.47	0.50	0.29	0.27

Chapter 5

Lessons from the EU Relevant to ASEAN Integration in Services

5.1 The EU and Trade in Services: Some Contextual Considerations

The European Union (EU) is the most important global player in international services trade today.[1] The period since the 1990s has seen a constant rise in the service sector of the EU economy. Services play a major role in EU growth, jobs and exports, accounting for over 70 percent of Europe's gross domestic product (GDP) and a similar proportion of aggregate employment. Cross-border services trade represent 25 percent of the EU's global trade – a level some 20 percent above the world average.[2] In recent decades, the expansion of EU services trade has exceeded service output growth by a sizeable margin.[3]

---

[1] Three main sectors accounts for two-thirds of the total trade in services, transport, travel and other business services (financial services, computer and information services) Statistics Eurostat: http://epp.eurostat.ec.europa.eu/statistics_explained/index.php/International_trade_in_services

[2] Ibid.

[3] Eurostat, 'European Union International Trade in Services. Analytical Aspects. 1997–2005', 2007 edition http://epp.eurostat.ec.europa.eu/cache/ITY_OFFPUB/KS-EB-07-001/EN/KS-EB-07-001-EN.PDF

Important defining characteristics of services trade are the immediacy and proximity of the relationship that it entails between the provider and the recipient (consumer) in many transactions. A derivative feature of services is that they are provided via various modes of supply that can trigger, and indeed often require, the mobility of production factors (capital and labour). In EU law, a specific approach was taken such that, in the very same sector, services can be subject either to the rules of the Treaty of Rome on freedom to provide services or to the freedom of establishment triggering a different legal regime.

Over the past decade, efforts have intensified within the EU to take full advantage of both intra- and extra-EU trade in services. Several strategies were adopted by the European Commission, culminating in the adoption of the Services Directive[4] at the end of 2006, followed by the Single Market Act in 2011. At the international level, the EU has concluded several bilateral trade agreements (BTAs) of a preferential nature (PTAs) and is currently engaged in negotiating new ones in which services are almost inherently a central component.

Since 2016, several major changes have occurred that put pressure on EU trade policy, including the field of services. The EU–Canada Comprehensive Economic and Trade Agreement (CETA) faced unprecedented and largely unanticipated challenges from a number of European national

[4] Directive 2006/123 of the European Parliament and of the Council of 12 December 2006 on services in the internal market [2006] O.J. L376/36 (Services Directive).

parliaments at the ratification change, chiefly over issues relating to Union versus Member State competence over investment rule making. The outcome of the United Kingdom's (UK's) Brexit referendum of June 2016, leading to its decision to leave the EU represents another major challenge for the orientation of EU trade Policy. If it becomes a new (non-EU) third country, the UK will have to negotiate a new trade relationship with its EU counterparts. Deprived of a country accounting for 28 percent of EU aggregate output and, significantly, its leading exporter of services, the EU27 will also have to reconsider its trade policy and negotiation strategy. Finally, the overall political context and aggressive trade policy orientation of the Trump administration in the United States pose additional policy-making challenges to the EU in pursuing its trade policy objectives.[5]

5.2 Building the European Internal Market for Services

Since its very inception, primary EU law has referred to services.[6] The Treaty of Rome does not offer a definition of what a service is, but nonetheless aims at liberalizing trade in services. To achieve this objective, EU law relies on the

---

[5] Towards a more responsible trade and investment policy, 14 October 2015, COM (2015)497: https://ec.europa.eu/transparency/regdoc/rep/1/2015/EN/1-2015-497-EN-F1-1.PDF

[6] 'While the European Union has always looked upon services as an essential part of the integration process, it has taken some time for the EU to devote much attention to them': W. Molle (2006), The Economics of European Integration (Farnham: Ashgate), p. 323.

economic notion of services, which, as Peter Hill aptly noted, can be defined 'as a change in the condition of a person, or a good belonging to some economic unit, which is brought about as the result of the activity of some other economic unit, with the prior agreement of the former person or economic unit'.[7]

At the core of the European project is the objective of establishing an internal market through the economic integration of the founding Member States' market. The project is framed as an international agreement,[8] its peculiar institutional and legal environments allowing such an objective to proceed in a dynamic manner.[9] The unprecedented ambition

---

[7] T. P. Hill, 'On Goods and Services', Review of Wealth and Income (1997).

[8] Rome Treaty establishing the European Economic Community. See O. Spiermann, 'The Other Side of the Story: An Unpopular Essay on the Making of the European Community Legal Order', *European Journal of International Law*, 10(4) (1999), 763–89.In this piece, the author establishes a clear link between the early case law of the ECJ and the specificities of the EU treaties. The potential of the preliminary reference allowed the Court to decide cases such as *Van Gend en Loos* v. *Nederlandse Administratie der Belastingen* (Case 26/62) [1963] E.C.R. 1 and *Costa* v. *ENEL* [1964] E.C.R. 585. The principles of direct effect and ECJ supremacy that were established in these cases created a new dynamic that the ECJ explored further. Scholars have also shown that ECJ judges were deciding more as national rather than international court members. See J. H. H. Weiler, 'The Transformation of Europe', *Yale Law Journal*, 8 (1991), 2403–83.

[9] All relevant ideas are already clearly embedded in the Schuman Declaration of 9 May 1950: http://europa.eu/about-eu/basic-information/symbols/europe-day/schuman-declaration/index_en.htm as well as in J. Monnet, Mémoires (Paris: Fayard, 1976), p. 642; J. Delors, 1992 Le défi (Paris: Flammarion, 1990), p. 250; speeches by Émile Noël in Hommage à Emile Noël (Office des publications de la Communauté, 1988), p. 176.

of the European project was recognized early on, as the region did not aim for 'just' free trade[10] but rather for a more advanced stage of economic integration via a customs union and, subsequently, a single internal market. In 1993, the objective was revisited and an extra level of integration was added with the aim of establishing a European Economic and Monetary Union.

The first version of the founding treaty mentions services, but for decades services were considered only as incidental to trade in goods. From the early 1990s, the economic weight of services grew significantly, entailing a notable policy shift towards greater regulatory activity and judicial activism on the basis of the primary law referring to services.

5.2.1 *The Instruments Used*

The establishment of a European-wide internal market for services required Member States tackling the obstacles to intra-EU trade and the fragmentation of the European market. Several instruments are available and used for the objective. Hard law is the central instrument, but it takes different forms; primary law (treaty), secondary law (regulation and directive) or case law. Soft law also plays an important role in the establishment of the internal market in services. Regular reports, strategies, white papers and communications are and

---

[10] As opposed to the other European regional trade project: the European Free Trade Association, created in 1960, or the original 'Outer Seven' (as opposed to the 'Inner Six').

were adopted, mainly by the European Commission but also by other EU institutions, to push forward the completion of the internal market in services.

Since the inception of the EU, several instruments have been included in the Treaty of Rome towards this end – namely a standstill clause as well as clauses on negative and positive integration. The standstill and negative integration clause included in the Treaty allowed the tackling of national obstacles to trade.[11] Both clauses introduced clear prohibitions for Member States and were recognized as having direct effect by the European Court of Justice (ECJ), which also gave a wide interpretation of their material scope. Positive integration clauses inserted in the treaty allow for harmonization of national regulations at the level of the EU. This instrument proved particularly efficient to advance the agenda of the internal market and to facilitate the de-fragmentation of the EU-wide services market.

However, it was the combination of the two instruments that ultimately allowed the establishment of the internal market to be achieved.[12] The active litigation of economic

[11] Early on, the ECJ gave a wide interpretation of the negative integration clauses, allowing traders to challenge an important number of obstacles to services trade. In the early 1990s, when case law began to rise in the services field, it gave a wide interpretation of the negative integration clause of the treaty on services.

[12] K. Mortelmans, 'The Common Market, the Internal Market and the Single Market, what's in a Market?', *Common Market Law Review*, 35 (1998), 101–36, at 120 on this point; and J. H. H. Weiler, 'Epilogue: Towards a Common Law of International Trade' in *The EU, the WTO and the NAFTA. Towards a Common Law of International Trade* (Oxford: Oxford University Press, 2000), pp. 201–32, at 223 on this point.

agents on the basis of the negative integration clauses echoed by a reactive ECJ prompted the removal of national measures constituting obstacles to services trade. The adoption of secondary law came afterwards, starting with sector-by-sector harmonization of national regulations on services and widespread recourse to the principle of mutual recognition (especially in regard to the recognition of diplomas). Only recently, in 2006, did the EU adopt a Directive that was not sector specific and covered services in the internal market.[13] Since the transposition of the Directive, new soft law instruments have been adopted to advance the objective further. Among them the most innovative is the EU Points of Single Contact, which allow entrepreneurs to have, for each EU Member State, one address (one web contact point) to access to find out the relevant formalities to set up a business.

5.2.2 *The Steps to Build the Internal Market for Services*

The first period of integration was quite long and specific to the EU, and as such of limited relevance to the Association of South East Asian Nations (ASEAN). Indeed, from its inception, services were included in the EU economic integration project. However, until the 1990s, services were largely accessory to trade in goods. The place of services is no longer accessory, as in the case of ASEAN. What might be interesting to consider during this period is how the different instruments were used in the European project.

[13] Services Directive.

The Origins: the First Soft Law Instrument: the Spaak Report

In June 1955, in the negotiating framework that would later lead to the signature of the Treaty of Rome, the governments of the soon-to-be six founding Member States of the European Economic Community (EEC) decided at the Messine Conference to convene an intergovernmental committee presided over by Paul-Henri Spaak.[14] On 21 April 1956, the committee presented a report that delineated all the foundations of what would subsequently become the internal market project in the Treaty of Rome signed in March 1957, and the main aim of which was to merge the six national markets.

The Spaak Report foresaw the establishment of a sound environment, in terms of competition, and the elimination of all forms of protectionism. The report also suggested tackling monopolies and states' subsidies as well as liberalizing all factors of production, capital and persons by allowing their free movement within the European internal market.[15] The report refers to both free movement of goods and of services. Chapter 3 of the report concentrates exclusively on services, with the following introductory remark: 'the importance and the growth of services is notable in the economies of the Member States'. A short enumeration lists

---

[14] P. H. Spaak, Report of the Heads of Delegation to the Ministers of Foreign Affairs. Intergovernmental Committee on European Integration (commonly known as the 'Spaak Report') (1956), p. 135; Spaak was the Foreign Affairs Minister of Belgium at that time.

[15] Spaak Report, p. 15.

examples of services such as transport, insurance, banking and financial services.

While preparing the Spaak Report, the committee members referred to the works of the Organization for European Economic Co-operation (OECE),[16] one of the aims of which was to liberalize services then commonly referred to as 'invisibles'. The Spaak Report advanced several proposals on services. The first and most important challenge was to tackle the liberalization of services that were important components of the production and trade in goods,[17] revealing the predominant perception at the time of the somewhat adjunct nature of services as primarily inputs into other economic activities rather than genuine activities in their own right.[18] Services were thus initially seen as incidental to advancing the main economic priority of the European project that concerned the liberalization of trade in goods.

The second key focus of the Spaak Report was the monitoring of Member States' regulation on services to avoid discrimination on the basis of nationality or residence.[19] The Spaak Report further considered the necessity of putting into place a system of recognition of diplomas and academic titles

---

[16] It is worth reminding ourselves of one of the objectives behind the creation of the OECE in 1948, which was the improvement of trade relations between its members. To achieve that, several codes on liberalization of exchanges, invisible transactions and capital movements were adopted.
[17] Spaak Report, p. 41.
[18] Goods are described by the Spaak Report as being of 'top priority'.
[19] This concern would be placed at the heart of the services-related articles of the future Treaty of Rome.

with a view to facilitating the cross-border movement of skilled labour. This point would assume significant prominence in the EU's positive integration (harmonization) agenda from the 1980s onwards, affirming the central market-opening role assumed by the principle of mutual recognition.[20]

The Founding Treaties: Hard Law Sources
Following the Spaak Report, the group of experts who drafted the Treaty of Rome (called the Common Market Group) finalized the articles on services. Despite attempts to include an article with a positive definition of services, the signed version of the Treaty did not feature such a definition. Chapter 3 of the Treaty of Rome contained seven articles that dealt with services but has since remained largely unchanged.

The *standstill clause* of former article 62 of the Treaty establishing the European Community was removed, as well as references to the transitional period, but otherwise the primary law articulation and references to *negative and positive integration* remained unchanged in the field of services liberalization. However, one important modification introduced since the Treaty's signature has been the use of the ordinary legislative process to adopt EU Directives in the services field. The following lists the relevant articles of the Treaty of Rome that govern services in the EU today.

---

[20] Mutual recognition was also used in earlier case law and secondary law in regard to the free movement of goods. For an extensive study of the principle in the field of services, see V. Hatzopoulos, Regulating Services in the EU (Oxford: Oxford University Press, 2012), p. 283 and onwards.

Chapter 3: Services
Article 56 of the Treaty on the Functioning of the European Union (TFEU)
Within the framework of the provisions set out below, *restrictions on the freedom to provide services within the Union are to be prohibited*[21] in respect of nationals of Member States who are established in a State of the Community other than that of the person for whom the services are intended. The Council, acting by a qualified majority on a proposal from the Commission, may extend the provisions of the chapter to nationals of a third country who provide services and who are established within the Union.

Article 57 TFEU
Services are to be considered to be 'services' within the meaning of this Treaty where they are normally provided for remuneration, in so far as they are not governed by the provisions relating to freedom of movement for goods, capital and persons. In particular, 'services' shall include activities of: (a) an industrial character; (b) a commercial character; (c) craftsmen; and (d) the professions.[22] Without prejudice to the provisions of the chapter relating to the right of establishment, in order to provide a service a person may temporarily pursue his activity in the State in which it is provided, under

---

[21] Authors' emphasis. The trigger of the negative integration clause is the prohibition on restrictions to free provision of services in the EU.

[22] There is no positive and comprehensive definition of 'services' in the Treaty of Rome, and it cannot be linked to any other positive legal source. It is a *sui generis* definition of the activity of services with reference to the necessity of remuneration and a cross-border element.

the same conditions as are imposed by that State on its own nationals.[23]

Article 58 TFEU
Freedom to provide services in the field of transport are to be governed by the provisions of the title relating to transport.[24] The liberalization of banking and insurance services connected with movements of capital are to be pursued in step with the liberalization of movement of capital.

Article 59 TFEU
In order to achieve the liberalization of a specific service, the European Parliament and the Council, acting in accordance with the ordinary legislative procedure and after consulting the Economic and Social Committee, shall issue directives. As regards the Directives referred to above, as a general rule, priority is to be given to the services that directly affect production costs or the liberalization of which helps to promote trade in goods.

Article 60 TFEU
The Member States are to endeavour to undertake the liberalization of services beyond the extent required by the Directives issued pursuant to Article 59(1) if their general economic situation and the situation of the economic sector concerned so permit. To this end, the Commission is to make recommendations to the Member States concerned.

---

[23] We see here reference to the mutually exclusive articles on establishment and provision of services and the reference to the temporary nature of the freedom to provide services.

[24] A specific chapter is inserted in the Treaty of Rome on transport, in Arts 90–100 TFEU.

Article 61 TFEU
As long as restrictions on freedom to provide services have not been abolished, each Member State is to apply such restrictions without distinction on grounds of nationality or residence[25] to all persons who provide services within the meaning of the first paragraph of Article 56 TFEU.

Article 62 TFEU
The provisions of Articles 51–54 are to apply to the matters covered by the chapter.[26]

Chapter 4: Establishment

Article 52 TFEU
The provisions of the chapter and measures taken in pursuance thereof are not to prejudice the applicability of provisions laid down by law, regulation or administrative action providing for special treatment for foreign nationals on grounds of public policy, public security or public health.[27]

The Treaty of Rome included two chapters on services: one entitled 'Freedom to provide services' and the other 'Establishment'. The approach pursued under the Treaty was to put in place two distinct legal regimes for the same economic activity.[28] As we shall see, the EU

---

[25] Discriminatory national regulations are prohibited by the treaty in the field of services also.
[26] Articles 51–54 are part of Chapter 2, on the freedom of establishment in the EU.
[27] This article establishes a closed list of justifications of restrictive national measures affecting the free provision of services.
[28] Both primary law and secondary law refer to services taking into account the two legal regimes. Many Directives and Regulations on services

construct did not pursue commitments by modes of supply, as is now found in the General Agreement on Trade in Services (GATS) or PTAs. Such terminology and categorical distinctions for negotiating purposes would come from the GATS negotiating process, which itself borrows from early attempts at developing rules for services in various preferential trade agreements.

In a landmark case, the ECJ clarified the differences that could be seen to distinguish the delivery of legal services in the EU under the agreed freedom to provide services versus the freedom of establishment.[29] Such differences lay principally in the duration of the economic activity in question, with the two legal regimes excluding each other mutually. An economic activity that is temporary in nature would be covered by the rules of the treaty dealing with the free provision of services. This characteristic is explained by the Court in the following terms in the Gebhard case: 'the temporary nature of the activities in question has to be determined in the light not only of the duration of the provision of the service but also of its regularity, periodicity or continuity. The fact that the provision of services is temporary does not mean that the service provider within the meaning of the Treaty may not equip himself (or herself) with some form of infrastructure in the host Member State (including an office, chambers or consulting rooms) in so far

include sections on freedom of establishment and free provision of services.
[29] *Gebhard* v. *Consiglio dell'Ordine degli Avvocati e Procurati di Milano* (C-55/94) [1995] E.C.R. I-4165, para. 27.

as such infrastructure is necessary for the purposes of performing the services in question'.[30]

The main difference between the two legal regimes is that, when covered by the freedom to provide services, the economic activity is subject to the regulation of the home country and if covered by the freedom of establishment it is the regulation of the host country that applies. The two regimes are mutually exclusive.

The Recurring Role of Soft Law Instruments
Between the 1960s and the early 1990s, several initiatives were taken to advance the integration of the European internal market. As early as 1961, the Council adopted two General Programmes aimed at removing all restrictions to the free provision of services and the freedom of establishment.[31] The Programmes had the same main focus as the Spaak Report and the Treaty of Rome – namely the liberalization of services 'as instruments for' free trade in goods.

In the early 1980s, a second Spaak Committee was convened by France and Germany to advance the European

[30] R. Wägenbaur, 'La libéralisation des prestations de service dans la perspective du marché intérieur', *Nuove tendenze del commercio internazionale* (Milan: Istituto Universitario di Studi di Torino, Giuffre editore, 1989), p. 163; M. Fallon, 'Vers un principe général de liberté de circulation? Pour une approche unitaire du droit du marché intérieur', *Annales d'études européennes de l'Université catholique de Louvain* (Bruxelles: Bruylant, 1996), p. 81; E. Steindorff, 'Freedom of Services in the EEC', *Fordham International Law Journal*, 11(1988), 372.

[31] These programmes were adopted unanimously by the Council and, despite their lack of legal force, they had an important political influence: [1962] O.J.2/32 and 36.

project.[32] The second Spaak Report underlines the importance of the internal market and the need to set up deadlines to remove restrictions thereto. According to the Report, a fragmented internal market hampers Europe's competitiveness on the global stage. The Report was the first political document to advocate, in a concerted manner, the need to establish an internal market for services.[33]

The second Spaak Report was followed by the ambitious White Paper of 1985. In this document (also a soft law instrument), the European Commission suggested that the Council set the end of 1992 as the target date for the completion of the European internal market.[34] It also suggested two orientations: the first relying more systematically on the principle of mutual recognition and the second adopting a new approach towards harmonization.[35] Some scholars have called this document 'utopic'[36] because of the numerous objectives

---

[32] P. Dabin, Le Comité Spaak 2 (dit Comité Dooge): Actes du Comité ad hoc pour les questions institutionnelles créé par le Conseil européen de Fontainebleau (25–26 juin 1984) (Bruxelles, 1985).

[33] The wording of the second Spaak Report is quite familiar today as the Lisbon Strategy in 2000, in Europe 2020 and in the 2011 Single Market Act; reference is made to the necessity for an effective and obstacle free internal market for services.

[34] COM (85) 310 final, 'Completing the Internal Market – White Paper from the Commission to the European Council' (Milan, 28–29 June 1985).

[35] The new approach departed from the idea that all aspects of trade should be harmonized at European level by identifying priority fields in which harmonization would be relevant.

[36] H. Schmitt von Sydow, 'The Basic Strategies of the Commission's White Paper' in R. Bieber, R. Dehousse, J. Pinder and J. H. H. Weiler (eds.), 1992: One European Market? (Baden-Baden: Nomos Verlagsgesellschaft, 1998), 79–106.

that it sets, as well as the exhaustive range of obstacles that it targeted for removal. Still, the document would prove to be decisive in the establishment of the EU internal market precisely because of its clear objectives but also because of the reasonable deadline that it set for their realization.[37] The White Paper recognizes the importance of services in the economies, especially at a time when the European manufacturing sector had begun its relative decline.

Following the White Paper, for the first time, Member States introduced amendments to the Treaty of Rome, leading to the Single European Act. Among other changes, the voting rule in the Council became a qualified majority for the adoption of secondary law in regard to the internal market (Article 114 TFEU).[38] This facilitated the adoption of secondary law and promoted the harmonization of internal market rules.[39]

Three years after the White Paper, in 1988, an impact assessment was commissioned regarding the completion of

---

[37] It is worth noting that the use of a deadline proved effective both for the internal market for goods and for the establishment of the custom union of the EU. As in AFAS, the setting of realistic but firm deadlines and of clear intermediary objectives were a successful mix in advancing the European integration project.

[38] J.-P. Jacqué, 'L'Acte unique européen', *RTDE*, 1986, 4, 575; G. Bosco, 'Commentaire de l'Acte unique européen', *CDE*, 1987, 45, 355; and S. Deniniolle, 'L'acte unique et le marché commun', Moniteur du commerce international, février 1988, n° 805/29, 17.

[39] Even today, the importance of the change in the voting rule in the Council is acknowledged as one of the key factors in the completion of the internal market by 1993: J. Delors, 'The Single Market, Cornerstone of the EU, Tribune', Notre Europe, 22 November 2012.

the European internal market. The resulting document, called the Cecchini Report, was critical in the emphasis that it laid on the potential of the service sector to advance the European economy in terms of both growth and employment. The Report pointed to a host of national regulations and practices that artificially inhibited the free provision of services and held back competition in the sector.[40] The Report concluded that 'much more significant growth is being artificially held back by regulations and practices which significantly inhibit the free flow of services and thus the free play of competition between companies supplying them'.

The continuity and coherence of the European project for completing the internal market proceeded very clearly from the adoption of the Treaty of Rome to the Cecchini Report. Over three decades, all the necessary political, institutional and legal efforts concurred to secure the defragmentation of national markets and the establishment of a Europe-wide services market.

The Case Law: The Input of the European Court of Justice

Until the early 1990s, litigation and ECJ decisions on services were limited. This changed progressively as the importance of services grew in the economies of Member States. The relevant articles of the Treaty of Rome were invoked more frequently by traders, economic agents and consumers within

---

[40] 'The European Challenge, 1992: The Benefit of a Single Market', Paolo Cecchini, Wildwood House, pour la Commission, 1988, Sommaire du rapport Cecchini, SEC (88) 524 final du 13 avril 1988: http://aei.pitt.edu /3813/01/000209_1.pdf

the Member States in the framework of domestic litigation. National judges started to refer preliminary references to the ECJ, asking for the interpretation of Articles 56 and 57 TFEU. For much of the recent past, the majority of questions that have been referred to the ECJ on the issue of free movement have concerned services-related issues.[41]

The Recognition of Direct Effect of Article 56 TFEU
However, a few important cases in the services field were decided earlier by the ECJ, which, as early as 1974, notably recognized the direct effect of certain treaty articles on services. As noted earlier, interaction between the provider and the recipient is essential to trade in services. Accordingly, recognition of direct effect has allowed stakeholders to rely on the Treaty articles and to challenge national measures that were contrary to EU law. The landmark case on this issue dates from 1974, when the ECJ recognized the direct effect of Article 56(1) and Article 57(3) of the Treaty of Rome treaty in the *van Bisbergen* case.[42]

Recognition of direct effect allowed for the more effective and speedy removal of national regulations restricting the free provision of services. Indeed, economic agents (both natural and juridical persons) could invoke Article 56 or Article 57 TFEU before national judges to challenge domestic

---
[41] The ECJ's annual report shows a steady decrease over the past decade in the number of cases brought to the ECJ on the free movement of goods, and an increase in cases relating to the free movement of services.

[42] In *Van Bisbergen* (33/74) [1974] E.C.R. 1299, a Dutch legal representative changed residence from the Netherlands to Belgium. The question arose whether this person could continue to represent his client in a pending litigation and whether Art. 56 TFEU could have direct effect.

regulations.[43] Without direct effect, the Treaty would have left them with the possibility of sending complaints to the European Commission requesting an investigation of a specific national regulation and its possible violation of EU law.

The Scope of Article 56 TFEU

The aim of Article 56 TFEU seems clear upon reading, as it states that national measures that restrict the provision of services are prohibited. However, the ECJ's interpretation of this article, and especially the concomitant scope of the prohibition, evolved over time. Such evolution highlights the central role assumed by the ECJ as a major actor in the European institutional landscape through the teleological interpretation that it has given to the relevant Treaty articles on services.

For example, the ECJ gave a flexible interpretation of the private, public or mixed origins of national measures. According to the ECJ, '[t]he abolition, as between Member States, of obstacles to freedom of movement for persons would be compromised if the abolition of State barriers could be neutralized by obstacles resulting from the exercise of their legal autonomy by associations or organizations not governed by public law'.[44]

---

[43] See Opinion of Advocate General Warner in *Debauve and Coditel* (52/79 and 62/79) [1979] E.C.R. 874.

[44] *Wouters* (C-309/99) [2002] E.C.R. I-1577, point 120, quoting *Walrave and Koch* (36/74) [1974] E.C.R. 1405, points 17, 18, 23 and 24; *Donà* (13/76) [1976] E.C.R. 1333, points 17 and 18; *Bosman* (C-415/93) [1995] E.C.R. I-4921, points 83 and 84; and *Angonese* (C-281/98) [2000] E.C.R. I-4139, point 32. Recently quoted in *International Transport Workers' Federation v. Finnish Seamen's Union* (C-438/05) [2007] E.C.R. 10779 and *Laval un Partneri* (C-341/05) [2007] E.C.R. 11767.

As early as 1974, the ECJ interpreted Article 56 TFEU as prohibiting all discrimination based on the nationality of the service provider.[45] According to that, both *de jure* (overt) and *de facto* (covert) discrimination are caught by the treaty prohibition – a distinction that the drafters of the World Trade Organization's (WTO's) GATS would subsequently adopt. This important distinction was further explained by a member of the ECJ:

> By overt discrimination, I mean discrimination which is expressed in the legislation itself, i.e. legislation which expressly applies different requirements to nationals of, or those residents in, another Member State. By covert discrimination, I mean discrimination which results from legislation apparently applying the same requirements, but where the effect of the requirements is to disadvantage nationals of, or those residents in, another Member State.[46]

In the early 1990s, the ECJ revisited the scope of the prohibition of Article 56 TFEU and widened it to all national measures restricting the free provision of services. This evolution of the Court's interpretation of Treaty provisions came about as the number of cases in the services field brought

---

[45] *Van Bisbergen* (33/74) [1974] E.C.R. 1299; *Seco* (62/81 and 63/81) [1982] E.C.R. 223 (discrimination on the basis of nationality) and *Debauve* (52/79) [1980] E.C.R. 833. It is settled law that discrimination can arise only through the application of different rules to comparable situations or the application of the same rule to different situations: *Lease Plan* (C–390/96) [1998] E.C.R. I–2553, point 34 and *Danner* (C–136/00) [2002] E.C.R. I–8147.

[46] Point 19 of the opinion of the Advocate General, *Säger* (76/90) [1991] E.C.R. 4221.

before it increased significantly. The Court underlined in its judgment that most violations to free provision of services were made not by discriminatory but through unduly restrictive national regulations. The new interpretation of the Court is the following:

> Article [56] of the Treaty requires not only the elimination of all discrimination against a person providing services on the ground of its nationality but also the abolition of any restriction, even if it applies without distinction to national providers of services and to those of other Member States, when it is liable to prohibit or otherwise impede the activities of a provider of services established in another Member State where it lawfully provides similar services.[47]

Recent judgments rendered in the services field show that the ECJ typically proceeds in steps, applying different tests based on discrimination, market access or additional cost or comparing the effect in law or in fact of national measures before it.[48]

The evolution of case law allowed several national regulations that were restrictive to free trade in services to be challenged while also advancing various aspects relating to the freedom of establishment of service providers. However, to this day, the question of Treaty interpretation remains

---

[47] Point 12 of the *Säger* case became a systematic opening in each case of the Court on services. It was also used by the EFTA Court on
12 December 2003: *EFTA Surveillance Authority/Island* (E-1/03), EFTA Court Report 2003, 143, point 28.

[48] *Mobistar* (C-544/03 and 545/03) [2005] E.C.R. I-7723. See also
J. Meulman and H. de Waele, 'A Retreat from Säger? Servicing or Fine-Tuning the Application of Article 49 EC', *LIEI* (2006), 226.

salient: are they intended to liberalize intra-EU trade or, rather, more generally to encourage the unhindered pursuit of commerce in individual Member States?[49]

Justifying Restrictions on the Free Provision of Services
The Treaty of Rome allows Member States to justify restrictions (non-tariff barriers) on free movement in certain specified circumstances. These justifications are specific to each freedom, for 'the freedom to provide services is one of the fundamental principles of the Treaty and may be restricted only by provisions which are justified by the general good and which are imposed on all persons *or* undertakings operating in the said State in so far as that interest is not safeguarded by the provisions to which the provider of the service is subject in the Member State of his establishment'.[50] In addition, 'such requirements must be objectively justified by the need to ensure that professional rules of conduct are complied with and that the interests which such rules are designed to safeguard are protected'.[51]

The key balancing notion of proportionality has also been clarified by the ECJ through its case rulings.[52] For

---

[49] As noted in its introduction, AG Tesauro, in his Opinion of 27 October 1993 in the case *Hünermund* (C–292/92) [1993] E.C.R. 6787.

[50] *Webb* (279/80) [1981] E.C.R. 3305, point 17.

[51] *Commission* v. *France* (220/83) [1986] E.C.R. 3663, point 17; *Mobistar* (C–544/03 and 545/03) [2005] E.C.R. I–7723.

[52] J. C. Moitinho de Almeida, 'La libre prestation de services dans la jurisprudence de la Cour de Justice des Communautés européennes', *Scritti in onore di Giuseppe Federico Mancini. Vol. II. Diritto dell'Unione europea* (Milan: Dott. A. Giuffrè Editore, 1998), 658; *Ahokeinen and Leppik* (C–434/04) [2006] E.C.R. 609, and developments in the Opinion of Advocate General Poiares Maduro at points 23–26.

example, the ECJ allowed for the maintenance of an important margin of appreciation for Member States when considering the proportionality of national measures that target public morality[53] or public health objectives.[54]

As noted earlier, the legal basis for doing so is Article 52 TFEU for the express and closed list of justifications for national measures caught by Article 56 TFEU. The three grounds are public policy, public security or public health, all of which can be maintained despite being subject to the scope of the prohibition arising from Article 56 TFEU. In addition to treaty-based justification, an open list of justifications has been developed by the ECJ as it builds up its case law on services.[55] Such justifications, labelled 'overriding reasons of public interest', include, for example, public morality, the protection of consumers and workers, intellectual property and the protection of national treasures with an artistic, historic or archaeological value,[56] as well as the protection of fundamental human rights.

The Court explained that 'national rules which are not applicable to services without discrimination as regards their origin are compatible with [EU] law only if they can be

---

[53] *Grogan* (C-159/90) [1991] E.C.R. 4685, point 20, and *Schindler* (C-275/92) [1994] E.C.R. 1039, point 61.
[54] Opinion of AG Bot in *Doulamis* (C-446/05) [2007], points 108 and following.
[55] S. O'Leary and J. Fernandez-Martin, 'Judicially-created Exceptions to the Free Provision of Services', *European Business Law Review* (2000), 347–62.
[56] *Seco* (62/81 and 63/81) [1982] E.C.R. 223; *Rush Portuguesa* (C-113/89) [1990] E.C.R. I-1417 and *Coditel* (62/79) [1980] E.C.R. 881.

brought within the scope of an express exemption, such as that contained in Article [52] of the Treaty'.[57] The ECJ further stated that

> as a fundamental principle of the Treaty, the freedom to provide services may be limited only by rules which are justified by imperative reasons relating to the public interest and which apply to all persons or undertakings pursuing an activity in the State of destination, in so far as that interest is not protected by the rules to which the person providing the services is subject in the Member State in which he is established. In particular, those requirements must be objectively necessary in order to ensure compliance with professional rules and to guarantee the protection of the recipient of services and they must not exceed what is necessary to attain those objectives.[58]

The two lists of justifications (treaty-based and case-law-based) do not apply to the same measures, as can be seen from ECJ case law. However, the open-ended nature of the list allows the Court to take into account new overriding reasons that Member States may deem necessary to introduce or maintain otherwise Treaty incompatible measures in the services field.

The Principle of Mutual Recognition

Quite early in its case law, the ECJ recognized the principle of mutual recognition in the field of free provision of

---

[57] *Mediawet* (288/89) [1991] E.C.R. 4007, point 11; and *Bond van Adverteerders* (352/85) [1988] E.C.R. 2085, at paras 32 and 33.

[58] *Säger* (C–76/90) [1991] E.C.R. 4221, point 15.

services.[59] According to this principle, the host country of the service provider should take into account the regulatory framework with which the services provider has already complied in its home country.[60] The approach taken by the ECJ has been to avoid instances in which services providers would be subject to dual regulatory burdens in home and host country markets.[61] However, host countries could always request additional regulatory requirements if they are justified and applied in a proportional manner.

Following the ECJ's decision, numerous secondary law sources on the provision of services relied on the principle of mutual recognition. Scholars have also reflected on the benefits of the principle on free provision of services and how it facilitates market access for services.[62] Some scholars have called the principle of mutual recognition 'the intellectual foundation, the step before the country of origin principle' that will be the cornerstone of the 2004 draft Services Directive.[63]

---

[59] Mutual recognition was also considered in the positive integration instruments on services – for example, the Directives on insurance and banking sectors all refer to the system of 'unique licence' delivered by the home country in which the services provider has his or her residence: K. Peglow, 'La libre prestation de services dans la directive 2006/123. Réflexion sur l'insertion de la directive dans le droit communautaire existant', RTDE (2008), 67–118.

[60] *Van Wesemael* (110–111/78) [1979] E.C.R. 35.

[61] *Schnitzer* (C–215/01) [2003] E.C.R. 14847.

[62] J. Pelkmans, 'Mutual recognition: economic and regulatory logic in goods and services', Bruges European Economic Research, 24 (2012).

[63] V. Hatzopoulos, Le principe communautaire d'équivalence et de reconnaissance mutuelle dans la libre prestation de services (Athens/Bruxelles: Sakkoulas/Bruylant, 1999); and Regulating Service in the European Union (Oxford: Oxford University Press, 2012).

5.2.3 Completing the Single Market for Services

By the end of the twentieth century, numerous measures were already in place in the EU with a view to suppressing most of the major obstacles to the internal market in services. All economic integration instruments included in the Treaty of Rome were used to this effect: litigation on the basis of negative integration clauses arbitrated before national courts and the ECJ[64] and an activist, pro-market opening, advocacy role of the European Commission both as guardian of the treaties and as the initiator of positive integration steps in the services field. The use of all the above instruments enabled the European project to reach a level of economic integration that is unprecedented in its breadth, and greater than that achieved under any other regional grouping. However, all has not been (or will ever be) finalized in the quest for EU market integration, as major obstacles continue to hamper the stated aim of taking full advantage of the European internal market for services.

---

[64] 'It is clear from the jurisprudence of the Court that any measure liable to prohibit, impede or render less advantageous the supply or use of cross-border services or cross-border establishment within the EU could constitute a barrier. This report therefore includes examples of barriers which are not simply prohibitions, discriminations or conditions which are impossible to meet, but various types of requirements which, if applied to companies from other Member States, would undermine the freedoms to establish or provide services. Some barriers are due to complex, burdensome or non-transparent regulation or practices; most are just due to the wide divergence of national rules': 'The State of the Internal Market for Services', COM (2002) 441 final, 30 July 2002, p. 13.

A New Set of Soft Law Instruments: the Strategies
In 1996, following the forward dynamic that was spawned by the Spaak 2 and Cecchini Reports, the Commission produced a document on the untapped potential of services for the economies of the Member States and as a source of employment in Europe.[65] A year later, the Commission produced an Action Plan on the Single Market, for the attention of the European Council.[66] This was followed in 1999 by the Strategy for the internal market, prepared for the European Parliament and the Council.[67] These documents, while less ambitious than the White Paper of 1985, paved the way for the European Council's adoption in 2000 of the Lisbon Strategy, the fundamental aim of which was to make 'the European Union the most dynamic and competitive knowledge-based economy in the world'.[68]

As part of the Lisbon Strategy, the Commission continued to explore possibilities for using the full potential of the internal market in services by producing a specific Strategy for the Internal Market for Services.[69] The Strategy put the internal market back at the heart of the European project,

[65] *Services: mode d'emploi* CSE (96) 6 final, 27 November 1996.
[66] Commission Communication, 4 June 1997 to the European Council – (Amsterdam).
[67] COM (1999) 624, 24 November 1999.
[68] European Council (Lisbon) – June 2000 and set 2010 as the target date for its objective. For an evaluation of the Strategy, see SEC (2010) 114 final, 2 February 2010.
[69] 'An Internal Market Strategy for Services', COM (2000) 888 final, 29 December 2000; and 'The State of the Internal Market for Services', COM (2002) 441 final, 30 July 2002, p. 13, which is the first stage of the Strategy.

emphasizing services trade most particularly, just prior to the major enlargement of the EU in 2004 and the tenth anniversary of the completion of the internal market in goods. The Lisbon Strategy featured various steps aimed at boosting EU-wide competitiveness, among them the identification of obstacles to intra-EU trade to which Member States and civil society stakeholders could react.

The Commission's report of 2002 noted that '[t]he overall aim (of the report) is to describe the realities of the Internal Market as seen by providers and users of services. It does not at this stage seek to assess whether any individual barrier is justifiable or not. A wide range of difficulties was identified that both services providers and consumers were facing.'

The Services Strategy put aside, for the first time, the sector-specific approach and considered services globally and in an interconnected environment. It suggested the establishment of a common regulatory framework but with enough flexibility to consider new and innovative types of services as well.

This proposed regulatory framework was presented by the Commission to the European Parliament and the Council in the form of a draft Directive on services in the internal market.[70] For the first time, an annex was attached,

---

[70] Commission – draft Directive to the EP and the Council on services in the internal market to be adopted following a co-decision COM (2004) 2 final, 13 January 2004 – [SEC (2004) 21] influenced by general follow-up documents on the Strategy for the internal market COM (2003) 238 final, 7 May 2003 and COM (2004) 22 final, January 2004.

on an 'Extended Impact Assessment',[71] which emphasized the benefits to be derived from greater intra-EU trade in services under the draft Directive. It would take two years to finalize the Directive, which, in its final version, was more modest than foreseen under the original draft. However, the Directive is widely considered a landmark piece of EU legislation.[72]

The Latest Hard Law Instrument: the Services Directive

The aim of the draft Services Directive was to establish a regulatory framework that can tackle the obstacles to the free movement of services between Member States and offer a reliable environment to both services providers and the recipients of services (consumers). In drafting the Directive, the European Commission took a pragmatic (if ambitious) approach, attempting to cover all services in a single instrument instead of adopting a set of instruments to cover each sector specifically.[73] The Directive aimed at creating a dynamic environment to tackle remaining obstacles to the free movement of services within the EU with a minimum of regulatory instruments (exercising so-called 'regulatory or judicial economy').

---

[71] *Extended Impact Assessment,* presented on the same day as the draft Directive, 13 January 2004, SEC (2004) 21.
[72] Directive 2006/123/EC, European Parliament and Council, 12December 2006, on services in the internal market [2006] O.J. L 376/36.
[73] The advantage of the framework Directive is underlined by the Commission, as it is in line with ECJ case law that is not sector-specific and also avoids overregulation in the services field: Recital 7 of the Directive.

For the most part, the draft Directive codified ECJ case law on the free movement of services and included an important principle as a central rule – that of the country of origin.[74] This principle aims to create a dynamic for tackling the remaining obstacles in the services sector[75] but without the need to adopt Europe-wide harmonized rules, such that each country can keep its own domestic regulatory frameworks so long as they broadly approximate EU-wide aims. However, the Directive called for further collaboration in the field of consumer protection. In practice, the principle applies as follows: service providers comply with the regulatory requirements of their home state[76] that are applicable to the services they supply. The country of origin principle allows the provider to offer its services in other Member States without additional regulatory requirements.[77] The draft Directive nevertheless included some exceptions and temporary arrangements in this regard.[78]

---

[74] Also called 'automatic mutual recognition principle', B. De Witte, 'Setting the Scene. How did Services get to *Bolkenstein* and Why?', EUI Working Papers, Law 2007/20, p. 8; V. Hatzopoulos, 'Que reste-t-il de la directive sur les services?', *CDE*, 2007, n 3/4, p. 303 and S. Micossi, 'Fixing the Services Directive', *CEPS Policy Brief*, 2006, n. 100, p. 7

[75] Those identified by the 2002 Report of the Commission and the case law of the ECJ.

[76] According to the case law of the ECJ, it is the Member State in which the services provider is established.

[77] The principle applies somewhat differently when the service activity is done under the freedom of establishment; indeed, the draft Directive relies on the existence of a single contact point to facilitate establishment in other Member States.

[78] COM (2004) 2 final, p. 4, Arts 17, 18 and 19.

In 2006, following difficult discussions in the European Parliament and the Council, the European Commission drafted a second version of the Directive,[79] signed in December of the same year. The final version of the framework Directive was less ambitious and innovative, compared with its original version.[80] For example, the material scope of the Directive is much reduced, and several sectors, among which are financial services, electronic communications, energy, social services, and gambling activities, are now excluded. The Directive did not replace Directives that apply to regulated services or certain specific services that are covered by separate (sector-specific) Directives.[81] The most important change was the removal of the country of origin principle, which made the draft framework Directive potentially dynamic, according to the impact assessment. Indeed, the principle was supposed to bring greater legal certainty to traders as it established, as a general rule, that the regulatory framework of the country of origin of the service provider should apply to intra-EU trade in services. The removal of the principle became necessary following debates in the European Parliament and public opinion reactions in certain Member States. These were clear signs of a lack of confidence and of the difficulty in triggering mutual trust, both of which are foundational elements of the country of origin principle. Disparities in national regulations might

---

[79] COM (2006) 160 final, 4 April 2006.
[80] The legal basis of the framework Directive is Arts 52 and 64 TFEU.
[81] We can consider this a *lex specialis* of the Services Directive (Directive 2005/36/EC on regulated services).

have been a reason for the removal of the principle from the Directive but, in any event, efforts were needed and remain necessary today in the EU to increase levels of trust in regulatory matters. This is an important point from the perspective of the ASEAN Economic Community, as the EU experience makes clear that trust requires sustained and regular interactions between relevant epistemic communities within Member States.

The final version of the framework Directive 'establishes general provisions facilitating the exercise of the freedom of establishment for service providers and the free movement of services'.[82] The Directive did not harmonize national law but served as an additional vehicle for negative integration. The purpose of the Directive is further to eliminate barriers to the freedom of establishment for service providers and the free movement of services between Member States. The Directive 'directs' the Member States to 'screen' their national legislation and remove obstacles to the freedom of services.[83] Ultimately, the Services Directive calls for rationalization of regulation in the services field.

However, according to the Directive, the free movement of services can be subject to host country requirements when justified by public order, public health, public security

---

[82] Article 1, paragraph 1 of the Directive. With such a limited impact, certain authors even questioned the need to keep the framework Directive: D. Gareth, 'The Services Directive: Extending the Country of Origin Principle, and Reforming Public Administration', *ELR*, 2007, 239.

[83] H. Merteen, 'A comparison of the services directive with the case law of the Court of justice: a case study', 4 (2006) *Griffin's view*, 141: http://papers.ssrn.com/sol3/papers.cfm?abstract_id=1537681

or environmental protection considerations.[84] For many observers, this closed list of justifications is the main innovation of the framework Directive, as it reduces the possible scope of restrictive national measures on the free movement of services to four grounds and arguably suppresses the open list of justifications created by the ECJ case law through the overriding concept of 'general interest'.[85] This has led some observers to argue that the Directive encouraged a deregulatory shift compared with the existing legal environment on services in the EU.[86]

Overall, the Services Directive that was signed in December 2006 was significantly less ambitious than the dynamic instrument initially foreseen by the Commission to advance the Lisbon Strategy and secure the removal of the remaining major obstacles to the free movement of services. However, if the ECJ revisits its case law on the justifications for restrictive national measures on services and does not accept any other justification beyond those listed in the Services Directive, important changes in the European regulatory environment for services providers may follow. Currently, ECJ case law recognizes a wide range of justifications that allow Member States' national regulations to limit or impede the free provision of services in the EU. If interpreted strictly, the wording of the Services Directive revisits the range of admissible justifications and limits them strictly to the four grounds listed in Article 16.

---

[84] Article 16, para. 3 of the Directive.
[85] *Corsten* (C–58/98) [2000] E.C.R. 7919.
[86] De Witte, 'Setting the Scene'.

A final interesting outcome of the Services Directive that is worthy of note and of relevance in an ASEAN context concerns the establishment of Single Contact Points (SCPs) at EU level.[87] According to the European Commission, the SCPs can help to bring the benefits of e-governance to businesses by providing them with comprehensive information on applicable regulatory requirements and allowing them to complete administrative procedures online, be it in their own countries or in any other EU Member State. They simplify the setting up and expansion of businesses in the Single Market. SCPs are part of the efforts made by Member States to cut red tape and modernize national administrations. They are a major step towards more efficient public online services and form an integral part of Member States' e-government agendas. Member States have invested time, effort and resources in designing and implementing the SCPs, which are now up and running in all Member States.

The Soft Law Instruments that Followed the Services Directive

Despite the difficulties encountered in adopting the Services Directive, the European Commission put forward a new action plan to maintain forward momentum in the operation of the European internal market.[88] The action plan followed

---

[87] http://ec.europa.eu/internal_market/eu-go and http://ec.europa.eu/internal_market/services/docs/services-dir/psc-charter_en.pdf

[88] COM (2011) 206 final, 13 April 2011, Single Market Act, Twelve levers to boost growth and strengthen confidence, 'Working together to create new growth', SEC (2011) 467 final and COM (2012) 573 final, 3 October 2012, Single Market Act II, Together for new growth.

up on a study carried out in 2010 at the behest of the President of the European Commission.[89] The study found that many obstacles continued to hamper the full realization of the benefits of the European internal market and cautioned that past achievements and the existing level of completion of the internal market should not be taken for granted. Another consideration was that, despite all the efforts in the field, mobility in the EU was still low compared with that in the United States, with studies showing that mobility in Europe was up to ten times lower than in the US, notably as a result of linguistic barriers.[90] The study therefore argued the need to boost the internal market.

The Commission produced fifty proposals for debate. In 2010, these were set out in a communication entitled 'Towards a Single Market Act ', with public debates taking place at European, national and local levels. The initiative generated more than 800 responses to the call for public consultations on the Single Market Act, reflecting the points of view of Member States, non-governmental organizations, social partners at national and European levels, local and regional authorities, industrial and professional organizations,

---

[89] The Monti Report: *A New Strategy for the Internal Market*, May 2010.
[90] E. M. Mouhoud and J. Oudinet, 'Migrations et marché du travail dans l'espace européen', Économie internationale, 105 (2006); X. Chojnicki, 'Les migrations intra-européennes sont d'ampleur limitées et se concentrent sur les grands pays', *Blog du CEPII*, blogpost 4 Septembre 2014; G. Cornilleau, 'La libre circulation des citoyens en questions', *Blog OFCE*, blogpost 8 June 2015. For a detailed and systematic study, see E. Recchi, Mobile Europe, The Theory and Practice of Free Movements in the EU (London: Palgrave Macmillan, 2015).

trade unions, businesses, consumer organizations, think-tanks, academics and many individuals.

The consultations revealed high expectations from civil society, in terms of the development of the Single Market's potential to foster growth and employment as well as its social dimension and the concomitant need to protect and preserve an adequate supply of public services. The Commission formalized the results of its consultation process through the Single European Act of 2011 that was followed by a second Act in 2012, both of which featured a number of actions directed towards the services sector.

In May 2012, the European Commission confirmed that all Member States had officially transposed the Services Directive into national law, and shortly thereafter released a Communication entitled 'A partnership for new growth in services 2012–2015'.[91] The Communication formed part of a wider 'Services package' advocated by the Single European Act. The 'Services package' adopted in June 2012 called for additional efforts towards an ambitious implementation of the Services Directive. According to the Commission in 2014, this 'would significantly improve the smooth functioning of the Single Market for Services, in particular for small- and medium-sized companies and for consumers. Enhancing competitiveness could lead to an estimated economic gain equivalent to 2.6% of EU GDP.'

---

[91] COM (2012) 261 final, 8 June 2012, followed in the same month by an impact assessment study of the Commission entitled 'The Economic Impact of the Services Directive: a first assessment following implementation', Economic Paper, 456.

Since the Directive's adoption and the deadline for its transposition into domestic laws in 2009, a fourth period has seen a continued push for deepening the internal market in services as a core policy concern of the EU integration agenda. The current phase combines continued reliance on consolidated case law on services and a more widely regulated European environment that still faces many challenges due to the limits of the horizontal Directive and the difficulties encountered in its transposition at the national level.[92]

At the end of 2015, an ambitious joint communication was issued by the European Commission, the European Parliament, the European Council and two European committees to upgrade the Single Market,[93] followed a little more than a year later by additional policy proposals. In the first half of 2016, the European Commission launched a broad set of public consultations on future directions in EU services policy. These were deployed across various sub-sectors, the most important of which were business services, construction services and insurance as well as the services sector in general. The policy orientations that emerged from the above

---

[92] The European Commission put in place unprecedented monitoring to ensure the correct transposition of the Services Directive in all Member States by the end of 2009. However, despite those coordinated efforts, the task has proven very difficult as the Services Directive requested that certain Member States change not only their regulations on services but also adapt their administrative procedures or organizations: K. Peglow, 'La libre prestation de services dans la directive n°2006/123/CE: Réflexion sur l'insertion de la directive dans le droit communautaire existant', RTDE (2008), 67–118.

[93] Reference to the Communication and the Press release in footnote 4.

consultations led to the formulation of four policy proposals by the European Commission in early 2017. These related to a new European Services e-card;[94] a proportionality assessment on national rules for professional services;[95] an improved notification of draft national laws on services;[96] and guidance for national reforms in the regulation of professional services. Since early 2017, legislative proposals have followed the EU legislative train[97] between the Council and the European Parliament (including consultations of Parliamentary Committees) with a view to complementing the Services Directive. During the latter phase, both soft-law and hard-law instruments were elaborated and used by the EU institutions to advance the completion of the Single Market in services. At the time of writing, the Juncker Commission is coming to an end, the agenda of the Single Market in services has not registered notable progress and the hard law instruments of the Services Package either are still under legislative review or have been set aside owing to a lack of consensus among Member States. The tepid progress achieved over the past decade has prompted some observers

[94] http://ec.europa.eu/DocsRoom/documents/20813
[95] http://ec.europa.eu/DocsRoom/documents/20504
[96] http://ec.europa.eu/DocsRoom/documents/20502
[97] For each proposal: www.europarl.europa.eu/legislative-train/theme-deeper-and-fairer-internal-market-with-a-strengthened-industrial-base-services-including-transport/file-services-e-card; www.europarl.europa.eu/legislative-train/theme-deeper-and-fairer-internal-market-with-a-strengthened-industrial-base-services-including-transport/file-services-notification-procedure; and www.europarl.europa.eu/legislative-train/theme-deeper-and-fairer-internal-market-with-a-strengthened-industrial-base-services-including-transport/file-proportionality-test

to speak of the 'un-singleness' of the EU Single Market in services.[98]

The Single Market in Services after Brexit
Since the British referendum and the decision of British citizens to leave the EU, an unprecedented legal situation is unfolding over the terms under which a Member State may leave the Union and the nature of ensuing trade ties.[99] One of the major arguments of the 'leave' campaign was for Britain to break away from the European internal market and the rules governing the four freedoms, particularly that governing the freedom of labour movement. The two parties have been engaged in complex negotiations over the nature of their future trade relations and the rules governing them, with the EU as the dominant trading partner of Britain on both the import and export sides. The nature of the post-Brexit trade relationship between the EU and Britain might vary widely, depending on the choice of integration model that is chosen. Among the options on the table are those characterizing the EU's links with Norway, Switzerland and Canada (i.e. a deep free trade agreement only) or trade rules that are anchored in WTO provisions. The complexity and starkness of implications deriving from the above choices has raised considerable uncertainty that weighs on the business and investment climates on both sides of the English Channel.

[98] F. Erikson and R. Georgieva, 'What is Wrong with the Single Market?' *European Center for International Political Economy*, 2016.
[99] The Art. 50 negotiation process and principles for the UK's departure from the European Union: https://ec.europa.eu/commission/brexit-negotiations_en

5.3 The EU and Global Trade in Services[100]

As the world's leading exporter of services, the EU assigns to services trade and investment liberalization a central place in its trade diplomacy. The aims that the EU pursues with third parties in the services realm are essentially different and more recent than those enshrined in the EU's six-decade-old foundational treaty. Indeed, while the Treaty of Rome laid down clear and ambitious aims for the internal market and intra-EU trade in services, the legal sources from which the EU derives its international negotiating agenda are both more recent and modest. Indeed, the EU agenda on international trade in services came later, and gained significant traction only once the broad contours of the EC-1992 Single Market objectives came into being – a process that coincided with the launch of the Uruguay Round negotiations on trade in services towards the end of the 1980s.[101]

The EU's approach in services trade has been, and remains, broadly anchored in the pursuit of negotiating advances under the multilateral framework contained in the WTO's GATS, a body of rules the development of which the EU helped to shape. While the EU continued to profess its faith in the WTO process, and in fact maintained for a while a moratorium on its participation in preferential trade

---

[100] In contrast with intra-EU trade, international trade in services covers all major trading relation of the EU with third countries (countries outside the EU).

[101] P. Eeckhout, 'Constitutional Concepts for Free Trade in Services' in G. De Burca and J. Scott (eds.), *The EU and the WTO. Legal and Constitutional Issues* (Oxford: Hart Publishing, 2001), p. 212.

liberalization initiatives in the early years of the Doha Development Agenda, the protracted stalemate in WTO talks since the mid-2000s has prompted the EU to respond to private sector pressure and engage in a large and growing network of bilateral, regional and, most recently, plurilateral, initiatives aimed at WTO+ rule making and market-opening advances in the services field.[102] Several such initiatives concern ASEAN Member States, with agreements already concluded with Singapore and Vietnam and under negotiation with Indonesia and Malaysia.

5.3.1 The EU and a Multilateral Agreement for Trade in Services

The EU's growing interest in services as an engine of growth and pro-competitive regulation and its decision to lend support to what remained initially a predominantly American push to place services on the global trade agenda paralleled the rising tide of intra- and extra-EU services trade that was observed from the middle of the 1970s onwards. The American position found increasing (albeit uneven) echo within the EU.[103] The then United States Trade

---

[102] As we shall see throughout this part, the reasons, circumstances, timing and content of the EU's trade agreements EU vary a great deal, and seem to concur with the findings of Craig VanGrasstek in 'The Political Economy of Services in Regional Trade Agreements', OECD Trade Policy Working Papers, 2011, 112, who speaks about the EU's trade agreements as 'multifaceted undertakings'.

[103] In the United States, influential businessmen advocated the inclusion of services in the Trade Act of 1974: G. Feketekuty, International Trade in

Representative (USTR), William Brock, advanced a two-pronged agenda focusing in turn on the development of a body of multilateral provisions and an institutional framework to govern international services transactions, followed by a process aimed at securing the reduction or elimination of obstacles, both discriminatory and non-discriminatory, to international trade in services.[104] The American efforts proved successful, as services were placed on the agenda of the General Agreement on Tariffs and Trade (GATT) ministerial meeting in Punta del Este in September 1986.[105]

The EU would ultimately join the United States in advocating the inclusion of services in the multilateral trading

Services: an Overview and Blueprint for Negotiations (Cambridge, MA: An American Enterprise Institut/Ballinger Publication, 1988), appendix 300–1.

[104] W. E. Brock, 'A Simple Plan for Negotiating on Trade in Services', The World Economy (1982), 237–8 in H. B. Malmgren, 'Negotiating International Rules for Trade in Services', *World Economy* 8 (1985), p. 19 and M. Gibbs and M. Mashayekhi, 'Services: Cooperation for Development', *Journal of World Trade Law* 22 (1988), 86. Some authors contested this approach as unnecessary. According to them, services do not need a separate agreement since they were either embodied in goods or persons: H. G. Grubel, 'All Traded Services are Embodied in Materials or People', World Economy, 3 (1987), 319 and C. J. Berr and L. Reboud, 'Les services' in T. Flory (ed.), *La Communauté européenne et le GATT. Évaluations des accords du cycle d'Uruguay* (Apogée, publication du centre de recherches européenne de l'Université Rennes I, 1995), p. 120.

[105] R. J. Krommenacker, 'Multilateral Services Negotiations: From Interest-Lateralism to Reasoned Multilateralism in the Context of Servicization' in E. U. Petersmann and M. Hilf (eds.), *The New GATT Round of Multilateral Trade Negotiations – Legal and Economic Problems* (Deventer: Kluwer, 1988), p. 457.

system but with a number of specificities reflecting, *inter alia*, the mixed competence prevailing in services regulation between the Commission and the Member States; the still dominant presence of state-owned service providers in key service sectors (e.g. energy, telecommunications, postal services and air transport); the more defensive attitudes of Southern European Member States towards an ambitious liberalizing agenda; the lack of a clear intra-EU road map for full market integration in services (which would soon be articulated in the EC-92 Single Market drive); and calls for key sectors, particularly the audio-visual and cultural industries, to be left outside the negotiations in light of their sensitive nature.[106]

Despite the strong reluctance of numerous developing countries, services were placed on the Uruguay Round's negotiating agenda agreed by ministers in Punta del Este in September 1986,[107] which called for the 'progressive

---

[106] The specificity of the EU position is still topical today, and is high on the agenda of any EU negotiations in the field of international trade in services.

[107] The Uruguay Round ministerial declaration [MIN(86)/6] at Punta del Este was a very carefully drafted declaration: 'Negotiations in this area shall aim to establish a multilateral framework of principles and rules for trade in services, including elaboration of possible disciplines for individual sectors, with a view to expansion of such trade under conditions of transparency and progressive liberalization and as means of promoting economic growth of all trading partners and the development of developing countries. Such a framework shall respect the policy objectives of national laws and regulations applying to services and shall take into account the work of relevant international organizations. GATT procedures and practices shall apply to these negotiations. A Group of Negotiations on Services is established to deal

liberalization' – and, if possible, abolition – of non-tariff barriers that inhibit international trade in services.[108]

At the time of the Uruguay Round's launch, a number of scholars had suggested that the EU legal framework be used as a model for the progressive liberalization of trade in services.[109] However, it quickly became obvious that the objectives of the multilateral journey initiated in Punta del Este, which aimed to secure progressively freer trade and investment in services through periodic negotiating rounds, was significantly less ambitious than the EU's internal quest to integrate the markets of its Member States via a *sui generis* institutional and legal environment.[110]

---

with these matters. Participation in the negotiations under this Part of the Declaration will be open to the same countries as under Part I. GATT secretariat support will be provided, with technical support from other organizations as decided by the Group of Negotiations on Services.'

[108] E. U. Petersmann, 'The Transformation of the World Trading System through the 1994 Agreement Establishing the WTO', *European Journal of International Law*, 2 (1995), 200. The author lists the types of restrictions to trade in services that should be tackled, especially with regard to market access. C. D. Ehlermann and G. Campogrande, 'Rules on Services in the EEC: A Model for Negotiating World-Wide Rules' in Petersmann and Hilf (eds.), *The New GATT Round of Multilateral Trade Negotiations – Legal and Economic Problems*, pp. 481–98.

[109] Ehlermann and Campogrande (1988), p. 484.

[110] We refer here to the unprecedented decision-making process of the EU (the use of qualified majority in the Council), as well as the judicial system presented in the Treaty of Rome. We also have in mind the founding principles of EU law, i.e. direct effect (*Van Gend en Loos* (26/62) [1963] E.C.R. 1) and supremacy (*Costa* v. *ENEL* (6/64) [1964] E.C.R. 585) which create a unique regional legal environment in the EU that knows no parallel at the multilateral level.

The Uruguay Round negotiations in services proved challenging for the EU from the outset, as it needed to clarify its own mandate. Indeed, since its inception, the Treaty of Rome has included a legal basis for the negotiation of international trade agreements within the ambit of the EU's common commercial policy (CCP). However, the relevant chapter of the Treaty referred to trade in goods and not in services.[111] An opinion was requested from the ECJ to establish the nature of the EU's competence in the services field and decide whether the EU only (i.e. exclusive Community competence) or the EU and Member States (i.e. shared competence) should characterize the conduct of the negotiations.

In Opinion 1/94, the ECJ considered the definition of services being contemplated under the multilateral negotiations, which referred to four modes of supplying services. The ECJ established that '[a]s regards cross-frontier supplies, the service is rendered by a supplier established in one country to a consumer residing in another. The supplier does not move to the consumer's country; nor, conversely, does the

---

[111] F. Jacobs, 'The Completion of the Internal Market v the Incomplete Common Commercial Policy' in Kostadinidis (ed.), *The Legal Regulation of the EC's External Relations after the Completion of the Internal Market* (Dartmouth: Aldershot, 1996), pp. 3–18. Some authors have suggested the need for a flexible interpretation of this chapter of the Treaty of Rome, since international trade is constantly evolving: P. Eeckhout, *The European Internal Market and International Trade: A Legal Analysis* (Oxford: European Community Law Series, 1994), p. 399 and C. W. A. Timmermans, 'Common Commercial Policy (article 113 EEC) and the International Trade in Services', *Du droit international au droit de l'intégration. Liber Amicorum Pierre Pescatore* (Baden-Baden: Nomos Verlagsgesellschaft, 1987), p. 684.

consumer move to the supplier's country. That situation is, therefore, not unlike trade in goods, which is unquestionably covered by the common commercial policy within the meaning of the Treaty.' However, the ECJ noted that '[t]he same cannot be said of the other three modes of supplying services covered by the GATS, namely, consumption abroad, commercial presence and the presence of natural persons ... [which] are not covered by the common commercial policy.'[112] The Treaty of Rome Treaty was amended in the light of the ECJ's opinion and, since 1997, the CCP has referred to trade in both goods and services.[113]

The Uruguay Round produced a services agreement – the GATS 1994 – that lay outside the scope of the GATT 1994. Presented in a separate, parallel document, the GATS largely echoes the structure of the original GATT but with several important distinctions that are uniquely tailored to meet the specificities of services trade. Negotiated in the heyday of the Washington consensus and of Francis Fukuyama's proclaimed 'end of history', the GATS has a wide scope, with all services (including audio-visual services) being covered by the final agreement.[114] Article 1 of the GATS states that

---

[112] ECJ 15 November 1994, Opinion 1/94, E.C.R. p. I-5267, points 44 and 46.
[113] The relevant article is Art. 207 TFEU, the former Art. 133 of the EC Treaty, paragraph 4 of which sets apart audiovisual and cultural services as well as social, education and health services.
[114] Article I, paragraph 3(b), 'except services supplied in the exercise of governmental authority': G. Feketekuty, 'Assessing and Improving the Architecture of GATS' in P. Sauvé and R. Stern (eds.), *GATS 2000. New Directions in Service Trade Liberalization* (Washington DC: Brookings Institution Press, 2000), p. 104.

'trade in services is defined by the supply of a service' through four modes of supply: cross-border supply; consumption abroad; commercial presence; and movement of persons. However, the Agreement affirms the pragmatic principle of 'progressive liberalization', affording scope for parties to schedule specific commitments on national treatment and market access (subject to any scheduled limitations thereto) while retaining considerable regulatory immunity in non-scheduled sectors, sub-sectors and/or modes of supply. Additionally, the GATS features a number of annexes that deal with sectoral (e.g. finance, telecommunications, maritime and air transport) or horizontal (labour mobility and most favoured nation (MFN) exemptions) specificities, all of which are subject to renegotiation through periodic multilateral negotiating rounds.[115]

Article VII of the GATS codifies the principle of mutual recognition. As noted earlier, such a principle was a centrally important means of promoting regulatory approximation in intra-EU trade in services. Entitled 'Recognition', Article VII of the GATS encourages parties to take into account the 'education, experience, licences, certification obtained from a particular country'. Article XVI of the GATS establishes the cornerstone concept of 'market access', which is once more a notion that is familiar within the intra-

---

[115] The architecture was considered by some scholars as 'à la carte' and potentially less effective: P. Sauvé, 'Regional *versus* Multilateral Approaches to Services and Investment Liberalization: Anything to worry about?' *Regionalism and Multilateralism after the Uruguay Round* (1997), 429.

EU trade environment.[116] The GATS, alongside agricultural talks, foresaw a built-in negotiating mandate, such that, eighteen years down the road, the fate of services negotiations resumed prior to (and subsequently incorporated into) the late 2001 launch of the Doha Development Agenda has yet to be sealed.

5.3.2 *The EU and Bilateral Agreements on Trade in Services*

As noted above, an important derivative consequence of the stalled Doha Round has been the surge of preferential agreements of a bilateral and regional and often trans-regional nature, such as the Comprehensive and Progressive Trans-Pacific Partnership (CPTPP), most of which now routinely extend to services. At the end of 2017, some 152 services-related PTAs had been notified to the WTO, which was half as much as the number obtaining in 2012.[117] The above trend is one in which the EU has been particularly active around the

---

[116] Some scholars have underlined that, for the first time, a multilateral trade agreement targets more than discriminatory obstacles to trade, but they have also regretted the lack of definition of the concept of market access: B. Hoekman, 'Services and Intellectual Property Rights' in S. Collins and B. Bosworth (eds.), *The New GATT. Implications for the US* (Washington DC: The Brookings Institution, 1994), pp. 85 and 89. The concept of market access was considered in the litigation on gambling WT/DS285; cf. comments on the litigation: 'Gambling – with Regulation and Market Access in the GATS', *Legal Issues of Economic Integration* (2005), 231–4.

[117] See the WTO RTA database at: http://rtais.wto.org/UI/publicsummary table.aspx

globe in recent years. In pursuing services liberalization along preferential lines, the EU has had several key policy motivations.

One important subset of agreements can be categorized as either precursors to EU accession or responses to neighbourhood policy impulses. To varying degrees, such agreements help EU trading partners to converge towards the *acquis communautaire*, prompting them to embed EU compatible or proximate features in the domestic laws and regulations of EU negotiating partners. Talks towards the creation of so-called Association Agreements of which Deep and Comprehensive Free Trade Areas (DCFTAs) form important constituent parts and which typically extend to services trade have been initiated with a diverse set of actors in the EU's immediate periphery.

A second impulse guiding the selection of partners with whom the EU has entered into PTAs extending to services relates to the policy aim of neutralizing the preferences granted to the EU's major trading partners and competitors, particularly the United States. Agreements fitting this pattern, almost invariably negotiated or concluded *after* the completion of a PTA between the United States and key trading partners of the EU, responds to the need of EU business interests to enjoy the same degree of preferential access that is afforded to US firms in third-country markets. Agreements of this type include those signed with Mexico (concluded in 1997 in the wake of the North American Free Trade Agreement (NAFTA) of 1994 but whose generally modest provisions and commitments in the services field were added in 2001 and upgraded in a renegotiation concluded in April 2018); Chile,[118] in which a considerably more ambitious and innovative agreement in the services field entered into force in 2003, fresh on the heels of the US-Chile FTA that was concluded in 2002; and South Korea, in which the first of a newer generation of comprehensive EU PTAs with extensive disciplines and provisions on services trade and investment was negotiated in parallel with the US-Korea FTA but which actually entered into force before the latter agreement in July 2011.

In 2012, the EU also completed negotiations on an FTA with the Andean countries of Peru and Colombia, both of which had previously signed FTAs with the United States that came into force in 2009 and 2011, respectively. Meanwhile, following the failed attempt to negotiate a bloc-to-bloc agreement with the ten Member States of ASEAN, the negotiation of which was halted in March 2009, the EU embarked on a series of bilateral negotiations with four ASEAN Member States – Indonesia, Malaysia, Singapore and Vietnam – concluding agreements with the latter two. In December 2016, the EU completed negotiations with Singapore on an FTA that featured an ambitious services chapter (which can once again be seen as neutralizing the preferences granted by Singapore to the United States in an FTA that entered into force in 2004). The EU–Vietnam Agreement was concluded.

On the bilateral front, the EU has also been negotiating with a number of major trading partners. These include

---

[118] The text of the agreement can be found at: http://eurlex.europa.eu/Lex UriServ/LexUriServ.do?uri=OJ:L:2002:352:0003:1439:EN:PDF

Canada, with which the EU concluded the CETA in late 2013, the negotiation of which was launched in May 2009[119] and which promised several novel advances in the EU's treatment of services and investment in PTAs, notably the first-ever adoption of a negative list approach to market opening in services markets (in respect of both cross-border trade and investment in services). The EU is Canada's second-largest trading partner, while Canada is the EU's eleventh-biggest trading partner. The year 2018 also saw the EU conclude what constitutes its largest-ever bilateral agreement, agreeing to the terms of a comprehensive pact with Japan, the world's third-largest economy.

A pending PTA of importance in the services field is that which the EU has been negotiating, so far inconclusively, with India since 2007. Finally, the EU launched negotiations, which were subsequently suspended, with the United States on what would have represented, if successfully concluded, its most ambitious ever bilateral PTA. Services trade and the quest for trade- and investment-facilitating regulatory convergence and cooperation were indeed at the core of the proposed Transatlantic Trade and Investment Partnership (TTIP) talks that got under way in

---

[119] Joint Report on the EU and Canada Scoping Exercise, 2009: http://trade.ec.europa.eu/doclib/docs/2009/march/tradoc_142470.pdf See
L. Biuković and J. Mathis, 'Enhanced Regulatory Cooperation in the Canada: EU Comprehensive Trade Agreement' *Legal Issues of Economic Integration* 1 (2012), 1–2 and, more preciously on services in the CETA, J. Anthony VanDuzer, 'A Critical Look at the Prospects for Robust Rules for Services in Preferential Trading Agreements', *Legal Issues of Economic Integration*, 1 (2012) 29–49.

July 2013 among the world's two dominant forces in services trade.[120]

The quest to deepen bilateral trade relations with the United States went back to the 1990s, when, in 1995, parallel to the conclusion of the Uruguay Round and the entering into force of the GATS and the NAFTA, the EU and the United States decided to launch the New Transatlantic Agenda (NTA). The NTA's main objective was the creation of a New Transatlantic Marketplace (NTMA) whose core focus would be to tackle trade-inhibiting non-tariff barriers and to promote the liberalization of services trade on the basis of the 'home country' principle. Such a non-legally binding agenda progressed slowly, and the ambitious NTMA objective was eventually shelved, giving way to the Transatlantic Dialogue that was focused on regulatory dialogue and the quest for mutual recognition agreements in the goods trade area.

The Doha Round stalemate revived interest in renewed transatlantic trade talks. At the end of 2011, a High Level Working Group on Jobs and Growth was jointly established by the EU's Trade Commissioner and the Office of the USTR, whose final report was issued in early 2013[121] calling for a re-launch of transatlantic trade discussions and the negotiation of a comprehensive, legally binding, agreement on trade

---

[120] For more data, see http://ec.europa.eu/trade/policy/countries-and-regions/countries/united-states/

[121] The interim report: http://trade.ec.europa.eu/doclib/docs/2012/june/tradoc_149557.pdf The final report: http://trade.ec.europa.eu/doclib/docs/2013/february/tradoc_150519.pdf

and investment issues[122] for which the European Commission secured a negotiating mandate from the European Council in June 2013.[123]

A third set of PTAs covering services that the EU has been involved with has sought to achieve economies of scale in rule making and market opening through negotiations conducted on a trans-regional, bloc-to-bloc, basis. Such a strategy, pursued to date with ASEAN (subsequently abandoned), the member countries of the Common Market of the South (Mercosur; still ongoing) and Central America (via the EU–Central America FTA) has generated mixed results. As noted earlier, when faced with a regional grouping that is characterized by a marked diversity of income levels and implementation capacities,[124] in 2009 the EU dropped the idea of a bloc-to-bloc compact with ASEAN in favour of a series of bilateral PTAs with selected ASEAN Member States.

Negotiations with the Member States of Mercosur, which were launched as far back as 1999 and resumed in 2010 after a three-year hiatus, have encountered recurring challenges since their inception, owing largely to seemingly unbridgeable divides on issues linked to agricultural trade.

---

[122] An independent economic impact assessment of the TTIP was also carried out and presented in 2013: http://trade.ec.europa.eu/doclib/docs/2013/march/tradoc_150737.pdf

[123] For information on the negotiation guidelines, see: http://europa.eu/rapid/press-release_IP-13-548_en.htm

[124] ASEAN is characterized by extreme gaps in per capita income levels, there being a 45 to 1 ratio (in PPP terms) between Singapore, the regional grouping's richest Member State, and Myanmar, its poorest.

To date, the FTA agreed in June 2012 between the EU and the member countries of the Central American Common Market has been the only successful bloc-to-bloc agreement that the EU has completed. Interestingly, the latter agreement came in the aftermath of the FTA that was concluded in 2004 between the five members of the Central American Common Market, the Dominican Republic and the United States (CAFTA-DR), such that, beyond the objective of negotiating on a bloc-to-bloc basis, preference neutralization imperatives could also be argued to lie behind the EU's negotiating strategy in Central America.

A fourth and final set of PTAs that address services that have entered into force or been pursued by the EU relates to a series of negotiations that the EU has had to initiate in the wake of an adverse ruling regarding the WTO (in)compatibility of its non-reciprocal trade relationship with countries from the African–Caribbean-Pacific (ACP) grouping. Such a ruling by the WTO's Dispute Settlement Body prompted the EU to pursue a series of reciprocal economic partnership agreements (EPAs) with seven regional groupings of ACP countries – five in Africa, one in the Pacific and one in the Caribbean.

To date, the 2008 CARIFORUM[125]–EU EPA[126] is the only agreement that features services and investment

---

[125] Antigua and Barbuda, Bahamas, Barbados, Belize, Dominica, Dominican Republic, Grenada, Guyana, Haiti, Jamaica, St Lucia, St Vincent and the Grenadines, St Kitts and Nevis, Suriname, Trinidad and Tobago.

[126] The text of the EPA: http://eur-lex.europa.eu/LexUriServ/LexUriServ.do?uri=OJ:L:2008:289:0003:1955:EN:PDF

disciplines to have been concluded with ACP countries.[127]

[127] A number of factors may be seen as explaining why, among all ACP regional groupings, the CARIFORUM countries were both willing and able to conclude a comprehensive EPA with the EU. Chief among these were the strong commitment manifested to negotiating an EPA by the region's political leadership and the high level of technical preparation on offer in the region, honed largely in the context of the failed Free Trade Area of the Americas (FTAA) negotiations. A complex set of dynamics served to reinforce such a commitment. There was, firstly, the region's desire to bind existing levels of access to the EU market and to preclude the possibility that such preferential access become the target of WTO dispute settlement procedures. Secondly, the region deliberately sought to expand its access to the EC's lucrative services market. Thirdly, the region needed to diversify its export base and derive higher value from its exports in the face of the combined effects of preference erosion and the decline in EC agricultural support policies for Caribbean producers of bananas and sugar. Fourthly, given that the process of intra-Caribbean regional integration was considered by many as suboptimal and suffering from an implementation deficit, the EPA's emphasis on regional groupings was seen as offering a desirable boost to the CARIFORUM integration process. Fifthly, by supporting the creation and/or strengthening of regional regimes in a number of disciplines such as, *inter alia*, competition policy, government procurement, services and investment, the EPA came to be seen as offering a tool with which to advance CARIFORUM competitiveness, promote productive capacity and innovation in new products and production systems. Sixthly, the region as a whole bought into the EPA's 'signaling' properties, viewing it as a powerful means to reassure foreign investors and development partners over the region's commitment to continued economic reforms. Another factor that facilitated the conclusion of a comprehensive EPA was that the negotiations pitted two partners that had both reached an advanced stage in their own internal process of regional integration, including in terms of the requisite machinery of regional inter-governmental cooperation. In addition, CARIFORUM was not as troubled as other ACP regions by the problem of overlapping regionalism, in which member countries are part of

The CARIFORUM–EU EPA marked a new sort of PTA, as both sides agreed to open their markets but in an asymmetric manner, taking into account the marked differences in economic development levels between the Parties.[128] The agreement features a number of novel advances in the services field, notably in its treatment of labour mobility, its detailed provisions on tourism services (including competition-related provisions to be applied in the sector), as well as significant doses of aid for trade linked to the implementation priorities of the CARIFORUM parties.[129]

> different integration groupings. CARIFORUM's capacity to negotiate a comprehensive EPA was furthermore facilitated by the fact that the region had already acquired significant experience in negotiating trade issues in several negotiating fora. Within the CARICOM grouping, the negotiation of the Single Market helped to identify barriers to internal trade as well as highlight the sectors with the greatest export potential. Hence, CARICOM Members had a head start in identifying their key negotiating priorities, both offensive and defensive. Likewise, the negotiation of the CARICOM-Dominican Republic FTA provided further insights on the level of existing barriers to trade within the CARIFORUM region and clear indications of what the future liberalization agenda should look like within the sub-region. All of these above processes, together with experience gained in multilateral negotiations at the WTO, contributed to improving the quality of the region's negotiating skills and boosted the region's comfort level in dealing with many of the policy areas, old and new, that would become subject to EPA negotiations.

[128] A. B. Zampetti and J. Lodge (eds.), *The CARIFORUM-EU Economic Partnership. A practitioner's Analysis* (Kluwer, 2011).

[129] P. Sauvé and N. Ward, 'The EC–CARIFORUM EPA: Assessing the Outcome on Services and Investment', European Center for International Political Economy (ECIPE), 2009.

5.3.3 The EU and a Plurilateral Agreement on Services

The lack of forward movement in the Doha Round and increasing frustration over the quest for an explicit multilateral consensus in the WTO prompted a number of countries, including those of the EU, to contemplate an agenda of 'progressive liberalization' of services trade outside the GATS framework.

In early 2012, a group of WTO members dubbed the 'Really Good Friends of Services'[130] agreed to launch a plurilateral negotiation on services.[131] The main idea behind the latter initiative was to (re)create a dynamic in the centrally important and vibrant field of services and achieve a critical enough mass of participants and trade coverage for the resulting negotiations to be ultimately embedded within the WTO and its benefits extended to all WTO Members on an MFN basis. As the world's two leading services exporters, the United States and the EU could expect to reap the largest

---

[130] Australia, Canada, Chile, Colombia, Costa Rica (joined end of 2012), European Union, Hong Kong, Iceland, Israel (joined end of 2012), Japan, Mexico, New Zealand, Norway, Panama (joined end of 2012), Pakistan, Peru (joined end of 2012), Singapore (left the group in July 2012), South Korea, Switzerland, Taiwan, Turkey (joined end of 2012) and the United States.

[131] Also called a 'new type of services agreement': J. R. Vastine, 'A New Form of Services Trade Agreement Moving Ahead in Geneva: The International Services Agreement', *Economic Policy Vignette, 2012-11-04*, Center for Business and Public Policy, McDonough School of Business, Georgetown University, 9 September 2012 November: www.gcbpp.org/files/EPV/Vastine_ISA_11042012.pdf

gains from a possible plurilateral agreement,[132] which, because of its perceived exclusionary, club-like nature, was roundly criticized in emerging country circles.[133]

The EU tried to strike a more open stance towards the plurilateral negotiations, encouraging broad participation in the talks and the pursuit of a GATS-compatible set of rules so as to facilitate the agreement's future WTO anchoring. In so doing, the EU sought to avoid being seen as contributing to the further undermining of the Doha Round by participating in the plurilateral initiative.[134] Rebranded as TiSA (for Trade in Services Agreement), the plurilateral agreement's negotiating process was formally launched in the spring of 2013.

The European Commission turned to the European Council for a negotiating mandate. The latter was granted in March 2013. Before the TiSA talks were suspended in 2016 owing to important differences of views on key negotiating issues, notably in the digital realm, the EU continued to underline the importance of persuading major non-participant countries, such as Brazil, China and India but also the ASEAN countries, to eventually join the plurilateral negotiations (including through the inclusion of a TiSA accession clause). The EU's position also advocated 'new and

---

[132] G. C. Hufbauer, J. B. Jensen and S. Stephenson, *'Framework for the International Services Agreement'*, Final Draft, Washington, DC, Peterson Institute for International Economics, 24 February, 2012, 22.

[133] R. K. Devarakonda, 'Tale of Two Approaches: the WTO Torn Asunder' *Ibsa news*, 2012: www.ibsanews.com/tale-of-two-approaches-the-wto-torn-asunder/

[134] Therefore the 'multilateralization' of the ISA is ultimately the way according to the EU.

improved market access commitments'. A major concern of the EU related to the scope to 'multilateralize' TiSA, whereby the core concepts, definitions and overall negotiating architecture of the GATS should be preserved in TiSA while deepening (GATS+) commitments and advancing new rules for services trade in the digital age.[135] The EU also decided to carry out a Trade Sustainability Impact Assessment and, in June 2013, the European Commission launched a public dialogue on TiSA to solicit private, academic and other non-governmental views on the proposed agreement.[136]

For the EU, the success of the plurilateral negotiations meant preserving the WTO *acquis*[137] while progressing through both the adoption of new rules of services trade governance and deeper liberalization commitments, including in sectors that were not yet subject to GATS commitments.[138]

---

[135] 'Negotiations for a Plurilateral Agreement on Trade in services' European Commission, MEMO/12/107, 15 February 2013: http://trade.ec.europa.eu/doclib/docs/2013/february/tradoc_150552.pdf

[136] The European Commission calls the ISA the 'Trade in Services Agreement' (TiSA): http://trade.ec.europa.eu/doclib/docs/2013/june/tradoc_151374.pdf

[137] D. Chambovey, 'Swiss Negotiator: Regional trade deals are good for multilateralism', *Euractiv*, 2012, October: www.euractiv.com/specialreport-free-trade-growth/swiss-negotiator-regional-trade-interview-515255

[138] For a fuller discussion of TiSA and its prospects, see P. Sauvé (2013), 'A Plurilateral Agenda for Services? Assessing the case for a Trade in Services Agreement (TISA)', NCCR-Trade Working Paper No. 2013/29 (May) (Bern: World Trade Institute): www.nccr-trade.org/fileadmin/user_upload/nccr-trade.ch/wp2/publications/TISA_P_Sauve.pdf

5.4 Implications for ASEAN: Tentative Conclusions

While the EU is the world's leading actor in the field of international trade in services, advances in the governance of services trade have been significantly greater on the internal EU front than in the Union's trade relations with third countries. This is to be expected, given the nature of the European integration process and its stated aim of achieving an internal market for services that is characterized by the deepest level of regulatory convergence and approximation on offer in any of the world's major regional groupings. This section has thus naturally drawn attention to differences in the legal sources, instruments and institutional settings and the strategic approaches to intra- and extra-EU trade in services. The recurring use of soft law instruments (programmes, communication and strategies) in the field must be also kept in mind. Such instruments were either preceding or following important hard law instruments.

Ever since the entry into force of the 1957 Treaty of Rome, the EU has adopted an increasingly complete arsenal of legal rules, tools and institutional means to advance the agenda of services liberalization and market integration within the EU, guided by the ultimate aim of creating an internal market for services. All the legal instruments available under the Treaty of Rome, from the 'standstill' clause to negative and positive integration clauses, were and remain necessary to liberalize intra-EU trade in services and establish an internal services market. Equally important has been, and remains, the active role of key institutions such as the

European Commission, which has advanced a set of Directives to pry open service markets in services, and the ECJ, the critically central task of which has been to interpret negative integration clauses and ensure compliance with relevant EU law.

The depth and range of legal instruments and institutions deployed in the EU in pursuit of market integration objectives knows no equivalent. The uniqueness of the EU's achievements always needs to be borne in mind in pondering whether, how and to what extent the lessons from the EU's ongoing experiment in market integration are replicable in other regional settings and policy contexts. In most instances, and notably in ASEAN, whose Member States have collectively affirmed a desire to establish a fully fledged economic community on the basis of a detailed integration blueprint, the EU model is not easily transposable, resting as it does on a degree of pooling of regulatory sovereignty that few regional groupings appear capable of replicating or even aspire to. It also bears noting that EU advances relate in no small measure to the Union's 'first mover' advantages, with progress rooted in more than 60 years of policy- and rule-making experimentation on the internal front and close to three decades of external experimentation. Such a path has afforded all EU stakeholders – Member States, the European Commission, regulatory agencies, the ECJ and private actors, considerable space in which to learn by doing, make mistakes, learn from them and fine-tune an evolving governance regime for services production, trade and investment.

While its aims have, of essence, been more modest on the global stage, the EU has nonetheless engaged the world through all possible negotiating means at its disposal – multilaterally in the WTO's GATS, and preferentially through a series of bilateral, regional, plurilateral and bloc-to-bloc agreements aimed at affording EU services and service providers wider and progressively freer markets in which to operate while also harnessing the gains to be had from the reciprocal opening of the EU's internal market to efficient third-country services and service suppliers. With six decades worth of accumulated knowledge in prying open services markets at its disposal, the EU has unprecedented experience in the setting of norms and standards with which to tackle a field of considerable regulatory complexity and diversity such as services. Such attributes naturally afford the EU important weight in shaping the texture of international trade negotiations in the services field.

Chapter 6

Concluding Thoughts

The Member States of the Association of South East Asian Nations (ASEAN) set themselves the ambitious aim of establishing a region-wide economic community by 2025. In striving to achieve this objective, this volume addressed a number of factors, internal to both ASEAN's integration process and the region's deepening ties with a dense layer of external economic partners, that lend support to the conclusion that service sector reforms, and trade and investment in services more particularly, will and must continue to occupy a place of choice in ASEAN collective efforts.

The region's rapid economic advance and the steady rise in living standards achieved in recent decades, anchored as it has been in external demand and through insertion into regional and global value chains, could not have proceeded without steady improvements in the efficiency with which the region's underlying services ecosystem has underpinned productivity growth in upstream and downstream industries. While such efficiency gains have often resulted as much from unilateral than from negotiated policy efforts, more institutionalized policy approaches have been exerting an increasing influence on the regional grouping's policy path since the late 1990s. The growth of China and India, the competitive threat that both pose and the concomitant pressures to retain investment attractiveness relative to the two regional hegemons and to place regional ties on a firmer, and more predictable, legal footing, have hastened the trend towards more treaty-centric forms of trade and investment ties in ASEAN. The region's emergence as an increasingly important source of outward foreign direct investment (FDI) further explains the growing shift towards – and rising homegrown political demand for – negotiated (i.e. treaty-based) forms of reciprocal market opening within the region and beyond.

The road ahead confronts ASEAN Member States (AMS) with numerous (and simultaneous) challenges with which other successful middle-income emerging nations are also contending in a world of heightened production fragmentation and significant trade policy turbulence. These include the need to move up value chains and escape the 'middle income trap' through continued improvements in product and process innovation and sustained gains in labour productivity. It also entails coping with the demographic transition that significant improvements in living conditions tend to usher in, while also addressing the derived demand for enhanced social safety nets. It also implies responding to increasingly assertive middle-class demands for better overall governance and the improved delivery of a range of services with public good characteristics, such as health, education, transportation, press and Internet freedoms. And it also implies deciding on whether ASEAN's future is best served through continued cohesion and concerted collective action or through greater freedom for individual Member States to join other preferential groupings potentially affording third countries ASEAN+ outcomes.

Moving forward, and as development levels continue to rise, the AMS will confront the need to rebalance what for most of them will be continued high dependence on external markets with more endogenous sources of (consumption-based) growth. Much like neighbouring China, such rebalancing of essence will entail a shift, which is already well under way in the majority of (but not all) AMS, towards a more service-centric development model. It is also one that may result in a progressive slowing of economic growth, given that productivity rises in services are harder to come by. This only heightens the need for ASEAN countries to speed up needed structural reforms in product and labour markets and continue to invest in the human capital of their citizens so as to endow them with the skills required to integrate successfully into a world economy that is characterized by ever-accelerating change and technology-fused disruption.

In meeting the ASEAN Economic Community's (AEC's) Blueprint 2025 objectives, AMS face the additional task of devising policy paths flexible enough to accommodate and reconcile continued steep gaps in income levels and implementation capacities across the regional grouping. Among ASEAN's many unique characteristics is the remarkable diversity of development levels characterizing its membership, by far the greatest of all the world's major regional groupings. The region's long-standing and novel practice of promoting deeper integration in a progressive manner and on the basis of variable geometry approaches should continue to serve it well. Such flexibility will prove especially important given that service sector reforms raise complex issues of regulatory convergence and approximation for which the strengthening of regulatory institutions and enforcement capacities are often critical prerequisites.

As AMS states pursue their agreed 2025 journey in the services field, a number of distinct policy issues need to move up the regional policy agenda. A first challenge relates to the production of a regional public good that is singularly lacking in the services realm: data. While ASEAN is hardly unique in this regard, the current paucity of empirical evidence on two-way trade and investment flows within and beyond the region in the services field and its disaggregated sectoral composition impose genuine limits to informed economic analysis and the formulation of trade and investment policies. Similarly, the lack of region-wide data on intra-industry trade and especially on the services content of exports (be they natural resources, agro-food or manufactures) as well as on the movement of service providers, without which any assessment of the policy traction generated by the various mutual recognition agreements otherwise agreed by AMS cannot be conducted, all need to be remedied through deeper collaboration among the region's under-resourced statistical agencies.

A second challenge arising in services concerns the need, today readily acknowledged but not yet effected, to update the ASEAN Framework Agreement on Services (AFAS) rule book. This should be done in a manner analogous to the major facelift performed in the investment field a few years ago through the adoption of the ASEAN Comprehensive Investment Agreement (ACIA). AMS cannot arguably meet the deep integration targets that they have set for themselves in the services field without revisiting the incomplete and outdated set of rules governing services trade among them. An exercise aimed at embedding a number of best practices in services regulation, many of them already practised by ASEAN as a whole or by individual AMS under various preferential agreements entered into with key trading partners since AFAS was devised in 1994, has become a critical necessity. Such a process could usefully anchor the region's integration process in a modern and comprehensive set of disciplines rooted in the regulatory realities of a world of trade in tasks and digital growth.

Advancing an ambitious and forward-looking services agenda with an outdated rule book is likely to prove problematic and inadequate for dismantling the many unduly burdensome or outright restrictive measures maintained behind borders that are likely to frustrate the attainment of ASEAN-wide objectives. The professed reluctance of AMS to litigate the removal of measures impeding the freer flow of services and service providers, and the lack of a supranational legal architecture through which to challenge non-compliance with region-wide commitments, arguably increase the need for a rule-making overhaul, particularly as regards disciplines on trade- and investment-inhibiting non-discriminatory regulatory conduct. Two-way interaction and dialogue is needed between the nascent ASEAN Trade in Services Agreement (ATISA) process and recent negotiating advances regarding disciplines on domestic regulation in services made at the WTO in Geneva.

The unfolding digital revolution and the need to address significant digital divides within and between ASEAN Member States call for stepped-up efforts towards enhanced regional digital governance. The question arises, as it does elsewhere, including at the World Trade Organization (WTO) in the context of ongoing plurilateral discussions on e-commerce, of the extent to which trade and investment diplomacy, alongside other policy domains, can be harnessed to this end. The ATISA talks currently proceeding would do well to draw on the increasingly rich harvest of provisions on digital governance found in latest-generation PTAs, starting perhaps with the Comprehensive and Progressive Trans-Pacific Partnership (CPTPP) to which four key AMS accounting for a predominant share of aggregate regional services trade are already bound.

The unfurling digital revolution is one towards which ASEAN countries cannot stay passive. The far-reaching changes arising from the so-called 'new industrial revolution' requires sound policy responses. Calls for liberalizing imports of intermediate inputs (goods and services), reducing trade and establishment costs through trade and investment facilitation, establishing a digital governance regime, strengthening intellectual property (IP) protection, and enhancing the performance of investment promotion agencies (IPAs) can all be expected to increase.

Digital technologies enable new forms of services trade by making it technologically feasible and fostering the emergence of new ways of delivering services. This is the case of information and communications technology (ICT)-related services (services related to the production, use and maintenance of ICT); Internet-enabled services (services that used to be non-tradeable, but can now be provided over the Internet); and digital services (such as cloud computing). Digitalization is also contributing to the wider and deeper 'servicification' of manufacturing. Producing goods now relies on the greater use of service inputs, such as engineering, sales or research and development undertaken in house or outsourced, domestically and internationally. This is often coordinated through digital networks. In parallel, services are also increasingly being embedded in goods and new forms of complementarities between goods and services are arising: smartphones allow access to an ever-wider range of services. Moreover, manufacturers also increasingly themselves produce and sell services. Data and associated digital technologies are also powering a manufacturing revolution built on digital services. At the same time, the growing service content of manufacturing activities, and of goods more generally, enabled by the digital transformation complicates the way in which trade policy (which is often still based on a distinction between goods and services) is applied. All are policy challenges that AMS will need to confront in deepening their e-ASEAN journey, harnessing the potential of digital technologies and addressing far-reaching internal gaps in infrastructure, institutional and regulatory regimes and levels of digital literacy and entrepreneurship. For gains from digital technologies to materialize, constraints to the adoption of technology must be overcome, notably in relation to market access and skills. Workers require new skills to operate new technologies. By some estimates, approximately 35 per cent of skills demanded for jobs across industries will change by

2020.[1] This represents a drastic and rapid change to which education and vocational training systems in ASEAN will need to adapt.[2]

A further challenge that the region faces concerns the need to raise the bar higher on the services liberalization front. Despite the progress achieved under the various market opening packages pursued (but not always fully implemented) under AFAS to date, the region continues to maintain a high overall level of restrictiveness in services trade and investment relative to the rest of the world. This not only contradicts the stated aim of realizing an economic community but also acts as a punitive tax on region-wide economic efficiency. The fact that AMS have chosen to cap *intra-ASEAN* foreign equity limitations at 70 per cent in the context of a *completed* AEC sums up such policy ambivalence – a stance paradoxically taken with regard to the most important mode of supplying services across borders. This volume's review of ASEAN-wide competitiveness, logistics and governance-related performance points to areas in which stepped-up collective and country-specific efforts need to be made to keep pace with regional competitors and enhance the regional grouping's doing business and investment climate performance and rankings. Progress in freeing-up region-wide labour mobility will also be required to give life – and

---

[1] The estimate from the World Economic Forum (2016) is based on a survey of large global and national employers that was conducted in the first half of 2015.
[2] See Batshur Gootiz (2018), '*Services Negotiations in Southeast Asia: Implications for Low-Income Countries in the Region*' (Geneva: International Centre for Trade and Sustainable Development).

commercial meaning – to the mutual recognition agreements to which ASEAN Member States have agreed.

Meanwhile, care needs to be taken in ensuring that the multiplicity of external liberalization initiatives pursued or concluded by ASEAN collectively (e.g. the Regional Comprehensive Economic Partnership (RCEP)) and by individual Member States (e.g. the CPTPP and EU-Vietnam) in the services field do not afford third countries better access to ASEAN markets than that enjoyed by AMS under AFAS. In developing ATISA, AMS should agree to a most favoured nation (MFN) treatment clause targeted at avoiding such a risk and ensuring that any regionally agreed liberalization benefits, whether unilaterally decreed or agreed with external partners, are extended immediately and unconditionally to all AMS.

A final observation, already alluded to above, concerns the adequacy of the institutional architecture that the AMS choose to assign to the realization of a region-wide economic community in a field in which obstacles to market integration stem primarily from diverging and often non-discriminatory domestic regulatory practices. ASEAN's institutional architecture is a (deliberate) far cry from the supranational forms of pooled regulatory governance and policed liberalization practised by the Member States of the EU in pursuit of a single market for services.

The building of the European internal market has been, and remains – much like the call for the establishment of a single production area within ASEAN – a work in progress. The EU experiment has been ongoing for six decades – a long march that has required the constant involvement of European institutions, Member States and economic agents as well as consumer organizations. The agenda for the completion of the EU internal market in services has progressed thanks to an important set of legal sources available at the EU level with the Treaty of Rome, the Services Directives, a number of sector-specific Directives, and decisions taken by the ECJ in striking down national measures deemed inconsistent with the Single Market's stated aims. Without the above set of legal instruments and the constant interaction of relevant European institutions, it is doubtful that the EU's internal market in services could have deepened as much as it has. However, the recurring and necessary role of soft law instruments is not to be neglected in the field and their use in an EU context shows how complementary they can be to the hard law instruments that serve the establishment of the internal market in services.

The European experience holds potentially important lessons for the quest for deepened service market integration within ASEAN. In pursuing deeper integration in services within ASEAN, the AEC Blueprint affirms the collective desire of AMS to limit their policy toolkit to only the first of the EU's market opening arsenal: the provisions found in the Treaty of Rome. The EU experience suggests that AMS may need to brace themselves for occasional bumps along the road to an integrated services market and single production area so long as they fail to adopt the necessary panoply of policy instruments and enforcement means to effect meaningful market opening within the regional grouping.

This latter point underlines the need to look at the AEC as a long-term journey in services liberalization, with first 2015 and, now, 2025, as important – if possibly far from final – steps along a path. Such a path is one that is likely to be characterized for some time by significant learning by doing externalities and confidence-building steps as well as by the continued coexistence of variable geometry hard law alongside various theatres of soft law cooperation as the ASEAN Economic Community progressively takes shape in an environment of marked diversity of incomes, governance capacities and collective preferences.

INDEX

AANZFTA. *See* ASEAN–Australia–
　New Zealand Free Trade
　Area
ABIF. *See* ASEAN Banking
　Integration Framework
ACFTA. *See* ASEAN–China Free
　Trade Agreement
ACIA. *See* ASEAN Comprehensive
　Investment Agreement
ACJEP. *See* ASEAN–Japan
　Comprehensive Economic
　Partnership
AEC Blueprint 2025. *See* ASEAN
　Economic Community
　Blueprint 2025
AFAS. *See* ASEAN Framework
　Agreement on Services
AFAS 7th Package, 115–125
　in Brunei Darussalam, 196
　in Cambodia, 196
　commitment packages in,
　　202–204
　　ASEAN+ PTAs compared to,
　　203–204
　in Laos PDR, 196–197
　liberalization in
　　levels of, 193–197
　　sectoral, 203
　in Malaysia, 196–197
　in Myanmar, 196–197
　in Philippines, 196–197
　in Singapore, 196–197
　subsectors committed in, 154
　in Thailand, 196–197
　in Vietnam, 196–197
AFAS 8th Package, 126–133
　in Brunei Darussalam,
　　126–127, 196
　in Cambodia, 127
　in Indonesia, 127–128
　in Laos PDR, 128
　in Malaysia, 128–129
　in Myanmar, 129–130
　in Philippines, 130–131
　in Singapore, 131
　subsectors committed in, 154
　in Thailand, 131–132
　in Vietnam, 132
AFAS 9th Package, 133–147
　in Brunei Darussalam, 134–135
　in Cambodia, 135–136
　in Indonesia, 136–137
　in Laos PDR, 137–138
　in Malaysia, 138–139
　in Myanmar, 139–141
　in Philippines, 143–145
　in Singapore, 141–142
　subsectors committed in, 154
　in Thailand, 145–146
　in Vietnam, 146–147

INDEX

AFTA. *See* ASEAN Free Trade Area
aggregate output trends, in services trade, 8–10
   for agriculture, shifts away from, 8–10
   for GDP, 8–10
agriculture
   in Indonesia, 8–10
   in Malaysia, 8–10
   in Myanmar, 8–10
   services trade aggregate output trends in, 8–10
   in Singapore, 8–10
AIA. *See* ASEAN Investment Agreement
AIFTA. *See* ASEAN-Indian Trade in Goods Agreement
air transport services, 93–94
air travel sector, in PIS, 97
AKFTA. *See* ASEAN–Korea Free Trade Agreement
AMS. *See* ASEAN Member States
APEC. *See* Asia-Pacific Economic Cooperation
APTA. *See* Asia-Pacific Trade Agreement
AQRF. *See* ASEAN Qualifications Reference Framework
ASEAN Banking Integration Framework (ABIF), 92
ASEAN Community, 78–79
ASEAN Comprehensive Investment Agreement (ACIA), 2, 66, 87
ASEAN Economic Community (AEC) Blueprint 2015, 1, 2
   AFAS and

   liberalization policies and, 78–85
   MRAs and, 109
   liberalization of trade services under, 78–85, 148–159
   targets of, 150–151
   liberalization policies and, 78–85
   MRAs and, 109
   in STRI database, 42
ASEAN Economic Community (AEC) Blueprint 2025, 1, 84–85, 158, 296–298
ASEAN Framework Agreement on Services (AFAS), 2, 54–98. *See also* AFAS 7th Package; AFAS 8th Package; AFAS 9th Package; liberalization
   ABIF, 92
   ACIA and, 66, 87
   AEC Blueprint 2015
   and liberalization policies and, 78–85
   MRAs and, 109
   AFTA and, 54–55
   AIA and, 54–55, 66, 87
   aims and purposes of, 54–57
   economic cooperation, 55–56
   elimination of trade restrictions, 56
   liberalization of trade, 56–57
   AQRF, 114–115
   articles and provisions in, 57–69
   MFN provisions, 62–64, 73–75, 220–221
   scope of, 64–65
   ATIGA and, 54–55
   ATISA and, 54–55, 65, 84

306

INDEX

CEPT Scheme and, 54–55
commitment packages in, 91. *See also* AFAS 7th Package; AFAS 8th Package; AFAS 9th Package
   air transport services, 93–94
   compared to GATS commitments, 120–121
   financial services, 92
cooperation policies in, 55–56, 77–88
   ASEAN Community through, 78–79
CPTPP and, 96
denial of benefits under, 70–75
GATS and, 56–69
   commitment packages in, comparisons between, 116–125
   MFN provisions in, 62–64, 73–75
minus-X formula in, 75–77
   inclusiveness as principle in, 76–77
MNP Agreement, 109–114
   effectiveness of, 113–114
   exceptions and limitations of, 110–113
   objectives of, 109–110
   Schedules of Commitments in, 111–113
modalities of, 88–98
MRAs in, 69–70, 98–109
   AEC Blueprint 2015 and, 109
   ATPRS, 109
   implementation of, 102–109
   in liberalization policies, 83

   scope of, 99–102
   types of, 100–102
negotiating history of, 88–98
PIS in, 84, 94–98
   air travel, 97
   e-ASEAN, 95–96
   healthcare, 97
   logistics, 98
   tourism, 96–97
reciprocity in, 210
rules of origin in, 70–75
Singapore Declaration of 1992, 77–78
in STRI database, 42
with third country partners, 208–211
ASEAN Free Trade Area (AFTA), 54–55
ASEAN Investment Agreement (AIA), 54–55, 66
ASEAN Member States (AMS), 2–3. *See also specific countries*
   in bilateral PTAs, with third countries, 211–216
   future of, 295–296
   methodological approach to, 2–3
   in optimal regulatory convergence area, 50–51
ASEAN+ preferential trade agreements (ASEAN+ PTAs), 159–167, 176–185. *See also* AFAS 7th Package
AANZFTA, 160–161, 190–191, 201–202
ACFTA, 160, 187–189, 197–199
ACJEP, 161–162

307

INDEX

ASEAN+ preferential trade (cont.)
   AIFTA, 161
   AKFTA, 160, 189–190, 199–201
   ASEAN–Hong Kong,
      China Free Trade
      Agreement, 162
   commitment packages in,
      186–195, 202–204
      AFAS 7th Package compared
         to, 203–204
      Hoekman Index for, 186–187
   liberalization in
      level of, 192
      sectoral, 192
      of services, 190
   RCEP, 162–167, 183–184
   FTAs and, 162–167
   rule-making in, 204–205
ASEAN Qualifications Reference
   Framework (AQRF), 114–115
ASEAN Tourism Professionals
   Registration System
   (ATPRS), 109
ASEAN Trade in Goods Agreement
   (ATIGA), 15
   AFAS and, 54–55
ASEAN Trade in Services
   Agreement (ATISA), 2,
   158, 299
   AEC Blueprint 2025 and, 1, 84–85,
      158, 296–298
ASEAN–Australia–New Zealand
   Free Trade Area
   (AANZFTA), 160–161,
   190–191, 201–202
   Hoekman Index and, 229
   MFN clauses in, 221–222

ASEAN–China Free Trade
   Agreement (ACFTA), 160,
   187–189, 197–199
   Hoekman Index and, 228
ASEAN–EU PTA, 181–182
ASEAN–Hong Kong, China Free
   Trade Agreement, 162
ASEAN–Indian Trade in Goods
   Agreement (AIFTA), 161
ASEAN–Japan Comprehensive
   Economic Partnership
   (ACJEP), 161–162
ASEAN–Korea Free Trade
   Agreement (AKFTA), 160,
   189–190, 199–201
   Hoekman Index and, 229
Asia-Pacific Economic Cooperation
   (APEC), 182–183
Asia-Pacific Trade Agreement
   (APTA), 175, 179
ATIGA. *See* ASEAN Trade in
   Goods Agreement
ATISA. *See* ASEAN Trade in
   Services Agreement
ATPRS. *See* ASEAN Tourism
   Professionals Registration
   System
Australia, bilateral agreements with,
   210–211

Bandar Seri Begawan
   Declaration, 158
bilateral agreements, 176–185. *See
   also specific agreements*
   with Australia, 210–211
   in EU trade in services, for global
      trade, 279–287

INDEX

liberalization of trade services in, 206–207
in PTAs of AMS, with third countries, 211–216
with Singapore, 211
Brexit, single market for services after, 270
Brock, William, 272–273
Brunei Darussalam, 47–48
AFAS 7th Package in, 196
AFAS 8th Package in, 126–127
AFAS 9th Package in, 134–135
PTAs in, 168, 179–180
Bulgaria, 49

CAFTA-DR. *See* Central American Common Market, Dominican Republic and the United States
Cambodia, 47–48. *See also* Services Trade Restrictiveness Index database
AFAS 7th Package in, 196
AFAS 8th Package in, 127
AFAS 9th Package in, 135–136
PTAs in, 175–176
Canada. *See* EU–Canada Comprehensive Economic and Trade Agreement
CARIFORUM-EU EPA, 285–287
Central American Common Market, Dominican Republic and the United States (CAFTA-DR), 285
CEPT Scheme. *See* Common Effective Preferential Tariff Scheme

CETA. *See* EU–Canada Comprehensive Economic and Trade Agreement
commercial services, export and import of, 12
commitment packages
in AFAS, 91. *See also* AFAS 7th Package; AFAS 8th Package; AFAS 9th Package
air transport services, 93–94
compared to GATS commitments, 116–125
financial services, 92
AFAS 7th Package, 202–204
in AFAS 7th Package, ASEAN+ PTAs compared to, 203–204
in ASEAN+ PTAs, 186–195, 202–204
AFAS 7th Package compared to, 203–204
Hoekman Index for, 186–187
in GATS
comparisons with AFAS commitments packages, 116–125
Hoekman Index for, 116–119
Common Effective Preferential Tariff (CEPT) Scheme, 54–55
Common Market of the South (Mercosur), 284–285
Comprehensive and Progressive Trans Pacific Partnership (CPTPP), 4–5, 180–181, 183–184, 216–218
AFAS and, 96

309

INDEX

Comprehensive (cont.)
  MFN clauses in, 224–225
  in STRI database, 34
  TPP and, 182–183, 216–217
cooperation
  in AFAS, 77–88
    aims and purposes of, 55–56
    ASEAN Community through, 78–79
  APEC, 182–183
  in optimal regulatory convergence area, 45–46
Corruption Perceptions Index rankings, 49
CPTPP. See Comprehensive and Progressive Trans Pacific Partnership
cross-border trade, trends in, 12

Deep and Comprehensive Free Trade Areas (DCFTA), 280
denial of benefits
  under AFAS, 70–75
  under GATS, 70–75
digital technology, 299–301

e-ASEAN sector, in PIS, 95–96
ECJ. See European Court of Justice
EEC. See European Economic Community
EFTA. See European Free Trade Area
employment trends, 10
  FDI as influence on, 10
Enhanced Trade Index (ETI), 25–28
EU. See European Union

EU–Canada Comprehensive Economic and Trade Agreement (CETA), 232–233, 281–282
European Commission, 265–270
European Court of Justice (ECJ), 172
  mutual recognition principle, 255–256
  restrictions on free provisions of services, 253–255
  single market for services in, 257, 260
  trade in services cases, 234, 236–237, 248–256
European Economic Community (EEC), 238
European Free Trade Area (EFTA), 223
European Union (EU). See also single market for services; trade in services; Treaty on the Functioning of European Union
  ECJ, 172
  EFTA, 223
  GATS in, 271–272

FDI. See foreign direct investment
financial services, 92
foreign direct investment (FDI)
  employment trends influenced by, 10
  in services trade, 17–18
  investment inflows, 18
free trade agreements (FTAs)
  under GATS, 67
  RCEP and, 162–167, 183–184

310

INDEX

GATS. *See* General Agreement on Trade and Services
GATT. *See* General Agreement on Tariffs and Trade
GDP. *See* gross domestic product
General Agreement on Tariffs and Trade (GATT), 274–276
General Agreement on Trade and Services (GATS)
  AFAS and, 56–69
    commitment packages in, comparisons between, 116–125
    MFN provisions in, 62–64, 73–75
  commitment packages in comparisons with AFAS commitments packages, 116–125
  Hoekman Index for, 116–119
  denial of benefits under, 70–75
  in EU, 271–272
  EU trade in services under, in global trade, 277–279
  FTAs under, 67
  liberalization of trade services under, 118, 148–159
  gains under, 120–121
  MFN clause in, 219–220
  rules of origin in, 70–75
  services liberalization in, 118
  Singapore and, 74
Global Competitiveness Index Rankings, 30
global trade in services, with EU, 271–290

through bilateral agreements, 279–287
governance indicator rankings, 52
gross domestic product (GDP), in services trade, 8–10

hard law instruments
  under Services Directive, 260–265
  trade in services in EU through, 240–245
healthcare sector, in PIS, 97
Hoekman Index, 116–119, 123–124, 186–187, 227
  AANZFTA and, 229
  ACFTA and, 228
  AKFTA and, 229
Human Development Index rankings, 50

inclusiveness principle, in minus-X formula, 76–77
India. *See also* Services Trade Restrictiveness Index database
  IT services in, 15–16
Indonesia, 47–48. *See also* Services Trade Restrictiveness Index database
  AFAS 7th Package in, 196–197
  AFAS 8th Package in, 127–128
  AFAS 9th Package in, 136–137
  agriculture services trends in, 8–10
  foreign ownership restrictions in, 153
  PTAs in, 168
  service liberalization in, 22

311

INDEX

information technology (IT) services, export trends for, 15–16
investment promotion agencies (IPAs), 299
IT services. *See* information technology services

Japan, PTAs in, 180–181
Judicial Independence Index rankings, 51

Laos PDR. *See also* Services Trade Restrictiveness Index database
  AFAS 7th Package in, 196–197
  AFAS 8th Package in, 128
  AFAS 9th Package in, 137–138
  PTAs in, 175–176
liberalization, of trade services, in AFAS, 77–88, 202–203. *See also* AFAS 8th Package; AFAS 9th Package; preferential trade agreements
  under AEC Blueprint 2015, 78–85, 148–159
  targets of, 150–151
  in ASEAN+ PTAs
  level of liberalization, 192
  sectoral liberalization in, 192
  of services, 190
  assessment of, 148–159
  future applications of, 158–159
  bilateral agreements compared to, 206–207
  under GATS, 118, 148–159
  gains under, 120–121

Hoekman Index for, 116–119, 123–124
improvement strategies for, 301–302
level of, in selected trade agreements, 207
MRAs, 83, 157
for non-ASEAN partners, 209
PIS and, 84
progress reports on, 85–88
for services, 115–147
7th Package, 115–125, 193–197
subsectors committed in, 154
license rejection, in STRI database, 42
Lisbon Strategy, 246. *See also* Spaak report
Logistics Performance Index (LPI) rankings, 25
logistics sector, in PIS, 98
LPI rankings. *See* Logistics Performance Index rankings

Malaysia, 47–48. *See also* Services Trade Restrictiveness Index database
  AFAS 7th Package in, 196–197
  AFAS 8th Package in, 128–129
  AFAS 9th Package in, 138–139
  agriculture services trends in, 8–10
  IT services in, 15–16
  New Zealand–Malaysia Free Trade Agreement, 215–216
  PTAs in, 169

INDEX

Member States of the Association of South East Asian Nations (ASEAN). *See also* ASEAN Member States
    AEC Blueprint 2015, 1, 2
    AEC Blueprint 2025, 1
    aims and goals of, 1
    growth models by, 1–2
Mercosur. *See* Common Market of the South
MFN treatment. *See* most-favoured nations treatment
minus-X formula, in AFAS, 75–77
    inclusiveness as principle in, 76–77
MNP Agreement. *See* Movement of Natural Persons Agreement
mode of supply, 36
most-favoured nations (MFN) treatment, 62–64, 218–225, 302
    in AANZFTA, 221–222
    in AFAS, 62–64, 73–75, 220–221
    in AFAS provisions, 62–64, 73–75
    in CPTPP, 224–225
    in EFTA, 223
    in GATS, 219–220
Movement of Natural Persons (MNP) Agreement, 109–114
    effectiveness of, 113–114
    exceptions and limitations of, 110–113
    objectives of, 109–110
    Schedules of Commitments in, 111–113
MRAs. *See* mutual recognition arrangements

multilateral agreements. *See also specific agreements*
    in EU trade in services, with global trade, 272–279
mutual recognition arrangements (MRAs)
    in AFAS, 69–70, 98–109
    AEC Blueprint 2025 and, 109
    ATPRS, 109
    implementation of, 102–109
    in liberalization policies, 83
    scope of, 99–102
    types of, 100–102
    liberalization of trade services and, in AFAS, 83, 157
Myanmar. *See also* Services Trade Restrictiveness Index database
    AFAS 7th Package in, 196–197
    AFAS 8th Package in, 129–130
    AFAS 9th Package in, 139–141
    agriculture services trends in, 8–10
    PTAs in, 175–176

NAFTA. *See* North American Free Trade Agreement
New Transatlantic Agenda (NTA), 283
New Transatlantic Marketplace (NTMA), 283
New Zealand–Malaysia Free Trade Agreement, 215–216
North American Free Trade Agreement (NAFTA), 280–281

313

NTA. *See* New Transatlantic Agenda
NTMA. *See* New Transatlantic Marketplace

OECE. *See* Organization for European Economic Co-operation
Open Markets Index, 29
openness in services markets, 28–42. *See also* Services Trade Restrictiveness Index database
optimal regulatory convergence area, in services, 43–53
  AMS performance, 50–51
  cooperation in, 45–46
  Corruption Perceptions Index rankings, 49
  costs of, 45
  definition of, 45–46
  governance indicators, 47–48
  Human Development Index rankings, 50
  income gap levels, 49
  innovation-related indicators, 47–48
  Judicial Independence Index rankings, 51
  PTAs and, 43–44, 46
  Regulatory Enforcement Index Factor 6, 52
  regulatory indicators, 47–48
  under Rule of Law Index, 52
  selected governance indicator rankings, 52
  signalling properties of treaty instruments, 43
Organization for European Economic Co-operation (OECE), 239

per capita income levels, 32
optimal regulatory convergence area, 49
Philippines, 47–48. *See also* Services Trade Restrictiveness Index database
  AFAS 7th Package in, 196–197
  AFAS 8th Package and, 130–131
  AFAS 9th Package in, 143–145
  foreign ownership restrictions in, 153
  IT services in, 15–16
  PTAs in, 170
PIS. *See* priority integration sectors
plurilateral agreements, 176–185. *See also specific agreements*
  in EU trade in services, global trade and, 288–290
preferential trade agreements (PTAs), 43–44, 46, 159–176, 177–226. *See also* ASEAN+ preferential trade agreements; bilateral agreements; plurilateral agreements
  APTA, 175, 179
  ASEAN–EU PTA, 181–182
  bilateral agreements in, with third countries, 211–216
  in Brunei Darussalam, 168, 179–180

INDEX

in Cambodia, 175–176
in Indonesia, 168
in Japan, 180–181
in Laos PDR, 175–176
in Malaysia, 169
in Myanmar, 175–176
in Philippines, 170
ratification of, 172
in Singapore, 170–173, 179–180
in Thailand, 173, 179–180
in Vietnam, 174
primary law, 243–244
priority integration sectors (PIS), 94–98
  in AFAS, 84, 94–98
    air travel, 97
    e-ASEAN, 95–96
    healthcare, 97
    logistics, 98
    tourism, 96–97
  air travel, 97
  e-ASEAN, 95–96
  healthcare, 97
  liberalization of trade services and, in AFAS, 84
  logistics, 98
  tourism, 96–97
PTAs. *See* preferential trade agreements

RCEP. *See* Regional Comprehensive Economic Partnership
reciprocity, in AFAS, 210
Regional Comprehensive Economic Partnership (RCEP), 162–167, 183–184

Regulatory Enforcement Index Factors, 52
Romania, 49
Rule of Law Index, 52
rule-making, in ASEAN+ PTAs, 204–205

SCPs. *See* Single Contact Points
secondary law, 243–244
Services Directive, 260–270
  freedom of establishment in, 261
  hard law instruments in, 260–265
  SCPs in, 265
  soft law instruments after, 265–270
services trade, 12–19. *See also* liberalization; optimal regulatory convergence area; trade in services
  aggregate output trends, 8–10
  for agriculture, shifts away from, 8–10
  for GDP, 8–10
  employment trends, 10
  FDI as influence on, 10
  general trends in, 12–17
    for commercial services, 14–16
    for cross-border trade, 12
    for IT services, 15–16
    for tourism, 17
  investment in, 17–19
    through FDI, 17–18
  trade integration trends, 10–12
    export and import of commercial services, 12
  value chains, 19–28
    ETI and, 25–28

INDEX

services trade (cont.)
  Global Competitiveness Index
    Rankings and, 30
  LPI rankings, 25
  Open Markets Index and, 29
  Services Trade Restrictiveness
    Index (STRI) database,
    31–42
  AEC Blueprint Goals, 42
  AFAS commitments in, 42
  CPTPP and, 34
  license rejection, 42
  by mode of supply, 36
  per capita income levels and, 32
  policy distance in, 34
  regional groupings, 41
  by sector, 37, 40, 41
  in 2008, 33
  in 2012, 33
Singapore, 47–48. *See also* Services
  Trade Restrictiveness Index
  database
  AFAS 7th Package in, 196–197
  AFAS 8th Package in, 131
  AFAS 9th Package in, 141–142
  agriculture services trends
    in, 8–10
  bilateral agreements with, 211
  GATS and, 74
  IT services in, 15–16
  PTAS in, 170–173, 179–180
  USSFTA, 212–215
Singapore Declaration of 1992,
  77–78
Single Contact Points (SCPs), 265
Single Market Act (2011), EU, 246,
  266–267

single market for services, in EU,
  257–270
  after Brexit, 270
  in ECJ cases, 257, 260
  European Commission and,
    265–270
  under Services Directive,
    260–270
  freedom of establishment
    in, 261
  hard law instruments in,
    260–265
  SCPs in, 265
  soft law instruments after,
    265–270
  soft law instruments for,
    258–260
  soft law instruments
    after Services Directive, 265–270
    for single market for services,
      258–260
    trade in services in EU through,
      238–240, 245–248
Spaak Report, 238–240, 245–248
STRI database. *See* Services Trade
  Restrictiveness Index
  database

TFEU. *See* Treaty on the
  Functioning of European
  Union
Thailand, 47–48. *See also* Services
  Trade Restrictiveness Index
  database
  AFAS 7th Package in, 196–197
  AFAS 8th Package in, 131–132
  AFAS 9th Package in, 145–146

INDEX

foreign ownership restrictions
   in, 153
PTAs in, 173, 179–180
third country partners
   AFAS with, 208–211
   in bilateral PTAs, with AMS, 211–216
   in EU trade in services, global trade and, 271
TiSA. *See* Trade in Services Agreement
tourism sector
   ATPRS, 109
   in PIS, 96–97
   in services trade, 17
TPP. *See* Trans-Pacific Partnership
trade agreements. *See* bilateral agreements; free trade agreements; multilateral agreements; plurilateral agreements; preferential trade agreements; *specific agreements*
trade in services, in EU, 231–233. *See also* Treaty on the Functioning of European Union
   ASEAN and, 291–293
   under CETA, 232–233, 281–282
   characteristics and features of, 232
   in ECJ cases, 234, 236–237, 248–256
   extra-trade, 232
   in global trade, 271–290
      through bilateral agreements, 279–287
      under GATS, 277–279
      under GATT, 274–276
      through multilateral agreements, 272–279
      through plurilateral agreements, 288–290
      with third countries, 271
   internal market construction for, 233–270, 302–304
      through hard law sources, 240–245
      instruments for, 235–237
      through soft law, 238–240, 245–248
      through Spaak Report, 238–240, 245–248
      through White Paper, 246–248
   intra-trade, 232, 271
   under Single Market Act, 232
   under Treaty of Rome, 233–234, 236, 238, 241, 243–244
Trade in Services Agreement (TiSA), 167, 289–290, 298
trade integration, trends in, 10–12
   export and import of commercial services, 12
Transatlantic Trade and Investment Partnership (TTIP), 282–283
Trans-Pacific Partnership (TPP), 182–183, 216–217
   US withdrawal from, 217
Treaty of Rome
   EU trade in services under, 233–234, 236, 238, 241, 243–244
   primary law under, 243–244
   secondary law under, 243–244

317

INDEX

Treaty on the Functioning of
European Union (TFEU),
240–245
  Article 52, 243–245
  Article 56, 241, 249–253
    recognition of direct effect of,
249–250
    scope of, 250–253
  Article 57, 241–242
  Article 58, 242
  Article 59, 242
  Article 60, 242
  Article 61, 243
  Article 62, 243
  in ECJ cases, 248–256
Trump, Donald, 217
TTIP. *See* Transatlantic Trade and Investment Partnership

United States (US), withdrawal from TPP, 217
Uruguay Round, in GATT, 274–276
US. *See* United States

US–Singapore FTA (USSFTA), 212–215

value chains, 19–28
  ETI and, 25–28
  Global Competitiveness Index Rankings and, 30
  LPI rankings, 25
  Open Markets Index and, 29
Vietnam, 47–48. *See also* Services Trade Restrictiveness Index database
  AFAS 7th Package in, 196–197
  AFAS 8th Package in, 132
  AFAS 9th Package in, 146–147
  PTAs in, 174
  service liberalization in, 22

White Paper, 246–248
World Justice Project, 52
World Trade Organization (WTO), 288–289
  GATT, 274–276